SIMON KENTON

His Life and Period

1755–1836

BY

EDNA KENTON

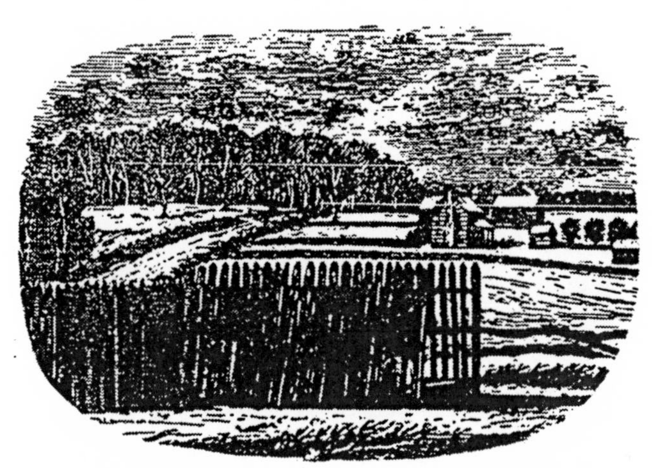

PRINTED IN THE UNITED STATES AT
THE COUNTRY LIFE PRESS
GARDEN CITY, N. Y.

FIRST EDITION

Printing Statement:

Due to the very old age and scarcity of this book, many of the pages may be hard to read due to the blurring of the original text, possible missing pages, missing text and other issues beyond our control.

Because this is such an important and rare work, we believe it is best to reproduce this book regardless of its original condition.

Thank you for your understanding.

TO

MAURICE DUNLAP KENTON

AND MABEL RUTH KENTON REBER

THE OTHER CHILDREN OF RUTH RICE

AND JAMES EDGAR KENTON

"IT IS NOT ENOUGH
THAT A MAN SHOULD BE GREAT, BUT
THAT HE SHOULD ALSO COME
AT THE PROPER SEASON."

*From the fragments of
John D. Taylor's manu-
script biography of
Simon Kenton*

Illustrations

K. Bodmer fect

Je certifie que les personnages ont été dessinés par J F Millet

Illustrations

TEXT ILLUSTRATIONS

Introduction

THE DRAPER COLLECTION OF MANUSCRIPTS

OF THE three men whose names stand always first on the long honor roll of Kentucky's pioneers, Daniel Boone and George Rogers Clark have had many biographers; their place in the foreground of their period is fixed. But the man whose services were unique not only in Kentucky's settlement but in the whole history of colonial border warfare, who performed in the background and "on his own hook" a continuous series of varied, self-assumed labors over a space of forty-two years, and for whose bones two states contended for a generation after his death, has never had the tribute of a "Life" of his own. For more than a generation, beginning with Theodore Roosevelt and William Hayden English, historians of this period and biographers of Clark have noted increasingly the prime importance of Simon Kenton to his time, and they have evidently endeavored to add to the scanty data afforded by the two minor sketches of him that exist. But with only one or two exceptions they have failed and the net result has been only a common amazement that so little is known of the man who played an "unparalleled rôle" in the settlement of Kentucky and Ohio.

Yet since 1838, when Lyman Copeland Draper began his great collection of manuscripts relating to the settlement of the middle states, there has been lying among them a group of Kenton Papers which steadily grew until, at Dr. Draper's death in 1891, they filled thirteen large folio volumes, supplemented by thirty-three volumes of "Draper's Notes," a great mass of which bears directly on Simon Kenton and his associates.

Dr. Draper was one of a number who planned to write Kenton's life; but he was a collector, not a writer. "I can write nothing," he said once to a close associate, "so long as I fear there is a fact, no matter how small, as yet ungarnered." But from the beginning to the end of his collector's life Simon Kenton the man and Simon Kenton the border figure interested him to the last detail. Just a week before his death he received the final Kenton Paper—an old Ohio cabinetmaker's painfully written account of his midnight order on April 29, 1836, to make for the old dead fighter "a good raised lid Black walnut or cherry Coffin," and of the simple funeral the next day. But by then Draper himself was a dying man and except for one isolated chapter in first draft, his "Life of Simon Kenton," whose preparation had extended through half a century, was never written.

The first sketch of Kenton's life and services—"which our feelings, his merits and the usefulness of history unite in claiming at our hands"—appeared in Humphrey Marshall's *History of Kentucky* in 1812. Marshall's authority for the statements he made there was undoubtedly Kenton himself.

In 1820, while Kenton was imprisoned for debt at Washington, Kentucky, John Bickley and Thomas Pickett issued "Proposals for publishing the memoirs of Gen. Simon Kenton," whose proceeds were "to relieve his wants and extradite him if possible from his difficulties." They had many conversations with him of which they took copious notes. But the notes never became a book.

At some time during the next ten years all these papers were turned over to John D. Taylor of Maysville, Kentucky, and they were evidently very full, for his stated purpose was "to embody and arrange, acting rather as compiler than an author." How much he made use of them we are likely never to know; all the papers disappeared and Dr. Draper searched for the lost notes and Taylor's lost manuscript for a number of years. He finally recovered seventeen pages of Taylor's manuscript from an old law office desk in Terre Haute, Indiana, where they had lain for an unknown period. But the Bickley and Picket notes had vanished completely.

The Reverend John A. McClung, however, had access to them while they were in Taylor's possession and to whatever existed before 1830 of Taylor's manuscript. On these he drew freely for his own thirty-two-page sketch of Kenton, published in his *Sketches of Western Adventure* in 1832.

In 1835 Colonel John McDonald, who when a boy was trained by Kenton in the fine art of Indian fighting, published in a Western paper a series of four biographies of pioneers, which in 1838 were issued in book form as *Biographical Sketches:* Kenton's story covered seventy pages. These two slight memoirs and the Marshall notice are the sources for all of the multitudinous little accounts of him that have followed.

But other "Lives" were planned, and one at least was written. Among the Kenton Papers is an amazing old blood-and-thunder biography by the Reverend Asal

Owen, grandnephew of Simon—it is dated April 5, 1858. The author had found it impossible to excite a publisher over the story of his "venerable old unkle," but this was exactly the sort of thing that interested Dr. Draper, who finally succeeded in getting possession of the manuscript. As the old preacher had been born in 1792 within sight of Kenton's Station and had been one of the party which migrated with Kenton to Ohio, all of his youth had been spent near his great-uncle, and "blood and thunder" though his life of Simon was, it had high value in throwing new or confirmatory light on a number of the clouded details of Kenton's career.

What might have been the most interesting of all the planned biographies was the one projected by Judge John H. James of Urbana, Ohio. Inspired by two days spent at Kenton's home in 1832 to collect material for a massive history of Ohio, also never written, he immediately planned to spend a month there, in order to take the fullest possible notes of his reminiscences.

> I intended [he wrote Dr. Draper in 1846] to write, at one heat, his life and Times in his own racy dialect . . . before another leisure offered, Gen. K's mind had become so much impaired as to memory that the proposed work was given up. I have often regretted it, for I was full of the purpose then, and would have pursued it *con amore*.

Judge James did, however, take down many pages of notes on Kenton's life as he told it—much of it verbatim, for Kenton's "racy dialect" and his markedly characteristic utterance delighted him. It makes a story in itself—Dr. Draper's efforts, from 1846 to 1889, to obtain these notes: first from Judge James through correspondence;

then in a personal visit when extracts were read to him; and later still, after James's death, from his children. Two years before his own death he succeeded in adding transcripts of them to the Kenton Papers, and here, more fully than anywhere else, we find Kenton's own statements on the Indian wars, his personal opinions of his old compatriots, and, best of all, the characteristically archaic quality of his habitual expression.

Lyman Copeland Draper is a figure as unique in the field of early Middle Western American history as James Boswell is in the field of biography. As Boswell stayed by Johnson, thinking nothing too trifling in speech or behavior for recording, so Draper stayed by his subject as it spoke through old documents and the lips of survivors or descendants of the dead; he saved everything it said and did.

His first interest was the seemingly simple one of correcting the fanciful histories of border warfare and the lives of the actors in them by rewriting them on a basis of more facts and less fiction; and the Draper collection of manuscripts began with an extensive correspondence among the survivors of the border days. About 1840 he began to make his famous "trips" or visits to them—Indians as well as white men—and to descendants and neighbors of the dead pioneers, from whose lips he took down what they said. From New York he branched into Pennsylvania, Virginia, Kentucky, Ohio, Michigan, western Canada, Indiana, Illinois, Iowa, and Missouri, traveling in all more than sixty thousand miles by whatever primitive means—on horseback, by stage, wagon, buggy, or boat.

He was the guest of those he came to interview, and among the thousand and one human touches we come on in the Draper manuscripts is the multiplied evidence of the friends he made in his consecrated journeyings. Babies were named for him, and long after he had come and gone, his hosts would write him, adding some belated detail to history or genealogy and asking when he was coming again. His persistent letters to key witnesses already drained dry under his expert questioning, subtly inviting them to renewed effort to recollect some dim date or distance, brought new interest into the lives of old men whose grandchildren had long since wearied of their tales; they sought out old comrades and formed temporary little groups in which old battlefields were redrawn, old battles refought and a collective memory invoked to reach some common conclusion. And then they sat down and laboriously began: "Sir, I find there were two distinct fights I have thrown into one." Or even more laboriously: "Sir, I am compelled to use both hands in writing—you may be sure I am in good earnest when I write."

In 1854 Dr. Draper went to Madison, Wisconsin, to become the head of the State Historical Society there. Three years later he computed that his collection of manuscripts amounted to "some 10,000 foolscap pages of notes of the recollections of warrior pioneers, either written by themselves or taken down from their own lips, and well nigh 5,000 pages more of original manuscripts, journals, memorandum books and old letters by near all the border heroes of the West." This covered the collection of but sixteen years; thirty-four years more of work were to multiply and remultiply its treasures. To-day the Draper collection of manuscripts lies in its steel chamber in the State Historical Society building at Madison, unsurpassed material on the region and period it covers.

Dr. Draper's dominant interest was in George Rogers Clark. That biography was to lead all the others he purposed to write—of Kenton, Boone, Brady, the Wetzels, Washburn, Sevier, Robertson, Sumter, Pickens, Crawford, Shelby, and Cleveland. But he never lost sight of Kenton's untold story. On all his trips he was persistently interviewing those of Kenton's old associates who survived, his own and their descendants and other relatives, and a large part of his thirty-three volumes of "Notes" centers about this buried figure.

He both visited and corresponded with William Miller Kenton over a long period of years, and through this son of Simon's came into possession of Kenton's Manuscript Statement taken down by Elizabeth his wife—chiefly concerned with his "Recollections of Gen. George Rogers Clark" but dealing briefly with his own early life and his Indian captivity. It would be hardly fair to omit this son from the list of his father's biographers; for when he sent Dr. Draper, in 1847, the fragments of the Taylor manuscript he had finally found, he wrote regretfully of the rest of the papers as probably "entirely lost," and of his lack of leisure—had he only time "to think with a view of thinking" about the details of his father's long evening talks with his friends he "might make it interesting." And then he launched into an extempore outline that formed the basis for years of correspondence: a finer skeleton to clothe with the flesh of facts than had come Dr. Draper's way so far. But he, like many of the others, grew impatient of "perfecting the book"; for the years went on, facts were garnered and regarnered, but the book never appeared.

In working with the Draper Manuscripts I was surprised to find how clearly the figure of their collector is shown through them, not only as historian but as psychologist. He had an uncanny gift for questioning and for invoking associations, a patient understanding of the tricks memory plays, and a real artistry in cultivating those little reservoirs of lost history. In his interviews he evidently tried to keep his victim racing under the straight rein of chronology, but he as evidently gave him the illusion of freedom, never failed to let him roam through the fields of memory when he was so inclined. When something seemingly quite unrelated to the topic in hand was recollected it was set down and later returned to again and again; under such culture it sometimes blossomed into a little historical flower. His letters of interrogation are marvels of directness, precision, and simplicity; they are of themselves almost history, so clearly do they divide the confirmed from the unconfirmed.

Simon Kenton was an illiterate man; he could sign his name but he could not write, so there is no first-hand material. His Manuscript Statement, his dictated letters, his many depositions for use in land cases (in no small number of which his own indubitable speech springs free above the legal phrases), the James Notes, the reminiscences of his children, William, Sarah, Mary, and Elizabeth, those of other relatives closely associated with him—notably the Arrowsmiths—and a few personal interviews reported by credible people are the nearest we have to original material. For the rest the reminiscences of friends and relatives, of old companions in arms, of men grown great as the West grew great who as boys were "Kenton's boys," trained by him in woodcraft, Indian sign, Indian scouting, and spying and warfare—all these build up the picture of a man so made for his time and so much a part of it that only from its people do we get his measure. Only here, in this great collection of papers of his period, in old faded letters and diaries and journals and notes, do these personal memories of him lie; they overflow from the Kenton Papers into other "papers" of other men and of two states; and their whole trend might be summed up in a sentence written by one of the men who remembered him: "He was the most *natural* man I ever saw or talked with."

EDNA KENTON

NEW YORK,
September, 1929.

Simon Kenton

Chapter I

KENTUCKY THE STRANGE LAND

TO THE south of the winding Ohio, along nearly eight hundred of the eleven hundred miles of its length, lies the ancient, cave-pierced land now called Kentucky, once called the Breathing Land, the Middle Ground, the Neutral Space, the Sacred Soil. Shaped by its natural boundaries like the half of a great oak leaf, it is to-day, except for the imaginary line that separates it from Tennessee, just what it was when its first map was drawn in 1755: on the right-angled east the Pine and Cumberland Mountains and the Big Sandy River; on the narrow west the Mississippi; and on the convolute north the white-capped Ohio, constantly in its course returning upon itself to flow repeatedly toward every point of the compass, yet all the while flowing irresistibly westward, key river of all the Colonial East to the Missouri-Mississippi and the Great West beyond.

Here and there on earth are little lands that we can only call quickening places for dream and fancy. There is a sweet poison in the very air that blows from these strange regions, infecting all alike to the spinning of myth and legend. Ireland is such a spot. Kentucky is another, for cave lands are always mysterious lands to their aboriginal inhabitants; they are the "breathing lands" of the ancients, through whose hollows, as through a body, the air of heaven is breathed in and out. Live beside Kentucky's Mammoth Cave for a winter and a summer and a winter. It will mean little to you at first that its great current of air flows inward. Suddenly, when summer comes, you will realize that its great current of air is flowing outward. And this will not mean much until winter comes again and, the year-long full breath finished, the inflowing current carries on the rhythm. Then you may begin to wonder, even though it is likely to seem to you no more than a very curious phenomenon, for to you the sun rises and sets in the heavens and the earth is merely a mass of matter with but one habitable surface. But to an aboriginal race through whose tradition and mythology stretches from tribe to tribe like a scarlet thread the belief in a hollow earth, into which the sun retreats at night to emerge at dawn, from which its vanished tribes have come forth in glory and to which they return when "gone to seed," a land of caves is a land where Time's divisions meet, where the past threatens the present, and where "talking men" may foretell the future. It is always a breeding spot for legend and myth.

The rough traders along the Ohio from the close of the Seventeenth Century onward were not sprung from a myth-making race, and at first they knew little of Kentucky except from its shore line; for the "Indian side" was the northern side, and they were mainly concerned with the quick barter of their English and French wares for Indian furs and then a safe return up river. They were a hardy crew, fearing neither God nor devil, immune to Indian legend, and not prone to disease. Yet they fell unwitting, easy victims to the contagion in the Kentucky air, and as the years went on became carriers of such a self-spun legend of it along the frontier that the distant land soon became a beckoning figure in a myriad gently fevered dreams and finally drew the dreamers to it in a wave of migration the like of which this country has never seen.

Of the Indian legends of the land the Ohio traders knew little, and of Indian tradition that explained the legends they knew less. They early learned that Kentucky was uninhabited but they did not learn why, else their own glowing legend of it might have taken a darker color. They did not know that by "assured tradition" "at first and in that place" had dwelt "a very long-ago people" who were "of a white color" and masters of arts unknown to the red man, who built great mounds and fortifications on both sides of the Ohio, and who were finally exterminated with great slaughter. They did not know that by "assured tradition" the mound-building people worshiped not the red man's sun but the moon, paradise of the spirits of "obedient females" who gratified their passion of curiosity in a ceaseless journey around the earth and with their wisdom made their worshipers wise. They did not know of other races and other wars that had come each "a long time ago" until at last, after the all-conquering Iroquois had swept down from the north, the land had become for vanquished and conqueror and onlooker alike the Middle Ground, the Neutral Space. They did not know it was a land less uninhabited than shunned, so reddened with human blood that it had become an "all-animal land," a "land of spirits," to be visited, to council in, to hunt upon, but never more to live upon. Strange to think of the Kentucky pioneers, in the dim light of Indian tradition, as barbarian invaders of a sacred land; stranger still to think of the Indians in that dim light as waging for a score of terrible years along the Ohio something like a holy war against the profaning whites.

Knowledge of Kentucky came slowly to the Ohio traders, since their range was the Indian side of the river. Sometimes they traded in midstream with passing hunting parties, sometimes on the northern shore, sometimes, leaving the great water for one of its tributaries, they paddled upstream a space to where some known Indian village stood. But now and then they followed Indian hunting parties into Kentucky and bartered at their camps for skins still warm from the great hunt, and on the long return trip up the river with their fur-packed canoes they camped at night on the southern shore and noted by day the figuration of the land. Their trained backwoodsmen's eyes saw all that could be seen, their backwoodsmen's sixth sense divined the probable nature of the unseen interior, and their inoculated fancy did the rest.

Half a century before the three men who were to play the major rôles in its settlement had been drawn by the legend of Kentucky to its center—and indeed before they were born—the gentle virus of the traders' reports of it began to spread rapidly along the Pennsylvania and Virginia frontiers. By 1725 these two colonies had extended their settlements close to the base of the Alleghany barrier and the game had retreated behind it. The dream of a Western Ocean "just behind the mountains" had long since faded, and the "Messipi"—intervening goal—was known to lie hundreds of savage-haunted miles to the west. What wonder that the restless frontiersmen listened so eagerly to the tale of an uninhabited land south of the Ohio, a new Canaan flowing with rivers of salt and bearing trees of sugar, whose loam was fine as flour to the hand!

Time gave time for the legend to grow. A few more years and Big Bone Lick was found and named and storied—graveyard of the elephant and the mastodon who had mired helplessly in the salty swamps and perished, whose great ribs made tent poles and their disjointed vertebræ camp stools and tables. The buffalo roads were discovered and the incredible herds that traveled them on their way to the salt licks; when they paused on their way to wallow in the shoals of the interior rivers no canoe could get upstream or down until the great beasts had shaken themselves free of water and mire and departed along their thunderous road.

These were the great animals, but there were lesser ones in fabulous numbers: elk and deer, panthers and bears, and birds of every sort from the ground birds—the turkey, partridge, pheasant, and quail—to the flowerlike humming bird, the flashing cardinal, and the heaven-spanning eagle. There were venomous snakes.

It was a land of rivers and creeks and gushing springs. It was a land of cane whose stalks were only lesser trees, of wild grasses that sprang to an enormous height, of nettles from whose fibers cloth might be spun. Its forests embraced an infinite variety of trees big of girth and of gigantic growth—the elm and oak, the ash and willow, the huge-bellied sycamore and cottonwood, the honey locust and the catalpa and the redwood tree, the fragrant spice wood and the walnut black and white, the pawpaw and the chestnut, the iron wood and the hoop wood, the hickory and the sugar maple. Its fruits were flavorsome and splendid—the wild strawberry and blackberry and raspberry, black and red, the wild cherry and hackberry and wild goose plum, the persimmon and mulberry—and every forest festooned with the wild grape vine. It was carpeted with wild rye, with prairie and buffalo clover, with the deep "blue grass" and with "Rich Weed," and it was spread with flowers strange and lovely and with familiar blooms so extravagant that they seemed strange—the trumpet creeper, Indian turnip, Solomon's seal, toad-flax and phlox, the May apple, fire pink and wintergreen, the blue wild lupine and spiked moth mullein, the bignonia vine and the poison ivy, the blue larkspur, the pink and white stonecrop, the trailing arbutus, and the great laurel. Even the forest became a giant's garden and perfumed land and river when the horse chestnut, the locust, the pawpaw, the willow, and the fox grape were in bloom.

Best and most incredible of all, the Indians did not inhabit it—so ran the story—and the restless frontiersmen, eager to press West, listened and believed and did not ask why. It seemed their good luck and that was enough, to know of such a land beyond the mountain barrier, so rich, so broad, so free from savage and tax gatherer alike, too far away to be concerned, as their settlements were beginning to be concerned, with the distant quarrels of a French and an English king. They could not know, those first dreamers of the beckoning land, how long it was to be before her first settlement would be made. They could not know that in the year it would be settled in the West, the Revolutionary War would have broken in the East, nor that this land of dream was fated not only to be the frontier outpost of the war while it lasted but to be the scene of a bitter aftermath of Indian warfare for years after the Revolutionary War had ended.

But time prolonged the dream—made poets of the pioneers. Colonel Richard Henderson's *Journal of an Expedition to Cantuckey in 1775*—the story of the building of Boonesborough—is the first record of daily living in a Kentucky settlement that we have. It is the journal of a man with fists, mostly brief and to the point. His entry for "Saturday, May 13" opens with this practical observation: "No scouring of floors, sweeping of yards, or scalding of bedsteads here." Then the mood of Kentucky falls suddenly upon him and he writes thus—though the dream breaks a little at the end:

> About 50 yards from the river, behind my camp and a fine spring a little to the west, stands one of the finest elms that perhaps nature has ever produced. The tree is produced on a beautiful plain, surrounded by a turf of fine white clover, forming a green to the very stock. The trunk is about 4 feet through to the first branches, which are about 9 feet from the ground. From thence it regularly extends its large branches on every side, at such equal distances as to form the most beautiful tree the imagination can suggest. The diameter of the branches from the extreme end is 100 feet, and every fair day it describes a semicircle in the heavenly green around it upwards of 400 feet in circumference. At any time between the hours of 10 and 2, 100 persons may commodiously seat themselves under the branches.

This divine tree—or rather one of the many proofs of the existence from all eternity of its Divine Author—is to be our church, council chamber, etc. Having many things on our hands, we have not had time to erect a pulpit, seats, etc.; but hope, by Sunday sevennight, to perform divine services in a public manner, and that to a set of *scoundrels*, who scarcely believe in a god or fear a devil—if we are to judge from most of their looks, words, or actions.

Through the twenty years of Indian war that followed, nothing shattered the dream. Though death lurked across the Ohio and might stride the stream at any hour, the land still inspired its swiftly increasing people to myth-making.

Little by little, bits of Indian tradition came to the ken of the white men, and that bit which persistently recurred, "of a very long ago people" who were white, most touched their fancy. Read the first histories of Kentucky—the first three—and see to what lengths their puzzled writers went to account for this tradition which almost they believed. John Filson, pioneer history-maker in 1784, suggested that these "white men" might have been descendants of ancient Carthaginian voyagers thrown by tempests on the Atlantic shore who had multiplied and grown strong and somehow pressed west. But he liked better to carry on the old Welsh legend of Madoc, son of Owen Gwynnedh, Prince of Wales, who in 1170 went west over the waters until he discovered "a fertile country," whereupon returning to Wales he set out again with a large colony to populate the new land and "was never more heard of." He plainly inclined to the opinion that the white men of Indian tradition were Madoc's men and cited many a rag tag of early explorers' tales of white Indians who spoke Welsh to prove it.

Or read *The Ancient Annals of Kentucky* by America's pioneer archæologist and prepare to be amazed, if any stories of the Lost Atlantis have come your way—particularly if you have read that if the great earth-wrapping continent ever existed and if any remnants of it are above the ocean to-day they are only the little island groups called the Canaries and Azores. For Constantine Rafinesque, writing in Kentucky in 1824, said that when "Peleg's Flood" split Atlantis and it went down into the White or Atlantic Sea, that part of it to the west which included Kentucky remained above water and "the Atlantes of the interior of America became insulated and separated from the Atlantic Empire." These—men of the Lost Atlantis—were the white people of Indian tradition. They lived on their nucleus-land while the new continent to be called America was in the making; they built the great earthworks along the Ohio for symbols of what had been once on earth and would be no more; and finally, except for "a few who escaped to the North," they surrendered their bones and blood to the ancient remnant of Atlantean land—Kentucky! So much did the learning of this little book impress Humphrey Marshall, Kentucky's first real historian, that he used *The Ancient Annals* entire for the introduction to the second edition of his history. Kentucky is a strange land and nothing has seemed too strange to explain it. From Carthaginian to Welsh to Platonic myth—they were all drawn on, and they only added to the sweet confusion.

But these were later myths born of books. It was

the earlier legend born of the land itself that first infected the border colonies with a fervid craze for Kentucky.

Time took her time to strengthen the legend and to breed her men against the day she would need them to play their parts in the prologue to the great Western drama. There were little premonitory shivers of the curtain—premonitory, that is, if the significances of coincidences could have been read at the moment. Wise men have said that if there are conjunctions in the heavens which astrologers can read, there are also conjunctions on earth whose signs and portents show themselves later to have been as marvelous as any in the sky. Certainly in two mid-Eighteenth Century years Kentucky's star was in the ascendent in the East. In 1752 George Rogers Clark was born, and in that year John Finley, trader with Thomas Kenton on the Ohio, entered Kentucky and marveled. In 1755, birth year of Simon Kenton and of the first map of Kentucky, Finley, out with Braddock's army, met Daniel Boone, twenty-one-year-old wagoner and blacksmith for the North Carolina frontiersmen who had come up to do their part in the French and Indian War.

From Finley, Boone first heard of Kentucky, and together they traced out a little picture map of the probable route from Boone's home to it. Twelve years later, never losing the vision of the fabled land, he tried to find it but failed. A year later Finley, itinerant land peddler then, knocked, as we say, by accident on Boone's Yadkin River door and in 1769 guided him through the Cumberland Gap into the golden land. Two years later Simon Kenton, sixteen-year old fugitive from Virginia, heard the story of Kentucky's cane-lands from one who could tell it from "the Indian side"—a white captive who had hunted happily with his friendly captors in the Middle Ground. The same year he entered it and succumbed to its spell. Four years were to pass before George Rogers Clark came down the Ohio, but by 1775 all three were in their own country, fashioned full-statured for their period and "come at the proper season."

Kentucky's "three men" were very dissimilar types, but each indispensable for her quick growth. She needed from her beginnings an organizer of her slender resources, an intermediary between her and the East, a fore-visioner of her measureless importance in the measureless destiny of the West, a practical general of her affairs in the large. All this she found in George Rogers Clark.

She needed a man who was himself a blend of the roving hunter and the farmer settler, a man who was a natural leader of rude frontiersmen, who could hold a primitive colony together, keep it harmonious, defend it and feed it and give generous aid to others; unless the blend balanced the man was useless. She found it in Daniel Boone.

She needed too a free agent, a man on his own, with the ability to adapt himself on the instant to whatever was, and with the will to act by a golden rule—to perform the duty laid by a free man upon himself. She found him in Simon Kenton, and for twenty years he never failed himself or her.

He was unique. He could take orders from others and give them to others, but he had a finer faculty—

he could give himself orders and command himself to perform them. This is why, in the old records, his figure so amazingly stands out; why too, perhaps, in later records it has sunk. A Napoleon or a Casabianca is never forgotten, but a man "on his own hook" (a phrase used over and over by his contemporaries to describe him) swims in his own sea, that is, his own time; his work is there and there is his record. It is doubtful if there was a man, woman, or child living between the Kentucky and Ohio rivers during the dangerous years but owed to him at one time or another, if not life, at least the chance of escape from attack, as he rode or ran along the settlement trails crying shrill warning of an Indian raid. He always remembered what others forgot, that tireless watchfulness was the price of life, and until peace was made and the land was comfortable, he stayed at his self-appointed post—guardian of the northern border.

Chapter II

EARLY LIFE AND THE FLIGHT FROM VIRGINIA
1755–1771

THE "old Kenton place" in Virginia—no landed estate this where Simon Kenton was born—lay in the northeastern part of Fauquier County, about forty miles from Dumfries and two miles south of the small hamlet of Hopewell where in 1744 the people called Quakers had established a Monthly Meeting. In this fertile little valley at the foot of Bull Run Mountain, on Mill Branch of Broad Run—headwaters of the Bull Run River—at some date unknown but probably before 1737, Mark Kenton, father of Simon, erected his log cabin on "rented land" and there reared his family.

Of Mark Kenton's ancestry there are no records, but of his nativity there is no doubt. He was a militant Irishman, probably of County Down, who knew Ireland's rank by right among the nations and impressed it on his progeny. Born only a few years after William III had broken the Irish revolt under Tyrconnell so thoroughly that for one hundred years to come the rebellious little island was to lie in a state of despairing peace under England's rule, the Kenton family records nevertheless memorialize thus the country of his birth:

Mark Kenton Senr. departed this life the 16th day of October, 1783, on his travel to Kentucky, within about 30 miles of Pittsburgh. He was born in the Kingdom of Ireland in the year of our Lord 1701 and March the 1st.

At what time or under what circumstances he came from Ireland to America is unknown. There is an old family tradition that he was one of three brothers born at a birth and that he and one of the others came to America at an early age. This triple birth has never been verified, for there are no records of the birth date of Thomas Kenton, Indian trader on the Ohio in the days of John Finley and David Duncan, whose descendants settled in Pennsylvania and Maryland. There appears to have been little if any contact between the two branches of the family in the early years, for Hopewell lay far from the traders' path between the Ohio and Philadelphia, which was Thomas Kenton's route for many years.[1] Later on, some of the Maryland descendants settled in Ohio, and one of them, William Kenton, received his education, such as the country afforded, by grace of his "Uncle Simon." Education was not free then; each child's learning was paid for at the rate of some two dollars a month; but Simon Kenton sent everybody to school in those early Ohio days, stray relatives and

[1]In the *Journals of James Kenney, 1758–1759 and 1761–1763* [a Quaker in charge of the trading store at Fort Pitt who made frequent trips to Hopewell to attend the Monthly Meetings there], Thomas Kenton's name is often mentioned as one "who informs us," more than the other traders, of the lively gossip of the country. Under date of March 19, 1761, Kenney writes: "Informed by Thos. Kenton that before ye Indian war, he being out here at a town a little way up ye Alegheny where the Indians found a Rat and killed it, that ye atiants of them seemed concerned, and told him that ye French or English should get that land from them, ye same prediction being made by their grandfathers on finding a Rat on Delaware before ye White People came here."

Indian children along with his own. He knew by then the disadvantages of not knowing his letters, but he had his own serene pride of knowledge at that, for one day he said to a small nephew boasting too much of his new power of reading, "Ah, child, reading a thing is only hearing it, but *seeing* is *knowing*."

There are several traditions also about the manner in which Mark Kenton came from Ireland to Virginia: one, that he was kidnapped in his boyhood by some ship's crew, brought to Virginia, and sold by the ship's captain to some planter for a term of years; another, that he came over voluntarily as an indentured man, and this is the likelier story, for in the first quarter of the Eighteenth Century the "Kingdom of Ireland" was a place to leave under any conditions. The system of indenture under which both men and women were imported into Virginia from England and the north of Ireland made it possible for poor men who could not pay their passage to go none the less to the Colonies; they entered into a contract under bond to work out their passage in the service of the landowner who had advanced the passage money. It was a business arrangement, and after the contract had been fulfilled, usually after four or five years of service, these men often took up lands of their own and became prosperous farmers and plantation owners who brought out indentured servants in their turn.

There is nothing, however, in the Fauquier County records to show that Mark Kenton was ever a landowner. He lived on what was originally the great Carter grant, which was divided, as it was surveyed, into small farms on which long leases were given, usually of "three lives" or ninety-nine years, at an annual rental of a few shillings an acre. He evidently paid certain taxes in Fauquier County up to 1778, for in the minutes of its court, under August 24th of that year, is this entry: "For reasons appearing to the Court, Mark Kenton is discharged from paying County levies for the future." No reason is given for this somewhat unusual act of grace; it was granted during the Revolutionary War, probably for some uncited service rendered by him. Two of his sons, Mark Junior and Benjamin, were in the service then, and there is a family tradition that at some time during the war he himself served as commissary, but the Revolutionary records do not show this. Probably his services, like most of those of his son Simon, who was operating extensively in Kentucky, Ohio, and Illinois at this time, were done "on his own," and so, like most of Simon's feats, failed to appear in the official reports.

Neither is there any record of the date of his marriage, but about 1737 Mary Miller, a young woman of Scotch-Welsh descent living in the neighborhood, became his wife, and on September 20, 1737, his eldest son William was born. Three daughters followed, Mary, Jane, and Frances, and two sons, Mark and John; then, in 1755, his son Simon was born. There were two younger children, Benjamin and Nancy.

Like many a man of his time, Simon Kenton has been given a variety of birth dates and birthplaces. According to his four biographers, he was born in two different counties, in two different years, in three different months, and on three different days of those months. Kenton himself always gave April 3, 1755, as his birth date and further impressed the month and the year by saying: "My mother always said I was born in the April before Braddock's defeat."[1]

Here then, seventh child of nine and son of a father who never rose above the tenant class, Simon lived for sixteen years. He himself seldom spoke of his childhood and youth, but by all the evidence most of his time was spent in ranging the country, learning, without knowing he was at school, the lay of the wilderness, Nature's signs of direction in trees, streams, and stars, fearlessness of solitude, and confidence in his ability to feel his way and make his own paths toward a goal. There were schools of sorts in the Bull Run Mountain settlement, and in them William and John and Mark Junior learned to read and write and do sums. Not so Simon. There is a persistent tradition that he attended school but half a day. Certainly he attended no more than he had to, played truant when he could, and learned nothing from books. To the day of his death he could neither read nor write; when he began to enter land in Kentucky he learned to scrawl his name mechanically; whatever else he knew he learned of himself from Nature and experience.

It was William, Simon's senior by eighteen years, who went to school when he could, improved every meager opportunity for acquiring "book knowledge,"

[1]Draper MSS.—5BB99, 8BB152.

Marshall says April 19, 1753; McClung says May 15, 1755; McDonald says "in the month of March, A.D. 1755"; but Taylor's MS., dictated by Kenton, and Kenton's family Bible, pension statement, and tombstone memorial say April 3, 1755. William Kenton, Simon's eldest brother, always insisted that Simon was two or three years older than he said, and in the various records of this branch of the family the birth is almost always given as 1752 or 1753.

worked shoulder to shoulder with his father during the hard years before and after Simon's birth; and it is through his children and grandchildren to whom he talked freely that most of the reminiscences of old Mark and the old home near Hopewell come. Living went from hand to mouth, with as little land cultivated as could be and the family live, and this was common to all classes in Virginia at that time. The Reverend Andrew Burnaby, traveling in 1759 through this very region, noted that the Virginians "are content if they can but live from day to day; they confine themselves almost entirely to the cultivation of tobacco; and if they have but enough of this to pay their merchants in London and to provide for their pleasures they are content."

Mark Kenton had no "merchants in London" to pay, and his pleasures were few. But there came a day in each year when the land rent was due, and with each spring preparations for payment began: the tobacco crop must be raised. Small wonder no more land was cultivated than need be, with the tools he had for working it. The plows were so primitive that father and son first had to loosen the rich valley ground with mattock and hoe—William had the reputation of being able to hoe an acre a day. This done, as he often told his children, the two family horses were necklaced with collars of corn husks and hitched tandem-fashion to the rude wooden plow by traces of hickory bark, which, tough as they were, snapped easily when the blunt plow point struck an underground root or stone: "it was a great stride in improvement when the bark traces were supplanted by rawhide tugs."

Then, with the father holding the plow and with Mary—eldest daughter—at the lead horse's head and William guiding the near horse, the deep overturning of the earth began, for the planting of tobacco and corn and "garden stuff." The garden stuff was for daily food; the corn was for daily bread and for a twelve-month grain supply for the horses, the pigs, and the cow; but the tobacco was the rent itself, to be delivered in Dumfries by Christmas of each year, and the surplus traded there for powder and lead and other annual supplies. The surplus crop need not be much, for, as William told his children, "If a family in the common walks of life could make and prize a single hogshead of tobacco, attach shafts to fellowes fastened at either end, and roll it with a horse to Dumfries for market, it could with the proceeds secure enough of plain clothes and the few necessary groceries for the family for a year's supply."

Mark Kenton's tobacco was rolled to Dumfries, not only because it was then the market place for all the country round but because there dwelt the landlord—not the manorial Carters now, but Richard Graham, wealthy Scotch merchant of the place, who, when the great grant was finally broken up and sold, bought several thousand acres which included the Bull Run Mountain tract where Kenton lived. There are proud old stories of "George Washington surveying this land" preparatory to its sale and of William Kenton, the learned son, assisting in the survey. However, at the close of each season, when the tobacco was cured and ready for market, and each tightly packed hogshead "of 800 or 1000 weight" had its lid driven in, a small wooden pin was inserted in each end and to these primitive axles shafts were fastened and made firm by a cross piece in front of each cask. Then, with a horse harnessed between the shafts, each hogshead was rolled forty miles to Dumfries for delivery. This always meant camping out over night, and this often meant "going along"; "sometimes a string of twenty or more teams might be seen rolling along their hogsheads for the Scotch town of Dumfries, and the road would become beaten down hard and smooth below the mountains."

When Simon was eight years old a small cloud of farm work impending gathered about his head, for in 1763 William, then a young man of twenty-six, tarried in Dumfries after the December rolling and married Mary Cleland, daughter of the Reverend Thomas Cleland and Mary his wife, who lived near that place. Three of his friends later married three of her sisters, which led years later to geneological complications, for eventually all four of the Cleland sisters came with their families to Kentucky, and Simon's two wives were the daughters of two of them.

With William's marriage and his removal to a farm of his own, Mark Kenton was left with four sons, all too young to take the place of his eldest; his oldest remaining son was but fourteen. He could not advance passage money for an indentured man, and he never owned slaves; he had to resort to the cheapest form of labor obtainable then—the seven years' redemptioner class, convicts sent out to the Colonies from the English prisons, whose services for seven years could be bought for fifteen or twenty dollars. He had them by pairs, mostly Irishmen, and with their aid raised his annual crops.

There is no evidence that during the next eight years Simon did more than chores about the place; he did these, because he did them for his family in Kentucky and Ohio quite naturally in later days. "He would pound enough hominy before day to cook a kettleful," says one of his daughters; from another, "He would not work—except to do chores." "On Lagunda," says another of his relatives, "Simon Kenton used to set bear traps of logs and catch them and cut occasional bee trees, but would never cut rails." "He told me," wrote the Reverend Thomas S. Hinde, "that he had never performed a regular day's labor in his life." One of his old neighbors at Zanesfield, Ohio, relates that Kenton once told him that there came a day when his father told him he must go to work and, giving him an ax, took him out to a tree and directed him to cut it down and make it into rail cuts. When the tree was down and one rail cut off, his father thought it was safe to leave him to finish the task. "No sooner had he disappeared than Simon concluded to sit down on the log and cogitate over the matter. Having a natural aversion to the tame drudgery of farm life and labor, he was not long in coming to the conclusion to which he gave earnest utterance—'Me work? No sir, I'll die first!'"

There are other evidences that he would not yield to the household authorities. He was too young while William lived at home to feel an idler's irritation at that good example, but his brother Mark developed into a responsible young man, an agent of sorts for Richard Graham, their landlord. Dressed one Sunday for the Holy Day and ready to ride away, he ordered Simon to saddle his horse and bring it up for him. Simon obeyed to the final flourish of the letter, but once in the yard, instead of dismounting and giving place to his brother, he whipped up and dashed off, and did not return for several days. He spent the time with some mountain neighbors and reappeared only after he had received word from his exasperated brother that if he returned with the sorely needed horse "he would not be hurt."

Search the old records as we may, there is nothing in the meager reminiscences of his youth to indicate any natural trend toward the life of peril and service he was to live. Nothing but his native gift for the absorption of forest lore. He would not go to school; he would not work; he had not even that fondness for hunting which marks the forest wanderer—he never hunted except from necessity or when it was the most dangerous work. And he seems to have had no sense of responsibility for anything or any one—he who was so soon to become the self-responsible pilot and ranger at large for the yet unplanted settlements of the Middle Ground. As passive an instrument as Nature ever molded to her ends, he moved through fifteen placid, do-less years and, seemingly a rather lonely fledgling in his family, he reached his sixteenth birthday, a tall, lithe, straight, auburn-haired, blue-eyed idler.

But an idler with a purpose for all that. At fifteen Simon had fallen in love and had suffered the humiliation of seeing his sweetheart married to an older man—and a better one. William Leachman had proved his title to that on the day he married Ellen Cummins, for when young Simon suddenly appeared during the wedding festivities and called the

KENTON'S FIRST VICTORY

FROM HARPER'S MAGAZINE, FEBRUARY, 1864.

bridegroom out, he was given a thorough beating in the presence of the entire neighborhood. Smarting under his disgrace, he retired to his temple, the forest, and there made a vow; then he went into private training for the coming combat that would prove him a man.

Shortly after his sixteenth birthday his father sent him across White Rock Ridge to borrow a neighborhood saw from the Leachmans. He found the elder Leachman building an outhouse and the younger one emerging from the forest, carrying the just-riven clapboards for it. The saw he had come for lay in the woods and he and William went back to get it. Once there, Simon, confident by now of his strength and considering this chance setting the best possible one for trying it out, proposed that they settle the old score without delay.

There were no coats to take off and without any preliminaries the famous fight began. It had not gone far before Simon discovered that he had overrated his powers. Once again he was getting the worst of it; he was soon brought to the ground and close to defeat. For a moment he did not struggle but lay passive under the blows, and suddenly one of those instinctive inspirations to unexpected action which always distinguished him was born—he freely admitted always that he would have been "mighty whipped" by Leachman had he not conceived and acted on his bright idea. For, seeing a small sapling not far away, he connected it in his mind's eye with Leachman's long queued hair; if he might but get his enemy's braid wound round the opportune tree, the day was his. So, seemingly still passive under the rain of blows, he began to lure Leachman toward the sapling by the most guileful of little movements, and suddenly with a startling leap knocked him close enough to it to wrap his hair about it.

Then long-suppressed rage had its way—Simon's flashes of terrible anger endured through his life—and he took full revenge for his old humiliation. Before long Leachman was lying senseless, with blood gushing from his mouth and nostrils, and Simon, suddenly brought back to himself, hurriedly released his foe from the sapling and raised him up against it. But Leachman fell limp to the ground and at last, after many futile efforts to revive him, Simon believed him dead.

Late that evening two fathers were searching for their sons. Leachman was discovered in the forest, still unconscious. He was carried home and when recovered enough told his story. But Simon had vanished—it was over twelve years before his parents heard of him again.

When the boy came out of his trance of horror he fled from the forest toward his home, but halfway there realization of his danger came over him. Leachman's father had seen them entering the forest together; sooner or later he would find his son's body and prove Simon the murderer. And again he fell into a trance of panic. He had often been told he would be hanged for the moles on his neck; he had never believed it until now.

He returned forthwith to the forest and lay there in hiding until night fell. Then, without gun or provisions or money, without hat or shoes, and with no clothes except those on his back—"a shirt and a pair of coarse tow linen pantaloons all stained with blood which he washed off with leaves and water"—he began, aged sixteen years and seven days, his westward flight.

Traveling all night, by daylight he had arrived at Ashby's Gap of the Blue Ridge, eighteen miles away, and his daughter Sarah says that when he reached it and paused to take "a longing, lingering look behind," he thought he could still recognize his father's house in the distance, which looked "not larger than a thimble." He stayed in the woods that day without food and traveled the next night. On the second day hunger forced him into the open. He fell in with some men clearing land, one of whom gave him a hat but offered him no food, and he was afraid to speak of his hunger lest he might be suspected of flight. "The next day he came to a cabin where there was a woman and two children—seeing him appearing she barred the door against him . . . she was baking a hoe-cake on an iron bake-oven lid . . . of this he begged a piece, which was generously given him. This was all he got that day."

At one place he worked in a corn field for a day or two, for his food, but his young nerves were so on edge that, seeing a man approaching from the path, he dropped his hoe and fled into the woods, where he remained until hunger again forced him to seek a cabin.

All the facts show that Simon in his flight deliberately planned to evade pursuit and discovery and that he displayed a considerable degree of cunning in choosing his route. For, instead of making directly for Redstone Old Fort by way of Nemacolin's Path and from there to Fort Pitt and the Ohio, he turned almost at right angles and sought the Cheat Valley region as one far less frequented by traders and movers. When he arrived at Warm Springs he had traveled more than one hundred and thirty miles in a southwesterly direction, which took him quite away from the Ohio.

Even on this circuitous route he continued to lie by during the day and to travel at night, for his extreme youth and poverty-stricken appearance made him an object of too curious attention from the few he fell in with. He lived on spring roots and greens and slept on a bed of dry leaves under a blanket of leaves. But the forest fare was meager and hunger pressed him hard. All too often he was forced to knock at some cabin door and ask for food, but the people's curiosity frightened him—he was not yet far enough from home to risk recognition.

And again invention served his necessity. Venturing to stop one day at a cabin for something to eat, he asked the name of the settler a day's journey on, and learning from his host's talk more than a little about the distant neighbor, presented himself there under the man's own name. So much interest was shown in a possible relationship that he sought and gained particulars of the next settler a day's journey on, and presented himself there under that cabiner's name. The little trick worked famously; he soon came to claim some distant relationship with all the families whose names he assumed, finding that they all gladly welcomed him. And thus he changed his name from day to day until at length, says his son William, "he reached one Butler, a clever man who was proud of claiming relationship with Sir Tobey Butler, of the Duke of Ormond's Butler family of Ireland. Butler was pleased with his newly found relative, kept him some time, employed him to work on his mill dam and farm."

This name Simon retained, and for nearly nine years, until he resumed his own proper name, he was known all along the border as "Simon Butler." Old depositions are filled with references to "Simon Butler, now Kenton"; "Simon Kenton, then Butler."

He stayed with his supposed relative until he had earned a gun; then, rested and refreshed and for the first time equipped for the wilderness, he resumed his journey, and near Warm Springs in what is now West Virginia, he met one day a man by the name of Daniel Johnson, "also an exile from his native state" —New Jersey. They fell into talk and soon agreed to pursue their journey together. This was luck for Simon, for Johnson had not only a gun but a pack horse loaded with provisions so abundant that he was not riding it. They took Johnson's course, and from Warm Springs plunged straight north into the Alleghany wilderness to the head of Cheat River. which they followed down until they came to Ice's Ford, not far from its junction with the Monongahela.

Here Simon lingered for some time, working at what he might for the sake of more clothing, more powder, more lead. And more food. And here he fell in with a party of four men, William Grills, Jacob Greathouse, and John Mahon and his brother, who were making ready to descend the Ohio on a hunting trip. Simon joined them eagerly enough, and helped to construct a large canoe in which they set off and descended the Monongahela as far as Provence's settlement in the neighborhood of Fort Pitt. They were all but on the Ohio, when they met with David Duncan, the Indian trader, who told the Mahon brothers that their father, whom the Indians had lately captured, was still alive, and how they could reach him. They immediately departed in search of him, and the hunting trip was abandoned.

Simon remained in the Provence settlement for several months, and probably visited Fort Pitt during that time. But he was back at Provence's in the fall, for then and there he met one day an old man and a young one, John Yeager and George Strader, and Yeager had a trip in mind. He had been captured by the Indians when a child and had lived with them for many years. He could speak several of their languages, knew their ways and their customs, had traveled with them summer and winter, had gone with them on many of their "great hunts" into the Kain-tuck-ee cane-lands. He told the young Simon, still sixteen, of this wondrous land, whose soil was of the richest, whose vegetation was the most luxuriant of all the lands he had ever seen. He retold the old story of Kentucky and its uninhabited lands, free to all who would hunt among its herds of buffalo and elk and deer, too great in number to be imagined. Many years had passed since he had last crossed the great river with the Indians, but he was confident he could guide them to the hunting grounds. He asserted that by going down the Ohio "for a few days" they would reach the old Indian crossing; they would know it bv the cane-lands that bordered the southern shore, and he would know it by the land itself, for the land itself was different from all the rest of the world.

The two boys listened to Yeager, as Boone in Braddock's camp had listened to John Finley, fascinated by the old legend that had fascinated so many others since its spinning days. They were hunters young and skillful; and here was a guide who knew the Indians, the marvelous land, and the ways of both. Without delay they laid their plans: Yeager would guide them to the cane-lands; once there, they would make their camp and he would tend it. They would do the hunting with rifles and traps and bring in the skins which Yeager would dress. When spring came they would carry their skins to the Ohio and be well on the way to fortune. For hunting was no less than fortune where great herds ambled unsuspiciously by an ambuscade.

Preparations for going into the wilderness were as simple in those days as preparations for staying at home. They laid in an extra hunting shirt or two—stout garments of linsey or dressed deerskin with their bosoms sewn as a wallet for carrying all their necessities—jerk, parched corn, tow for wiping the barrel of the rifle, sometimes "plugs"—the long down from turkey buzzards rolled and used for stopping the flow of blood and for dressing wounds. Their thighs were clothed in heavy drawers, which were met by leggins of buckskin, best of all defenses against briars and snakes. Moccasins covered their feet and dry leaves served for stockings. Only their headdress—a gay handkerchief or a cap—distinguished them from the Indians themselves in hunting array.

They built a canoe, filled it with blankets, provisions, ammunition, rifles, and as many traps for winter hunting as they could carry. Then they pushed out onto the Monongahela, bound for the great basin of the Three Forks where Fort Pitt stood. Not until its little stockade faded in the river mists behind them had they really begun their journey down the Ohio to the mysterious Middle Ground.

Chapter III

IN KENTUCKY
1771–1774

AT FIRST wooded hill slopes threaded with dusky water-bearing ravines held the great river to the channel so suddenly widened by the gathered torrents winding down for a thousand miles from the Blue Ridge, the Cumberland, and the Great Smoky. The hills gave way to bottoms and bottoms to palisades and these to hills again; islands thickened before them, and the beauty of the river lured them on, although Yeager's "few days" became weeks and the cane-lands lay still beyond.

They stopped at Logstown, a Shawanese village eighteen miles below Fort Pitt, and stayed a day or two with John Gibson, keeper of a small trading post there. History had been made there before them: twenty years had gone by since George Washington and Christopher Gist had lingered at "Loggestown" five days on their way to the French at Fort Le Bœuf. When the three left this place they left the last white settlement but one behind them, and at Beaver River they reached the apex of the great Northern Bend from whence the Ohio enters upon its great sweep to the southwest.

A little farther down they had Yellow Creek on their right, where even then Logan, the Mingo chief, had his camp; and Baker's Bottom on their left, scene all but set for the infamous murder of Logan's family. This would not be the cause, but it would be the precipitating incident for bringing on Lord Dunmore's war in which Simon Kenton was to play his part with George Rogers Clark, Simon Girty, and Daniel Boone. Already the meetings of these men in the Western wilderness were in the river air.

Seventy miles below Fort Pitt they hid their canoe and took a trail inland—for directions. "The Mingoes," said Kenton to Judge James in 1832, when the latter took his notes of their talks, "had a town at the Mingo Bottoms. No town on the Ohio in sight of a voyage down it." Arrived at the village, they lingered again and, "as it was a time of peace, they frolicked and danced with the young Indians."

They floated past Wheeling where Ebenezer Zane had just erected his fort—this was the literal frontier. But no more than twenty-five years were to pass before Zane was to cut his great road, "Zane's Trace," from this now frontier outpost to old Limestone in Kentucky, almost the foot of Kenton's Station, not only wagon but United States mail route from East to West.

They went by Big Grave Creek, incurious concerning the great mound beside it--sepulcher of the bones of an ancient Indian host fallen in one of the ancient battles for possession of the land; and they passed the hill through which broke Pipe Creek, again scene all but set for another slaughter of inoffensive Shawanese which would light another fire of anger for the Dunmore war.

They came to Captina Island, and to Captina

Creek where Washington had been the year before, where Clark and the missionary Jones were to be the year after, from where in less than three years Simon was to set out on his first Indian expedition into Ohio. At Graveyard Run on the Virginia side Clark was soon to make his first stake west of the Alleghanies; blaze a few trees, plant a little corn, do a little surveying for his neighbors, and in the evenings teach their children in a cabin on Fish Creek a few miles below.

They passed the mouth of the Muskingum where in 1749 Celeron with his little band of French soldiers had sunk one of his leaden plates on the western bank—"at the foot of a maple which forms a triangle with a red oak and an elm"—in his vain endeavor to turn English traders out of the Ohio Valley and to establish the right of the French king there; where in 1785 Fort Harmar was to be planted to turn the English and Indians out of the Ohio Valley and to establish the right of the United States there; where General Rufus Putnam and his band of Revolutionary veterans were to land from their clumsy flat boats three years later to found Marietta, "the Plymouth Rock of the West."

"The Delawares had a town near little Kenawha," said Kenton. It lay three miles below, and here again they stopped and "passed a few days very agreeably, hunting, fishing and dancing with the Indians." It was Simon's best possible introduction to the country and its people, for Yeager knew them and their language and Simon's young mind, like wax for receiving impressions, was again "going to school." This time it was not the school of Nature but the school of talk, the schoolmaster a plain frontiersman who had graduated from the Indian camps but who was as unconscious of teaching as his pupils were of learning. Under him Simon began to absorb the technic of savage art, and through it there developed in him a latent sixth sense that savages have—acute awareness of what passes—a latent seventh sense of prevision which was no more than taking into account all the probabilities that lay just ahead. The old woodsmen had these lost senses of man revived in them by the constant sense of danger and death. They slept on their guns; they were always prepared.

Simon's fear of the hangman had so unified his scattered forest lore that he made a brilliant escape from Virginia. Now, safe from the noose, he was in constant danger from the Indians, and he began to take on their coloration and arts—learned how to blend himself with a tree trunk and to stand as still; how to stalk a brush-strewn trail without cracking a twig; how to discriminate between the swaying movement of a bush stirred by the wind and one disturbed by a lurking enemy; how to move through the forest undergrowth more like air than a man; how to lie in ambush as stirless and as watchful as a snake; how to fight like a general and a private at once, in command of himself and obedient to his own command; how to read the subtlest message left by enemy or friend on the surface of the earth.

Here and now he began to acquire that characteristic habit of his which endured through his years, of keeping his eyes "generally directed to the ground, frequently interrupted by rapid glances which seemed like a flash to sweep the horizon and to include every object within the scope of his vision." Even when the Indian warpath and forest trail had given way to village and city streets, he continued to walk silently along them and to scan them as he walked. Even when none but neighbors surrounded him, he continued to interrupt his groundward glance with a quick survey of all that was about him, and then resume his careful noting of his "trail." The habit of forty-two years of constant alertness was not to be broken in the years that remained.

Since leaving the Muskingum, they had been passing interminable river bottoms, whose gently sloping beaches of sand or pebbles were sometimes barren, sometimes green and gold and red and purple with clumps of turned willow and maple, scrub oak and sycamore. The hills were fewer and not so high; they were set farther back and the river began to be studded with islands. Indian summer lay over the land and their campfire smoke blended night and morning with the autumnal haze of the low hills and hollows. Among the little islands they passed a large one—Blennerhasset; for nearly four miles they drifted by it. It was only forest then, but in less than a generation a great mansion was to rise there, filled with "French furniture and paintings and statuary"; where astronomy with a telescope and chemistry with a laboratory and "galvanism" with its new tools were to be the amusements of its rich young owner; where every traveler of importance coming down the Ohio was to be entertained; and where "culture" first nested in the West.

They came to the Big Hockhocking from whose mouth Lord Dunmore—with Simon along—was to march to the Pickaway plains at the end of his war and there conclude the treaty to which Logan, the Mingo chief, had refused his consent. Here began the Ohio palisades, springing fifty to sixty feet high from a wide, forested terrace, which dropped sharply in its turn to a boulder-strewn beach. The palisades darkened the river and the three floated in the far-flung shadows until they came to the south-sweeping Pomeroy Bend which for forty miles to come would be a swift succession of smaller bends twisting backward and forward upon each other too swiftly for more than dissolving views. They skimmed safely over Letart's Falls—rushing rapids between rugged shores. They passed Antiquity with its ageless rock carved by Indian hands and went by the mouth of the Great Kanawha, all ignorant that within a few weeks they would establish their camp there and there live until disaster overtook them.

But they had not reached the Kentucky lands until they passed the mouth of the Big Sandy. They began to float by great clay banks from which gushed countless springs, came to the Scioto, which Simon was to know so well, and, skirting the edges of the Three Islands, arrived at last at Limestone Creek—insignificant little stream but the future goal of countless pioneers and scene of Simon Kenton's greatest activities. Here, had they but known it, the cane-lands began, but for miles to come they lay inland; Yeager's Indian crossing that met the canebrake on the shore was still more than one hundred and fifty miles beyond them.

So they passed the hidden cane-lands by and a few miles below entered upon the Great Bend, another series of little bends so brief that pictures faded before they were seen. They floated by Snag Creek and Locust and Bullskin—all future scenes of Simon's forays, past the Little Miami which he was to know as well as Limestone, past Licking River and Cincinnati's hill, past Big Bone Creek, and after more than half a thousand miles of river travel arrived at last at the Kentucky's mouth, without finding any cane.

Only a few miles farther and they would have come upon the cane-lands they were seeking. But by this time Yeager's sense of distance was all awry, and with winter coming on they decided to return and note the southern shore more carefully, Yeager insisting they must have passed the canebrake in the night. So they turned upstream and, the weather continuing favorable, they stopped at various points to explore—at Licking, Bracken, Locust, Salt Lick and Kinnikinnick creeks, at Little and Big Sandy and Guyondotte, still seeking for the cane-lands but never finding them.

Winter was almost upon them when they reached the mouth of the Great Kanawha. They turned up that stream therefore and ascended it to the mouth of Elk River. Here they found a deeply worn buffalo trail which led them along the Kanawha to the salt spring. The location suited them; it was not too far from the Ohio to reach it in time of danger and it was at the same time far enough removed from Indians passing on it; they were close to a great game trail which would give them plenty of food and furs, and the luxury of the salt spring they could share with the forest animals.

So near the mouth of Elk River they erected their

shelter, a half-faced camp than which no better primitive quarters have been invented to this day. They found their huge fallen tree, cleared a square in front of it large enough for the cabin floor, and at the far

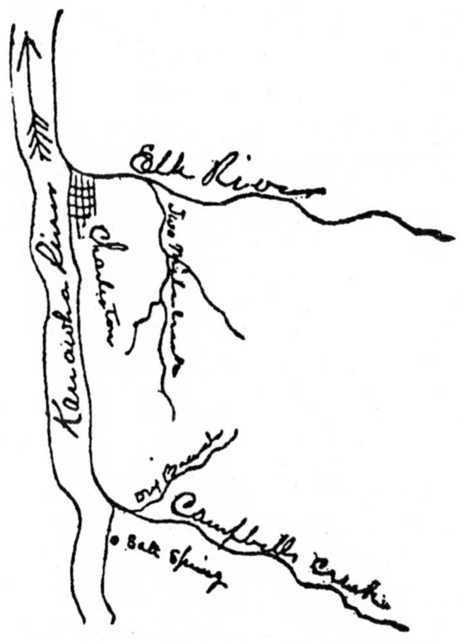

PLAT OF THE VICINITY OF SIMON KENTON'S HUNTING CAMP ON ELK RIVER, 1771-1773 FROM THE ORIGINAL BY J. P. HALE IN DRAPER MANUSCRIPTS,—IBB44

corners sunk two forked poles. They laid a twelve-foot pole in the forks, and laid other poles from it to the fallen tree. They piled this roof foundation with brush, dry grass, leaves, and sod, enclosed the two sides with bark and heaped logs, gathered moss and dry leaves for their beds, and their camp was done. Before its wide-open face they built their campfire, cooked their meals in the open, and at night lay down to sleep wrapped in blankets and furs with their bodies under shelter and their feet to the coals.

They made good killings that winter, and in the spring they heaped their skins in their canoe and went down to the Ohio where they waited for a trader to pass. With him, when he came, they bartered, exchanged their furs for clothing, ammunition, and corn, and then went back to the Elk where they lived another year in safety.

But sooner or later the Indians would come—it was the forest law. One day in March, 1773, Simon and Strader set out to pay their regular round of visits to their traps, and toward evening brought in what they had found, along with a fine turkey to roast for their supper. It was rainy and cold and they first dried their guns, wrapped them in blankets, and stacked them in the cabin out of the rain. Then they sat down at the cabin's edge before the evening fire, and while the turkey roasted on its pole above the blaze, they took off their leggins and moccasins and began to steam them slowly dry. Yeager was standing before his roasting fowl, clearly outlined by the fire, when suddenly the three, as one man, saw several Indians a few rods away, with their guns raised and in the act of firing. The two young men sprang to their feet; one named a place to meet and both then ran for their lives.

Just as they fled around the cabin the guns fired and Yeager was probably shot. Simon related that while he was running he cast a hasty glance back and saw Yeager take a step toward the Indians, either bewildered on account of a wound or with the intention of speaking to them in their own tongue and making quick surrender. But, said Simon, the Indians were close upon him and their tomahawks were raised.

Late that night the two fugitives met. They were without guns, without clothing except the shirts on their backs, and without provisions. But they did not dare return to their cabin; the Indians had not pursued—there was enough plunder in the camp to interest them—but they might linger. So the two set out as they were, barefooted and legginless, through the March woods toward the Ohio.

For three days they directed their route by the sun or the trees: "The moss on the north side of trees grows higher than on the other," said Kenton. "By them I could steer my course on cloudy days." But by the end of the third day their strength began to fail. The barren forests had yielded them nothing beyond a few roots; but they had passed the stage of ravenous hunger; exhaustion was taking its place. Their feet by then had become so inflamed from cuts and bruises that walking was agony, and their legs were raw from thorns and briars. Although they were sure they were then near the Ohio—and were indeed within six miles of it—they spent all of two days in covering that distance, for their feet were useless. Much of the time they lay exhausted on the ground, gathering strength—gathering desire even for strength—to crawl another few yards on their hands and knees.

At the end of the fifth day they crossed a path—"a trail where sugar water had been hauled"—and fortunately chose the turn that brought them within sight of a cabin, probably about six miles above the mouth of the Great Kanawha. Here they found a man and his wife who took the exhausted hunters in, and while the host supplied them with clothing from his scanty wardrobe, their hostess prepared food and fed them sparingly in spite of their ravenous cries for more. "Often," says John Arrowsmith, grand-nephew of Kenton and most reliable of witnesses, "have I heard him express his gratitude to that lady for her kindness, judgment, care, and control she exercised over them in that case. He said they would have eaten so much it would have killed them if they could have had their own way."[1]

At the mouth of the Kanawha at this time were six or seven canoes of explorers under the command of Joel Reese, among them William Grills, Jacob Greathouse, and the two Mahon brothers whom Kenton had met at Ice's Ford two years before and with whom he was to have made his first descent of the Ohio. The Mahons had returned from their search after their father and had come down with Reese. When this party learned from Simon and Strader of the Indian attack on their camp, it was immediately

---

[1]Kenton's two daughters, Mrs. Sarah Kenton McCord and Mrs. Elizabeth Kenton Thornton, and John Arrowsmith also, unite in giving this story of Kenton's rescue, which Taylor, McClung, and McDonald ascribe to traders or explorers on the Ohio. There is no difficulty in reconciling all the accounts except, as Dr. Draper points out, the matter of "the woman in the cabin, whether there was any woman at all." For there is no record of any white woman living on this part of the Ohio at this time. Some adventurous woman, however, may have escaped the notice of diarists and chroniclers of that time, and have been really on the spot. In any case, the family stories of this incident are firm and clear in their details.

decided to go down no farther but to ascend to the mouth of the Little Kanawha where Dr. Briscoe was attempting to make a settlement. Simon went up with them, and in order to get another rifle became hunter for the settlement there and worked out its price. By May it was paid for and he was again ready to join another exploring party.

They were coming fast now and he had his choice. Three groups of adventurers were at the Great Kanawha about to descend and Simon joined the first one, commanded by Dr. John Wood and Hancock Lee and numbering fourteen men. They lingered on their way, agreeing, said Kenton, "at the mouth of Tygert to survey and build cabins on to the mouth of Big Sandy. We proceeded on until we built one apiece."

The explorations continued throughout the trip. They were to have met Thomas Bullitt's party at the Scioto, but had word through the third party—the McAfees who passed them on the river—to meet him instead at the Little Miami. When they reached there they found his camp deserted, and supposing him taken by the Indians they turned promptly back. At the Three Islands they themselves narrowly escaped an Indian party, and going quickly on shore they abandoned their canoes and set out overland for Virginia, a trip never undertaken from this point before.

Simon, then aged eighteen, piloted the party through the wilderness.

It was a great feat for a boy with so little experience, and it won him no small fame on the border. The journey was long and fatiguing; at one time they had to halt for two weeks, waiting for Dr. Wood to recover from the bite of a copperhead snake. Food was scarce and they were out of luck in finding game from the beginning to the end of the trip. They lived on wild onions and young roots for the most part. Simon had his first taste on this journey of what the Indians esteemed a great delicacy, roasted wild turkey eggs just on the hatch. He had come triumphantly in with his catch; the contents surprised the feasters, but hunger prevailed over habit, and "Kenton used to say he had never had anything that relished so sweetly." It was all heavy going but the young pilot surmounted all the difficulties of illness, hunger, fatigue, and discouragement, and in the end brought his companions in safety to Greenbriar County.

He himself was not disposed to linger there—it was too near his home and the dreaded arm of justice to suit him. So he made again for the Monongahela country and there met for the third time with Greathouse, Grills, and the Mahons. They were planning another winter hunt along the Ohio, and again Simon joined in. Before they had their boat built two other adventurers, Samuel Cartwright and Joseph Lock, decided to go along. So seven men in a boat floated down the river until they came to the little string of cabins near the Big Sandy. There they settled and trapped and hunted through the winter and into the spring.

But by the spring of 1774 the Indians were restless and hostile, and though the little hunting camp on Big Sandy was left unmolested, the raids on the frontier became increasingly frequent. Doubtless an Indian war was inevitable, but if ever an Indian war was provoked by the whites Lord Dunmore's was.

He had his reasons and the clever initiating maneuvers took just six days. On April 25th he called on his local militia commandant, John Connolly, to embody men. On April 26th Connolly issued a letter to the borderers which amounted to a declaration of war against the Indians. On April 27th came the killing of two friendly Shawanese near Pipe Creek by Michael Cresap's party, among whom was Clark. It was then proposed to march against Chief Logan's camp at Yellow Creek and destroy it, but Logan was so well known as a friend of the whites that after a little discussion Cresap and Clark became ashamed of the project and abandoned it. On April 30th Logan's entire family was shamelessly massacred at Baker's Bottom by Daniel Greathouse and a large party of borderers. Kenton always stated most emphatically that Cresap, whose projected march against Logan's camp gave him for years the blame for the massacre, was not responsible for it. "I knew Cresap well," he told Judge James. "That family was killed by Baker and Greathouse."

The slaughter was complete: "There runs not a drop of my blood in the veins of any living creature," said Logan in his famous speech. Over night he changed from a friend to an avenger as cold as any inciter of an Indian war could have wished. His call to his warriors traveled like a prairie fire; it reached even the little hunting camp on Big Sandy. One McMahon had been out with some traders into Ohio after lost horses. "He gave me the word of the war breaking out," Kenton said to Judge James, "and we went back to Thomas's Fort together."

Chapter IV

LORD DUNMORE'S WAR
1774

SIMON KENTON was not the only one who went back to the fortified settlements in the spring of 1774. On his way up the river to Thomas's Fort he stopped at the Fish Creek settlement where Clark had been living. But it was deserted—all the cabiners' groups along the river had broken and scattered with the word that the Indians were rising. He went on to Ten Mile Creek and thence pushed on to Fort Pitt, arriving there some time in May.

His first contacts with people began here. And here, in McDonald's campaign and the Dunmore war, were laid the foundations for his two most enduring friendships. His range of affection was wide to have included in it the greatest general and the most famous white renegade of the West, but George Rogers Clark and Simon Girty were the two men in his life for whom his feeling of friendship was strongest.

"The first of my seeing George Rogers Clark," he dictated at the beginning of his Manuscript Statement, "was on the Ohio. Then, in 1774, we embodied at Fort Pitt. I had not much acquaintance with him until McDonald's (an old Brittoner) campaign—then he had Strother Crawford and several others whipped for telling the truth on him. This was at Becket's [Prickett's] Fort. I had some acquaintance with him which caused me to take notice of Clark."

Simon's first military experience was on McDonald's campaign against the Muskingum Indians, which set out early in June. "Jake Drennon and I," said Kenton to James, "were requested to raise a company; we did so, but afterwards acted as spies." Too bad he did not go into more detail as to the mustering of his company—the "truth" some of the men told on Clark remains one of the mysteries of history. It would appear, however, that he and Drennon failed to raise a full company; that the men who volunteered under them were incorporated into Clark's company with Kenton and Drennon acting as spies; that some of these men, including Strother Crawford, raised a tumult which Clark promptly put down, and that his technic in quelling revolt caused young Simon to "take notice" of him very particularly.

McDonald assembled his four hundred men at Wheeling, took them down in boats to Captina, and from there began his march inland through ninety miles of unbroken forest. It was Simon's first spying trip in Ohio.

Within five or six miles of the chief Indian town they came upon an ambuscade of half a hundred warriors and suffered a loss of two men killed and eight or ten wounded before they pressed on. By the time they reached the town the Indians there had deserted it and were lying in wait on the other side of the stream for the whites to cross over. But Simon and Drennon came on signs which showed where they had crossed, and detected them where they lay. Then the Indians sued for peace, but so many symptoms of treachery developed that McDonald burned their several towns along the Muskingum and destroyed all their crops.

Simon's feats of courage and daring on this campaign were so notable as to cause both McDonald and Clark to "take notice" of him. And Lord Dunmore likewise. For he promptly selected the nineteen-year-old boy, new figure on the border, to serve as spy in his coming campaign, and Clark also, along with experienced men like Cresap, Girty, Parchment, and others.

"In 1774," said Kenton to Judge James, "I was a Brittoner, and took the oath of allegiance at Fort Pitt."

Dunmore's plan to raise an army in two equal divisions, the experienced militia under him, the inexperienced backwoodsmen under Andrew Lewis, just exactly resulted, as matters fell out, in frustrating one of his aims in provoking the Indian war. He had intended to turn the restless colonists' attention from their grievances against England to troubles nearer home. He succeeded for a time, but not for long. For Lewis's men fought and won the Point Pleasant battle while Dunmore's wing lay inactive on the Pickaway plains. It was no more than a "pick-up" army, raw recruits every one as far as military discipline went, but every man of them a fighter from his heels to his head. Not a man—not even an officer—was uniformed; each wore his ordinary clothing—leggins and pantaloons of rough wool or buckskin, coarse hunting shirt and home-made cap of fur or of wool;

each carried his own weapons—rifle, tomahawk, and scalping knife; each rode his own horse or used his own legs; each was out to fight the Indians in the only way—the Indian way—and each knew that way. They made their own roads, transported their own provisions—beeves, flour, and salt—constructed their own canoes, and at the end of five weeks and one hundred and sixty miles of steady marching to the Elk River they knew how to move an army through the wilderness. At the end of the campaign Lewis's men knew that they *were* an army, and as the news of their victory filtered slowly through the Colonies, it strengthened instead of lessened the Colonists' resentment against their wrongs. It gave them confidence in their ability to rout a foe, whether redskin or red coat. The battle of Point Pleasant was fought for the crown, but as far as its effect upon the colonists went, it almost might be called the first battle in the Revolution.

During this period of preparation Simon had his single unfortunate experience of being held under suspicion as an enemy spy. Connolly sent him and two others with despatches to Lewis at the West Fork of the Monogahela, but on their way they were surprised and fired upon by Indians and became separated. Not finding Simon, the other two gave up their mission and returned to Connolly, but Simon went on by himself to Lowther's Fort and delivered the messages. When he appeared alone on so dangerous a mission, Lewis did not believe the account he gave of himself and had him detained at the fort until his own express could be sent to Connolly to discover the truth. Upon the messenger's return Simon was of course at once released and made his way back alone to Fort Pitt.[1]

Dunmore could have selected no spy better equipped than Simon to carry his last two most important messages to Lewis on the eve of the battle. For Lewis and his men were encamped at the mouth of the Great Kanawha, in a region which Simon knew as he knew his hand. These messages were insistent ones, for Lewis had already showed initiative by carrying out his first orders in the face of Dunmore's change of meeting place; he had already written Dunmore that it was too late to change his route from the Great to the Little Kanawha, that he would go on to Point Pleasant as first directed and would await further orders there.

Simon, Girty, and Peter Parchment left Dunmore's camp in September with orders to Lewis to come immediately up the river to the mouth of the Big Hockhocking. But Lewis had not yet reached Point Pleasant, so they left the despatches "by advertisment" in a hollow tree and returned with this word to Dunmore. Lewis reached the Point on October 6th with two detachments of men, and when he found and read the despatches he again disregarded them. His men were exhausted; it would be folly to leave before stockades for the beeves and provisions were built; folly likewise to leave before his third detachment arrived.

---

[1]In McDonald's sketch of Kenton he places this incident later—in October and at Point Pleasant, just before the decisive battle. But Kenton was on his way back to Dunmore then and he was also present at the Camp Charlotte treaty held later in the month. His arrest was prior to the campaign and possibly occurred in the last days of April or during May when the Dunmore war was in its hatching phase.

Two days later Simon, Girty, and one McCulloch appeared at Point Pleasant with reiterated orders from Dunmore for Lewis to join him on the Ohio side, eighty miles above. Lewis, angered, refused to go then. His men were still exhausted; his stockades were not built; his last detachment had not come up; to leave this place would be to leave the Virginia frontier open to the savages, and the Indian towns they had come to attack lay comparatively near. Under all these conditions he would not move, and Simon and his companions left the camp that night to carry back his decision. They thus missed the battle. The next day was Sunday, and Lewis and his army listened to "preaching" and continued to rest their tired bodies. Early the next morning Cornstalk and his thousand warriors surprised them, and the single battle of "Lord Dunmore's war" was fought and decisively won by Lewis's backwoods Americans.

Exactly one year before the battle of Point Pleasant, while Boone with his own and other families was traveling through Powell's Valley on his way to Kentucky, his eldest son James and a little squad of men were cruelly tortured and finally slain by a band of Cherokees and Shawanese. Most of the party returned to their homes, but Boone took his family on to Clinch River, and from there was despatched the following June with Michael Stoner into Kentucky to warn surveying parties in the interior that the Indians were out. He reached Harrodsburg, where James Harrod and thirty men were making improvements and erecting Kentucky's first station, paused for a day to make an improvement of his own, and then followed the string of surveyors to the Falls of the Ohio.

On his return to Clinch River he was prepared to join the Dunmore campaign, but instead stayed behind to defend the settlements there. In Lord Dunmore's speech at Fort Pitt he spoke of the tragedy of Powell's Valley as one of the inciting causes of the Indian war—which of course it was not. But at the Camp Charlotte treaty in October some of the year-old plunder of this massacre was delivered up—so far from Powell's Valley had it been carried by the roving raiders.

The Western wilderness, so trackless, so immense, had nevertheless its points of contact so coincidental that it sometimes came to seem to the children of fortune who roamed them that meetings in it were not born of accident but of some great design. Kenton's later captivity with the Indians was so marked by such coincidences as to appear afterward to him and to everyone a perfect series of fortuitous happenings. Some of them had their beginnings in the Dunmore war.

For at Fort Pitt he met the first of the men who were to rescue him from the stake—Simon Girty. At the Camp Charlotte treaty he met the second—Logan, the Mingo chief; he heard there Logan's famous speech, beginning, "I appeal to any white man to say, if he ever entered Logan's cabin hungry and he gave him not meat; if he ever came cold and hungry and he clothed him not." Four years later, on his way to Sandusky to be burned, Kenton was to lie two nights in Logan's cabin, fed and warmed and clothed by him and eventually saved through him. His fourth rescuer, raised up by Logan, he was not to meet until he appeared upon the final scene, clothed in scarlet and gold and great with authority. His third rescuer he always called the "grace of God."

But his first rescuer he always called a "good man." Strange words for the border's super-hero to say of the border's super-villain. Yet the Kenton Papers are filled with contemporary comments on Simon Girty which throw a new light on the man who has been so blackly painted in the border annals. Not only Kenton spoke well of him.

Their friendship was an extraordinary one, cemented by a curious pledge which, as Kenton told it, bears all the marks of some fraternal ritual: "Girty and I, two lonely men on the banks of the Ohio, pledged ourselves one to the other, hand in hand, for life or death, when there was no body in the wilderness but God and us."

Kenton heard from Girty the full story of his youth, of his capture and adoption by the Senecas, and of his life with them for eight years. Ten years before the Dunmore war he was surrendered to the English, and from that time on he was one of their Indian interpreters—evidently a good one, for his pay was a dollar a day. Trusted spy in the Dunmore war, he took the year after it the oath of allegiance to the British king. But in 1776 he was receiving "five-eighths of a dollar per diem" from the Continental Congress to interpret for the Six Nations at Fort Pitt. At the end of three months he was discharged for "ill behavior," but the ill behavior was evidently not serious enough to destroy the Americans' trust in him, for in February, 1778, he took part in General Hand's "squaw campaign" against the British and the Indians.

He had suffered a brief imprisonment the year before, when Alexander McKee's machinations with the British were being investigated and Girty was suspected of being involved in the plot. He made his escape from the guard house, just to show them, he affirmed, that he could, but returned voluntarily the next day and was again locked up. He was afterward examined and fully acquitted of the charge.

But on his return from Hand's campaign he was approached by McKee who was preparing to desert to Hamilton at Detroit, and was persuaded to join the deserters. On the 28th of March, 1778, McKee, Matthew Elliot, Girty, and a few others slipped out of Fort Pitt and made their way West. Girty's services from them on were with the British posts in the West, not with the Indians, and were largely those of an interpreter.

Kenton and Girty met rarely after their early Fort Pitt days. There is some evidence that they saw each other again there just before Girty's desertion, and that Girty told Kenton, if not his purpose, at least all his grievances against the Americans. Had it not been for Dr. Knight's "eye witness" account of Girty's behavior when William Crawford was burned at the stake six years later, Girty's name might never have been known in border annals except as the heroic rescuer of Simon Kenton. That was the beginning of his ill fame. Girty had lived with Crawford, but he was represented as brutally refusing to make any attempt at rescuing him and as watching with glee the slow process of torture. Nothing could have saved Crawford—his captors were avenging a massacre of their people as savage as that of Logan's family. But many papers in the Draper manuscripts go to show that Girty behaved in this case as in Kenton's; that he did, that is, all he could—offered property in the Indian councils for Crawford's release, and when that was refused tried to plan for his escape the night before he was burned. Mrs. McCormick, another of the prisoners who with Dr. Knight and all the others was compelled to witness Crawford's torture, defended all of Girty's actions then to the end of her life, said that he really did everything a mortal man could do to save Crawford. Another old manuscript narrative of the period—Jonathan Alder's—bears like testimony to his treatment of captives: "I have known Simon Girty to purchase at his own expense several boys who were prisoners, take them to the British, and have them educated. He was certainly a friend to many prisoners."

Kenton began to defend his friend then. But Girty's place in border history was soon fixed by the vivid writers of it. Canadian and British historians speak of him as "a refugee loyalist" but this page would be too short to list all the brief and simple terms by which American writers have described him. He was called devil, fiend, ghoul and butcher; he was "the notorious white renegade," "a man turned beast," "a creature so vile that even vileness disowned him and hid her face."

But Kenton's friendship never faltered. When he went to the Thames on his last campaign he broke off for a day "on his own" and visited Girty's home near Malden. But Girty was away and Kenton, brief deserter of a day for old friendship's sake, could not linger; he must catch up with his mess and go on.

He never saw Girty again, but he never forgot him, always spoke good of him, and to his latest years defended him. In his conversations with Judge James he mentioned Girty's name more often than Clark's; he seemed to be making an effort to explain his old friend through all his desultory two days' talk.

"Simon Girty was taken prisoner at the Little Cove at six years old," he said, "and in 1764 was brought back under Bouquet's treaty, when he was nineteen. The father and mother were killed—five sons, Jack, Thomas, Simon, George and James—the last three were prisoners and all raised as Indians—James more of an Indian than Simon.

"First knew Girty in 1774. Had seen him passing about before. Simon lived with Crawford—sometimes at Pitt and wherever he could get a living.

"Simon and McKee both joined us in the Dunmore war.

"Girty lived at Malden, became blind before his death, and died about the time of Harrison and Shelby's expedition.

"Sol. McCulloch was well acquainted with Simon Girty from 1800 to 1804, at which time he lived one mile below Malden and had a farm; he had two children, a daughter of eighteen, who married a Frenchman, and a son of 14. They were children of a white woman whom Girty had captured, but did not then live with her. He was then lame, from having had his thigh broke. He was the bravest looking man I ever saw—is said never to have had a wound. He lived here until the British evacuated Malden, when he went off. Was blind many years. He was an interpreter and received $1 per day from

British Government—could speak more Indian languages than any man I ever heard of. He was very friendly and kind to all Americans whom he had known or previously met with.

"James Girty had known me as well as any man could know another; but when he saw me a captive and about to be bound, he did not know me; while Simon was very kind to me and never ceased his efforts.

"Simon Girty told me he had been an Ensign, and was put in a guard house for being charged with having intercourse with the Indians; he said he left, that he could no longer remain with them. He was a man of sensitive feelings.

"McKee was a Pennsylvanian by birth, and looked as if of Indian descent. He was Indian agent at Fort Pitt.

"What became of him? Why, that was a kind of witchery business, as the Indians would think. He had a pet deer, and it came into his bedroom as he was rising from bed, and as he was drawing on his pantaloons, it ran at him, piercing his thigh with the tines of his horns, and producing death in a very short time.

"Solomon McCulloch was in Detroit in 1800 and witnessed a funeral dance in honor of McKee, composed of several hundred Indians, commenced in the morning and continued until next day. Young McKee, then a Capt. in the British army—a large man about 6 feet 3, with other officers joined in it. The death had then passed about three years before. Girty told him (McCulloch)that as long as he had been with the Indians, this was the third dance of the kind he had witnessed. They are made only for men of distinction among them.

"Girty often talked to him about his adventures, and the tears would roll down his cheeks and his voice be choked at a recurrence to some of the events in which he had been an actor. He had saved the lives of hundreds by diverting and restraining the Indians.

"Girty was anxious to see his brother Thomas who lived near Pittsburgh. McCulloch proposed to take him in disguise, but the dread of being hanged restrained him.

"The reason assigned for his becoming an enemy of the whites was the injustice done him in promoting an officer over [him] and refusing him the advancement to which he claimed of right to be entitled. The refusal was coupled with charges of secret intercourse with the Indians, and afterwards he was in some way imprisoned and guarded to prevent an escape, after which he told him he should certainly join them and be an enemy of his countrymen.

"In his last days he was very intemperate, and it was on this account that he and his wife did not live together. She bore a good character.

"Girty was a short thick-set man; piercing black eyes, black hair. He claimed that he had made every effort in his power to save Col. Crawford; and was finally answered by the Shawanoe chief, that it could be on one condition, that he should take Crawford's place at the stake. He then went for McKee, who had more influence than any other, but McKee was not in reach, and he went away to avoid seeing the sacrifice. But Dr. Knight says he was there and must be believed in preference."

Chapter V

HE FINDS THE CANE-LANDS OF KENTUCKY

1775

BACK again at Fort Pitt, Kenton received his discharge from the king's service—as Simon Butler, of course—and put up at David Duncan's tavern while he nursed his purpose and cast about for a man to help him carry it out.

His purpose was to find the fabled cane-lands of Kentucky. His fancy had been caught four years before by Yeager's tales of their marvels. Perhaps they were only tales. The search had been fruitless and Yeager was dead, but the fancy to find them persisted. For the time being he had enough of being one of a party; too many minds at work on a problem hindered the free work of one. This trip, his fourth descent, he would make on his own and feel his way after his own fashion. The search would be a blind one but he would make it unhurried.

He found his man in Thomas Williams, good hunter, good woodsman, with the good qualities of persistence and acquiescence. So in the late fall they embarked to float down what was now a dangerous river.

For two hundred miles and more it was the same story—no cane-lands. At Letart's Falls, however, they found a French trader who confirmed Yeager's glowing story and described the mouth of Limestone

Creek into which they were to turn and moor their canoe, then go inland a few miles until they came to a rise of ground where the cane-lands began. They went on, therefore, for nearly two hundred miles more, to within a few miles of Limestone, but, mistaking Cabin Creek for it, they halted at that stream and went inland—to find no rise of ground and no cane-land. Reëmbarking, they passed Limestone unnoticed and went down as far at Locust Creek where they stopped and explored for some days. Then, winter coming on, they turned their canoe up river and made for the mouth of the Big Sandy. There once again, on its Kentucky bank a few miles back from the Ohio, Kenton put up his camp, set his traps, and settled down for another winter of hunting.

Returning to the Ohio early next spring with his harvest of furs, he and Williams fell in again with the French trader they had met the fall before, who insisted that the cane-lands began near Limestone Creek and redescribed its shore line with all the details he could muster. Kenton listened intently and redrew his little mental map of the location. Then he exchanged his skins for supplies enough to last through many months, took corn for planting as well as parching, and for the fifth time descended the river.

He recognized the mouth of Limestone one afternoon: every detail of tree and sky line tallied; here too was the "point" stretching into the water—a landing port made by nature, "the best on the river." By the time they had made their camp it was late for exploring but Kenton's eagerness would not be restrained. In the late afternoon, under pretence of hunting, he set off alone up the creek for a mile or two, broke off toward the setting sun, came to rising ground, and soon found himself on the edge of the canebrake whose great dry stalks towered to double his height and whose young green ones were climbing swiftly to meet them. While he was surveying his new domain a young doe came by; he killed it and took it back to camp for supper, celebrating the end of his search with his favorite food: "the hams of a young deer were the best eating he ever enjoyed."

Now he took his leisure, explored at his pleasure and wandered about for several days seeking the finest location. But in the end he made his permanent camp near the spot where he first found the canebrake. And a permanent camp it was, even though he fled it twice and for eight years abandoned it. He hung about it; few months passed without his being somewhere in this region. He made it his crossing place for numberless Indian raids, always kept it in mind as the best of all sites for a station, and finally returned to put up his blockhouse there and there play his part during the last ten years of the Indian war.

So on the sixty-foot elevation above the two Right Hand Forks of Lawrence's Creek, about four miles from Limestone, near a fine large spring that gushed from the hillside, he and Williams cleared an acre of land in the center of the canebrake, erected a half-faced camp, and with some of the corn got from the Frenchman took "planting possession" of what was to be Mason County: they raised the first crop of corn ever cultivated by white men north of the Kentucky River.

As the days went on they established "tomahawk

rights" to their lands by girdling a few trees at the corners of the tract about their cabin and corn patch. With their tomahawks they tended their corn until it leafed, tasseled, and eared. Beside roasting ears and the roasted hams of young deer, they had their choice of birds and fish, and now and then caught a bear whose feet, roasted all night in hot ashes, turned by morning into the "richest conceivable delicacy." They had berries and fruits and could look forward to bread again—to hominy at least—when fall came and the corn hardened on the ear.

They widened their explorations of the country, marveling as they wandered that so rich a land was uninhabited. "The Indians," Kenton told James, "never made but two settlements in Kentucky—one on Slate Creek, and one at a place called Lul-bel-grud; and at both places they raised corn; what the name Lul-bel-grud came from I never heard, but it was named by Finley and Boone. I don't know how long ago it was, but the locust is a thrifty growth in Kentucky, and the trees were big enough to make ten rails, and the corn hills were plain to be seen there. They put mighty big hills to their corn."

What the name "Lul-bel-grud" came from is told in one of Boone's depositions.

> . . . in the year 1770, [he said (September 15, 1796)] I encamped on Red River with five other men, and we had with us for our amusement the History of Samuel Gulliver's Travels, whence he gave an account of his young master, Glumdelick, careing him on a market day for a show to a town called Lulbegrad.
>
> A young man of our camp called Alexander Neely, came to my camp one night and told us that he had been that day to Lulbegrad and had killed two Broddigings in their capital.

So it was that Lulbegrud Creek was named and so it is called to this day. There is more history in the depositions of the pioneers than has ever been taken out of them.

We speak of the "pathless forests," but they had their roads all the same. Kenton noted them and followed them. An Indian "war road" led from Cabin Creek to Lulbegrud Creek; a "buffalo road" touched at Lawrence Creek and ended at the great salt springs of Licking River, called later the Blue Licks from the color of the bubbling water. "When I first saw it," said Kenton in one of his depositions, "it was a deep pond of salt water and sand—the dryer the time the deeper the pond; the buffaloes tread it all up into a mire and prevented it running into the river . . . at different times the waters would overflow and leave a considerable quantity of sand in the places where the pond stood, when numerous small springs burst up all long . . . when the Buffaloes by treading it would soon make it a pond again." The flats on both sides of the river were crowded with buffalo come to lick the salty earth. At one time when he was there Kenton counted fifteen hundred pacing in single file to the Licks.

He crossed the Licking and on the other side fell in with another buffalo trail which led to the Upper Blue Licks where again was evidence of game the like of which he had never seen. He explored all the trails along Licking—war roads and buffalo traces alike—and what he did not know about Indian and animal sign he picked up then. War roads, he explained in one of his depositions, were distinguished by marks and blazes on trees—frequently there were rude drawings of animals or of men, of the sun or the moon; also, he said, they were *leading* roads—connecting lines from point to point—and except where they led along great rivers they were invariably forest trails. Buffalo roads, on the contrary, were found along ridges and creeks, were much wider, sometimes a hundred yards wide, and these were literally roads, with the earth tramped through to the bare rock and with the vegetation on either side utterly destroyed.

Nothing seemed to escape his young eyes; "points" and sky lines registered themselves without effort on his memory; he absorbed the figuration of the country as a sponge takes up water, but unlike a sponge he never seemed to reach the saturation point. He merely instinctively noted what he passed as he passed it—that was all. And it was enough, for his effortless notations went freely to their place, and later on when he needed them they rose freely to the surface of memory, little vivid pictures limned in years before. He was laying the foundation for an unsurpassed knowledge of the region which was to endure through his life. One of his most interesting depositions, made in 1823 for use in a land case which hinged on the location of two shifting salt springs at the Licks, is full of old geography, recalled clearly after a period of nearly forty years.

For months after they settled in the canebrake, Kenton and Williams believed themselves the only white men in the region. But embryo settlements were beginning to be made. By March of 1775 Harrod was back at his station site so suddenly abandoned the year before. On April 1st George Rogers Clark was at

Stewart's Crossing. "I have engaged as deputy surveyor under Cap'n Hancock Lee," he wrote his brother, "for to lay out lands on ye Kentuck, for ye Ohio company, at ye rate of 80£ year and ye privilege of taking what land I want." And again, on July 6th, from Leestown: "Colonel Henderson is [here] and claims all ye country below Kentucke. If his claim should be good, land may be got reasonable enough, and as good as any in ye world. . . . We have laid out a town seventy miles up ye Kentucke, where I intend to live, and I don't doubt but there will be fifty families living in it by Christmas."

Henderson and Boone reached Kentucky in April, fresh from the Watauga treaty just signed before twelve hundred Cherokees at the Sycamore Shoals and full of plans for the founding of Transylvania on the enormous tract Henderson and his company had bought from the Indians for ten thousand dollars in guns and goods.

Boonesborough began to go up this spring, however. A little later Benjamin Logan and his party were erecting St. Asaph's or Logan's Station. In May Haydon Wells and nine others landed at Limestone and in June the McConnells and McClellans were on Lawrence Creek at the "Indian Spring" across from Kenton's clearing. But they came and departed like woodpeckers; once their girdling of trees for locations and their stripping of trees for bark cabins was done, they were off, leaving behind them the first of the overlapping claims to Kenton's lands.

There is no evidence that Kenton met that year with any of these latter parties who improved so close to him; no evidence that any of them came upon his cabin and corn patch in the center of the canebrake. But other men than he were following the Indian roads and the buffalo traces and sooner or later he and they must meet.

One day while in a temporary camp at the Blue Licks, whither they had gone for game and salt, Kenton and Williams saw two white men coming along the trail from the Ohio. They were in great distress and their joy was great at finding men of their own color in the wilderness. They gave their names as Hendricks and Fitzpatrick, and related that while coming down the Ohio a sudden squall had overturned their canoe, spilling them, their guns, and all their supplies into the river. Reaching the shore with nothing but their lives, they had determined to go on to the "interior settlements." Of these Kenton knew nothing, and when he assured the strangers that he and his companion were the only white men he knew of in the country, Fitzpatrick gave up the adventure. Kenton told them of his small camp and invited them to join him, but only Hendricks elected to remain; Fitzpatrick's single wish was to return and that forthwith, even though he must go alone.

After a little consultation all was arranged. Hendricks remained behind at the Blue Licks, while Kenton and Williams returned with Fitzpatrick to outfit him from their small store, help him build a canoe, and see him on his way. Then, with a new interest in life, the presence of a third companion, they went back to the Blue Licks, arriving there on the evening of the fourth or fifth day after their departure.

But their camp was deserted and ransacked. Falling

FINDING THE REMAINS

FROM HARPER'S MAGAZINE, FEBRUARY, 1864

back into the woods and scouting cautiously about, they suddenly perceived smoke rising from a ravine not far off. They had no doubt that the Indians, so long in coming, had found them at last and, troubled and appalled, "thinking Indians were waylaid close by, cleared themselves." They stayed in the woods all night, prepared every moment for flight and becoming more certain with every hour that Hendricks had been taken. On the next evening they ventured to return and apprehensively sought out the ravine they had noted. The Indians were gone, but their fire was still smoldering and in its ashes they found Hendrick's skull and bones.

Depressed and dejected, they went back to their camp on Lawrence. This was the second camp attack in Kenton's experience so far, and each had resulted in the death of a companion. Each time he had fled for his life, on the good Indian rule of each man for himself. He could not have saved Yeager, but he was always to be haunted by the shadow of the untaken chance that he might have saved Hendricks, and his flight on this occasion was one of the two acts of his life for which he several times expressed bitter regret. Curiously enough, the other act for which he could not forgive himself was the killing of an Indian in battle. "For he was in my power, and I need not have done it," said Kenton.

They remained at their camp on Lawrence until fall, with no further molestation from the savages. But Kenton had several encounters with single Indians about this time. Once, while at the Blue Licks watching for deer and almost ready to shoot one, he heard a slight crackling sound behind him and discovered an Indian with his rifle raised and intent on the same deer. Kenton moved his own rifle around in a semicircle until he could draw a clear sight on the other hunter, who fell before he had fired.

Another time, while pursuing a trail up a high ridge, he encountered an Indian at its summit, just arrived from the other side. The meeting was so unexpected to both of them that each took to friendliness as the best way out. Each said "How-de-do," and each extended his hand. The Indian, discovering that Kenton had but little powder in his horn, poured into it one half of his own in proof of friendship, and after a little more pantomime and speech of the simplest they parted, each going down the trail the other had just ascended.

Kenton fell in with no other white men until fall; then, when alone at the Blue Licks, he was discovered by one James Galloway, who had been eight months in Kentucky with a hunting and exploring party from Pennsylvania and was on his way from the interior to rejoin them for their return voyage. Arriving on the south shore of Licking, he saw an Indian, as he supposed, sitting on a rock across the river, "busily employed in hammering flints for his gun." Putting himself behind a tree, he watched the man for some time until, seeing him put on his hat, he became convinced it was a white man, and called to him across the water. "The man immediately seized his gun and sprang behind a tree prepared to shoot." But, "on ascertaining through talk that they were friends and not enemies, each came to the water's edge and conversed for an hour or more with the river between them, inquiring each other's name, destination, the news, etc. The supposed Indian was Simon Kenton, afterwards celebrated for his skill and successes in fighting the Indians. He called himself Simon Butler."

In October Kenton and Williams met four white men at the Blue Licks. For there, according to Robert Patterson's manuscript narrative, "we met with Simon Butler and John Williams, who knew of no other white person in the country." And yet again at the Blue Licks, evidently after his meeting with Patterson, Kenton, taking to a tree while a herd of buffalo were passing, discovered someone treed a short distance from him. "Come out—show yourself," called Kenton, and the treed man replied with, "Come out yourself." Their common language was introduction enough; each promptly descended, and Kenton discovered his new friend to be John Hinkston, who had just put up a few cabins he called a station about forty miles from Kenton's camp.

Later still that year, and again at the Blue Licks, he met Michael Stoner and heard for the first time of Daniel Boone and Boonesborough. Stoner, chief hunter for Henderson's colony, was at the Blue Licks for game, and the meeting of the two men was another story of advance and retreat; of Kenton calling out and receiving a reply whose mixture of English and Dutch made him more than suspicious. He finally made out that the man's name was "Mich-el Stoner" and that he was from "Schpoon's Fort." Despairing of getting further information from him. Kenton took him back to his camp, where Williams "had better success in deciphering the old Dutchman's meaning; ascertained that *Schpoon's* first name was Daniel—

and at length made out the name of Daniel Boone."[1]

This word of new settlements in the interior roused Kenton's curiosity; then, too, winter was coming on, and he and Williams soon decided to break camp and make a round of visits. They had few treasures, but their ravaged hunting camp at the Blue Licks had made them secrete those they did not habitually carry with them. Among these were some extra shirts which they had tied up and hidden from the Indians in a hollow tree—as they hid extra knives and tomahawks from time to time far from their camp so that, if it were despoiled, they would not be entirely weaponless in the wilderness. They collected some of the knives, but upon going for the shirts "they found the raccoons had eaten off the string and the shirts had fallen down and rotted."

From Stoner's description of the localities of the new settlements and stations in Kentucky, Kenton contrived to make his way to them, and for several months he and Williams went from one to the other. "Thus," says Marshall, "he became acquainted with the first settlers in the country; to whom he was everywhere serviceable; and with whom he everywhere partook of danger, for the residue of that and the whole of the next year."

They settled finally for the winter at Hinkston's

---

[1] "The first white man Kenton met in Kentucky" varies in the old sketches of Kenton between Stoner and Boone. Kenton's daughter Sarah gave the above account to Dr. Draper, but his son William said "The first white man" was Boone. McClung says "a white man" in September; but Patterson, who did not meet him until October, writes that Kenton knew then of no other white man in Kentucky. Boone's son Nathan told Dr. Draper he always understood from his father that he first met Kenton at Boonesborough, and he is likely right.

blockhouse on the north side of South Licking. One of Kenton's depositions, made July 8, 1823, gives the list of his progressive "stands": "I first made a stand at Hinkston's blockhouse which was afterwards Riddle's Station, then to McClelland's fort where Georgetown now is, then to Harrodsburgh, then to Boonesborough."

At Hinkston's he hunted for the settlers, and going off one day to the Upper Blue Licks with two favorite dogs to hunt, witnessed a singular sight. There appeared suddenly along the trail a large buffalo bull, taking a solitary ramble over the icy road. The dogs made a rush and seized him by the ears, and all staggered down the hill together and skidded out upon the frozen river. Suddenly the ice gave way and all went through—dogs and buffalo together. Kenton said it was the greatest loss of his life—as it then seemed to him; for the dogs "used to sleep each on one side of, and guard him of nights when camped alone in the wilderness."

Chapter VI

KENTON AND CLARK
1776–1778

IN THE spring Kenton and Williams were back on Lawrence at their old camp, where Samuel Arrowsmith, earliest of the year's arrivals, joined them and began to clear an acre of land. Most of the preparations for his own spring planting Kenton left to Williams. He himself had other work to do, for exploring parties were coming down the river in dozens, and most of them were turning in at Limestone Creek, already known at Fort Pitt as the "landing port" for the interior settlements of Kentucky.

What it meant in those days to land on a strange shore and find there a tall, auburn-haired, blue-eyed, smiling young man, with a voice "soft and musical," who walked like an Indian and looked and dressed like one, who spoke confidently of trails and distances and the time it took to travel them, who knew exactly how to lead the newcomers to Harrodsburg, Boonesborough, McClellan's, Huston's, and Hinkston's forts, who knew all the men at all these stations, and who could give offhand all the facts of their numbers and achievements to date—what all this meant to the newcomers is not set down in history.

Nor is it told in Kenton's scant "biographies"; it has lain hidden for a century and more in old journals and memoirs and depositions of the Kentucky pioneers. "Major George Stockton deposes" that he landed at the mouth of Salt Lick early in April, 1776, and "found Simon Butler, now Kenton, in now Mason county." "John Virgin deposes" that he and a party of seven others "landed at Limestone the last of April or first of May, 1776—at Cabin creek were met by Simon Butler, now Kenton, who piloted them through the country." John McCauseland deposed that he and George Deakins, William Graden, and others landed at Limestone in April, 1776, "where they were met by Simon Butler, since Kenton, who then had a camp on Lawrence's creek at which camp they stayed some time: "They traveled out from the river for some distance along a war path—left said war path in a canebrake where Washington now is and went to Kenton's camp on Lawrence's Creek; explored the country, Butler conducting them." In June or July "Simon Kenton and his employe, Thos. Williams," went with Deakins, "a stranger in this country," to show him "where he might improve safely" on a small branch of the North Fork, and Williams was left there to assist Deakins in building a cabin, while Kenton returned to Mill Creek where he and Arrowsmith aided Jacob Drennon to set up a camp.

And besides these are many others. It would seem that comparatively few of the spring travelers landed at Limestone without meeting "Simon Butler," welcomer in chief for the land he loved and eager pilot of strangers into it. He was not attached to any station, owed no services to any one settlement—nor ever did. From this first year of his coming of age he was on his own hook; Kentucky was his settlement and this early he assumed the first of his own peculiar self-appointed duty to Kentucky and its settlers at large.

Since the Dunmore war the Indians had been passive. "Then, in 1776," says Kenton's Manuscript Statement, "the Indians became very harsh on us." The American Revolution was a year old and, incited by the British as well as by their own resentment against the white invasion of their hunting grounds, scattered Indian parties from over the Ohio began to creep through Kentucky. At first their mischief was confined to thefts of horses and the killing of cattle, but no one knew when or where they would strike to kill the settlers, and the smaller settlements began to take alarm.

When or where Kenton and Clark first met in Kentucky is not clear; certainly they did not meet in 1775. Clark left Leestown that fall for Virginia—but not to enlist in the Revolution on the seaward side. "It was at this period that I first thought about concerning myself with the future of this country," he wrote. Its future lay to the west, and the young nation's first problem, as he saw it, was to face the tangled status of Kentucky. He knew the details of the great Henderson grant with all its feudal ideals; knew the dangers under which its colonists must live just then as a colony separate from and unentitled to Virginia's protection. What their status was, or would be decided to be, or what they themselves wanted it to be was all too vague. But while Henderson's agents were asking the Continental Congress to validate his treaty with the Indians, Clark was asking Virginia to carve a new county out of her most westwardly Fincastle lands and call it Kentucky County. When Virginia asked for his letters of credit, he promptly said he would bring them, and started back to Kentucky to get an appointment as agent of the settlers with general powers to treat for them. He wrote on ahead asking for a council to be called at Harrodsburg on June 6th, and the Kentuckians were already enough concerned over their anomalous situation to call it.

According to Kenton's Manuscript Statement, he was in Leestown "about June, 1776." "I there heard," he said, "that the explorers of the country were requested to meet at Harrodsburg to select somebody to go to Virginia to see if they could not get some aid." He went on to Harrodsburg: "Then it was concluded that we ought to select two men, to apply to Virginia for aid, and we selected George Rogers Clark and John Gabriel Jones."

On his way back from Harrodsburg he met for the first time his good friend John Todd and gave him and his party word of Clark's mission. He told of this in his Statement and added some details of the Indian troubles:

"I and a few more had attempted to raise corn in Mason County, near Maysville that is now—there were John Lair and Robert Todd and Daniel Turner in a company and discovered their sign and hunted them up. I was the first that told that company what was in hand. I stayed all night with them, and returned to where Samuel Arrowsmith and I had planted some corn.

"A few days after they killed Joshua House at the

Upper Blue Licks, and took two daughters of Col. Callaway and one of Col. Boone at Boonesborough, and took two of Andrew McConnell's sons. It occasioned Arrowsmith and me to quit raising corn, and we went to Hinkston's settlement on South Licking. The explorers and us attempted to build a block-house. In a few days the Indians killed James Cooper and made several other attempts.

"McClelland had moved his family to where Georgetown now is. They broke at Leestown and at Hinkston's block-house. A number of explorers met at McClellan's and a party of us agreed to build a fort at McClellan's. There I met with the Todds again—and built the fort, expecting aid from Virginia."

But this was midsummer and aid from Virginia was long in coming—it did not reach them until the following January.

Kenton and Arrowsmith did not leave much behind them when they "quit raising corn" and went to Hinkston's. They had put in two acres, but the buffalo broke through the cane and what they did not destroy the squirrels and raccoons finished. Arrowsmith, come from Maryland not to explore but really to settle in Kentucky, had brought with him a good deal more than an ax and a gun. He buried his heavier implements at the camp—among them "two iron wedges and an iron pot," and from Boonesborough took the Wilderness Road back to Baltimore, near where his family lived. He intended to return with them immediately, but he became involved in the Revolution and it was eleven years before he saw Kenton or Kentucky again. Kenton's Station was then flourishing on the old campsite, and a day or two after his arrival, with a little digging he recovered his iron wedges and pot which some smearings of bear's grease put in good order for years of further service.

Clark and Jones had lost no time in setting out for Viriginia, for instead of being elected as free agents to treat for Kentucky, they had been elected as members of the Virginia Assembly, which hampered them somewhat, and they made all haste to get back before the Assembly adjourned.

But they were too late, and Clark sought out, therefore, Governor Henry to lay before him the Kentucky situation. The colony must have powder and lead, not only for its own salvation but also for Virginia's western defense. Henry sent him to the executive council of the state, which body made many demurs. Clark's request for ammunition could not be legally granted, it said; if it were given him the legislature when it reassembled would be within its rights in refusing to appropriate money to pay for it. The council asked Clark to assume the financial responsibility for its purchase and transportation, but with a good deal of finesse the young man declined to accept the burden, expressing regret that since aid must be had, Virginia's abandonment of this frontier settlement would compel him to seek it in other quarters.

This meant a good many things into which there is not space here to go, but it brought the council up with a good round turn, and on August 23d it issued an order for five hundredweight of powder to be delivered up to him at Pittsburgh for the use of the inhabitants of Kentucky. Five hundred pounds of powder is hardly enough to start a war to-day, but it meant the waging and winning of several wars in 1776. It meant much more: it meant Virginia's recognition of the country as a part of her own domain. And when the legislature reassembled Kentucky was formally organized as a county of the state, its boundaries and name just what they are to-day.

So, their mission highly accomplished, and with Clark's reputation so well established that his next demand for a commission to go against the British posts in the Illinois would be granted without too much parley, he and Jones left for Pittsburgh, from whence, writes Clark, "we set out with but seven hands in a small vessel and by the most indefatigable labor accomplished our journey."

This had been a dangerous year on the Ohio and a great part of their indefatigable labor was to keep the most constant of look-outs for Indian parties. "We passed the Indians in the night" says Clark, "or by some other means got ahead of them, for the day before we landed at Limestone, we plainly discovered they were pursuing us. We hid our stores in four or five places, scattered at considerable distances, and, running a few miles further down the river, turned our vessel adrift and set out by land for Harrodsburg to get an adequate force of men to return for the ammunition. We passed the Blue Licks and on the third day after leaving the river arrived at Hinkston's cabin on the west fork of Licking creek. While we were resting here, four men who had been out looking up land in that section came up and informed us concerning the situation in Kentucky."

At McClellan's Station, finding it too weak to

furnish men at the moment, Clark left Jones and five of his men behind, and with two others pushed on. "I met them crossing the country hunting Harrodsburg," Kenton told Judge James, and added, "That powder we got safely in."

But not without trouble and tragedy. While Kenton piloted Clark to Harrodsburg for men, John Todd and eight others returned to McClellan's, and Jones was imprudent enough to start with them after the concealed ammunition. On Christmas Day, while Clark was beginning his diary at Harrodsburg, the Jones party was fired upon at Johnson's Fork near the Lower Blue Lick by some forty Indians with Chief Pluggy at their head. Jones and William Graden were killed and two others were captured. When Clark and Kenton returned to McClellan's Station with the Harrodsburg men "they had the mortification of meeting the remnant of their defeated friends," and likewise of seeing Harrod and his men return hastily to their own station upon word that the Indians were abroad. On the 29th of December Pluggy and his men attacked McClellan's, and during the firing both Pluggy and McClellan were killed. But for the loss of their chief the Indians would have undoubtedly gone on to Harrodsburg; as it was, they retreated.

Kenton and Bates Collins undertook to track them and followed them almost one hundred miles to a point near Limestone where they saw the party had crossed. But they did not stop with this. Kenton knew from Clark where the precious powder was hid: "They lodged it on the islands above Maysville," he says in his Manuscript Statement. So, hastily making a canoe, they went up to the Three Islands, found it all safe, and returned with their good news to Harrodsburg. This was one of Kenton's record trips, for on the 2d of January, 1777—which would have given him but five days at the outside to make the trip whose shortest cuts covered more than one hundred and fifty miles—thirty men left under Harrod to bring in the powder and Kenton was of the party. They went by McClellan's, Blue Lick, and May's Lick, and struck the Ohio at Cabin Creek, where the Indian war road to the interior began. On their return some of them wished to take the short cut inland along the war road, but Kenton saw Indian sign along it that whispered of danger; the powder was too precious to risk and he advised against it, so they returned by the long roundabout way they had gone.

Back again at Harrodsburg they found a state of depression which even the sight of the powder could not lift. With the loss of McClellan, his station decided to break up and go to Harrod's, and if this fort was strengthened by numbers it was also weakened by them. By the end of January the refugees, including women and children, had arrived, and the station's resources were taxed to their limit to supply food for the new inhabitants. Logan's Station also broke up—all the settlements but Boone's and Harrod's were abandoned. Many who could returned to Virginia and Pennsylvania, and all the country held not more than one hundred and fifty white men capable of active service.

This was the winter that Kenton turned hunter—in the terrible year of "the three sevens," the "bloody year" of the border warfare. There was no more dangerous work; scouting and spying were child's play compared to it. He would slip out of the fort at night and go to the place where he intended hunting the next day. This meant a winter night alone in the woods and, but for infinite guile, a fireless one. But Kenton had guile and he knew the properties of white oak bark for burning without smoke and for retaining heat. He found his tree, stripped its bark, and sat down before it. Between his spread legs he dug a hole in the ground not larger than his head, and in it he "criss-crossed" fine strips of bark until it was filled. Then under his blanket he "made fire," and when the little pile was glowing he covered it with earth, leaving two air holes for draught. Then he went calmly to sleep, sitting against the tree, his hand always on his rifle.

In the morning, far from the settlement, the hunt began. Once the shot was fired and the game brought to earth, he lay concealed for a time before going after it. Then, dragging the dead deer to the nearest large tree, with his back protected by the tree and his gun leaning against it, he flayed the animal and laid its skin on the ground, piling onto it the quarters of meat as he cut them. And then, when another kill had heaped the skin to overflowing, tying it all up so that it made a back pack as heavy as he could possibly carry, he began the long return journey. Sometimes, when the distance between the fort and his hunting ground was not too great, "he would," says one of his grand-nephews, "steal off in troublesome times from the fort in the night, go several miles, hunt the next day, and the following night pack in two loads of meat—and so repeat these hunts as the wants of the garrison required, which indeed was constant—for they had little else on which to subsist." Indeed, wild meat without salt or bread was often their only food for weeks together.

With the breaking of winter the real fortification of Harrodsburg began; so far it was like all the rest—no more than a group of cabins. And when spring came Logan left Harrodsburg and reëstablished himself and his people at St. Asaph's.

Early in 1777 a commission arrived from Virginia, giving the command of the colony to Major George Rogers Clark, with authority to appoint his officers, and on March 5th the first militia of Kentucky was assembled and organized at Boonesborough and Harrodsburg. His appointments were—wrote Kenton to General Robert Pogue in 1821—"Daniel Boone, James Harrod and John Todd captains; Joseph Lindsay was then appointed commissary—Silas Harlan, Samuel Moore, Ben. Lynn, Thomas Brooks and myself appointed spyes. The whole country was then under the command of Major Clark, who was charged by the Governor of Virginia with the defense of the Western frontiers." The number and pay of Clark's officers was fixed; he was allowed nothing for spies. But he appointed them regardless, because he needed them so much, and for their payment he "pledged the faith of Virginia."

The very next day, because the Harrodsburg people were in extreme need of clothing, Kenton, John Haggin, and four others set out for the deserted clearings at Hinkston's, "to break out some flax and hemp which had been left at that place."[1] Haggin, riding

[1]"Used to gather nettles," Colonel Nathan Boone, Daniel's son, told Dr. Draper, "a sort of hemp, towards spring, when it became rotted by

ahead, discovered a party of Indians at the cabin—some of Black Fish's two hundred warriors just come over the Ohio to avenge Pluggy's death by wiping out the three stations left in Kentucky—and when Kenton heard this, with his characteristic caution he proposed a retreat. But when Haggin retorted that only cowards would think of retreating without giving the Indians a fire, all but "the Dutchman" dismounted, tied their horses, and prepared to steal upon the camp. The Indians, however, had caught sight of Haggin and had followed so swiftly that the whites were all but surrounded. Only the Dutchman was mounted; the rest took to their heels and all lost their horses.

Clark had told Kenton to take two men, after the flax had been dressed, and go on to Boone's Station with part of it. But during their flight from Hinkston's Kenton saw so many signs of a large Indian party out and evidently on their way to Harrod's that he sent the other five back to take part in its defence and went on alone to Boonesborough. He reached its neighborhood two days later but in the daytime, and knowing that it was highly probable Indians were here also, ready to pick off from tree tops any unwary person leaving or entering it, decided to wait till night to cross the clearing. He lay by for several hours, but finally grew impatient and took the risk of crossing in the daytime. He made the dash safely, but the delay quite likely saved his life, for a small detachment

---

the wet weather, and spin them, very strong—in rich lands grows four feet high: Nettles the warp, and buffalo wool spun the filling—both spun. For socks the buffalo wool alone was used—quite soft and wears very well."

of Black Fish's party had just crept up on some workers in the Boonesborough field, one of whom was killed and several wounded; their bodies were being carried into the fort when Kenton came in with his warning of the war party on the way.

The same morning on which Kenton and his party left for Hinkston's, Clark at Harrodsburg was fully apprised of an Indian party near by, for four men from the fort, making sugar at the Shawnee Springs, four miles northeast of the station, were attacked by some seventy Shawanese under Black Fish himself. Only one escaped to give the alarm, and the work of fortification went desperately on, aided late in the day by Haggin and his flax party from Hinkston's. That night the Indians encamped near by and early the next morning attacked, but the incomplete fort held its own against them.

Two other attacks were made later this month, on the 18th and the 28th, neither of which were successful. But Black Fish left some of his warriors there to annoy and to steal, and whenever possible to kill. This was the terror of the settlers' plight; an attack could be met—they knew then what they were facing. But the endless forest warfare, with the Indians—four or five were enough to carry on this guerrilla sniping—lurking in the woods surrounding the fort, sitting at their ease in the tree tops overlooking it, ready to pick off the workers in the fields or the hunters forced to go out in the face of death for food—this was the deadly terror that never lessened day or night. Fortunately for the poorly fortified stations, a severe March and April compelled Black Fish and his army to lie in wait. But they stayed in Kentucky, hampering the colonists in every way. Wood was needed for fire and to fortify, and corn must be planted now for food the next winter. So the colonists worked their fields with a guard set over the workers, and their woodcutters went into the forests with a guard over them.

Kenton was at Boonesborough when Black Fish and one hundred of his warriors attacked it at sunrise on April 24th. He and two others were standing with loaded guns at the gate, through which two men had gone out into the field, when the Indians suddenly fired and began to pursue from the forest. The men fled back to the fort; sixty yards from the gate an Indian overtook one of them, tomahawked him, and leisurely began to scalp him in sight of the fort—an insultingly clever ruse. For Kenton and his companions rushed up, shot the scalper down, and began to give chase to the others, while Boone, hearing the uproar, came out with ten men to aid. Then the main party of Indians, rushed these sixteen from behind, thus cutting them off from their refuge. Only eight riflemen were left in the fort—the rest were women and children.

One wonders after reading these old reminiscences of Simon Kenton whether any other Indian fighter of the border so uniformly conducted himself as Kenton did in such desperate encounters. Over and over, in the old accounts of this and so many other tight fights, this sentence recurs monotonously: "Kenton saw an Indian about to fire upon me [or a friend]: he fired first and the Indian fell." He was not concerned with any Indian, but with particular Indians about to fire. It was his way of multiplying his shots; he made his

SIGNATURE OF SOME OF THE KENTUCKY PIONEERS

REDUCED FACSIMILE FROM PETITIONS OF THE EARLY INHABITANTS OF KENTUCKY TO THE GENERAL ASSEMBLY OF VIRGINIA, 1769—1792
JAMES ROOD ROBERTSON, LOUISVILLE, 1914.

supernatural quickness and deadly aim do double duty; he killed his Indian and he saved his friend.

This engagement he began and ended so. As Boone rushed out, Kenton saw an Indian ready to fire on him; he fired first and the Indian fell. And when Boone, perceiving they were being cut off, gave the order to charge through the Indians back to the fort —which meant firing first and then, without taking time to reload, clubbing their guns and beating down the foe—Kenton charged in his own way; he took time, that is, to reload. He reloaded twice during the rush back, and this was the great test of a rifleman— to reload the clumsy old guns on the run. His last shot saved Boone again.

For among their seven wounded Boone had fallen, his leg broken by a shot. As an Indian stood over him with upraised tomahawk, Kenton, "everywhere present," says the old chronicles, not only shot him down, but, stooping and lifting Boone in his arms, performed one of the magnificent running feats for which he was famous. Hampered though he was with the weight of the wounded man, he darted and dodged, eluded the grasp of the Indians, and miraculously reached the gate. All the others, including the wounded, came close at his heels and somehow the gate was closed against Black Fish and his warriors, who, after lingering around the fort for a few days, quietly departed.

But for four weeks, until the next two attacks were over, the people at Boonesborough lived in a state of siege. Their cattle continued to be killed and their horses stolen; they could not cultivate their corn and vegetables; and no man knew, when Kenton and

Stoner went out to hunt, whether they would be seen ever again.

Black Fish had not relinquished his campaign, as the thefts at Boonesborough clearly showed. On May 23d he returned and, driven off then, renewed the attack the next day. On both these days Kenton was inside the fort and took part in its defence—Boone was still helpless.

Logan's Station, the weakest of the three now in Kentucky, was attacked May 30th, when the Indians opened fire on three women and four men going out to the field to milk. This siege was maintained, and Logan, knowing well that no aid could be given him by the others, slipped out of his fort one night and started overland to Virginia for succor. In three weeks he returned with word that relief would be sent out. Ammunition did arrive, but Kentucky needed men and for men they had to wait many weeks, for the Continental army had its own work to do in the East. At last, in the first of August, Colonel John Bowman arrived at Boonesborough with two Virginia companies numbering one hundred men. These served to ward off the Indians and to guard the inhabitants while they worked their fields and strengthened their forts. When Bowman returned to Virginia with his men there were at Boonesborough only twenty-two, at Harrodsburg only sixty-five, and at Logan's only fifteen men capable of service.

Kenton's secret services with Clark had begun with his spying expedition to the Three Islands to report on the safety of the powder caches there. He knew where they were and he knew their whereabouts from Clark. Whether he made the dangerous scout on

Clark's orders or on his own cannot be said; this can be affirmed, however: whether ordered or not he would have made it—and did.

Early in June Clark sent for him and three others of his best spies to come to him at Harrodsburg and council there; if he had ever doubted the necessity of conquering the northwest he doubted no longer. He began now to make his definite plans for his campaign and his first necessity was the obtaining of accurate information on the state of the British posts in the Illinois.

". . . he then spoke to Samuel Moore, Ben. Linn, and Si. Harland and myself," says Kenton in his Manuscript Statement, "to go in our own way and make a discovery. When we came to talk, we agreed that two were enough to go, and we drew lots, and Ben. Linn and Sam. Moore got it. They went and hired themselves to the Governor of the place [Kaskaskia] for hunters; and when they made discoveries to their satisfaction, they returned to Clark at Harrodsburg. Then Clark went to Virginia and got a command."

Clark left in the fall, hoping against hope that things would go fairly well. The Indian season was nearly ended; by November the colonists could count ordinarily on a few months of comparative peace while the Indians were in their winter camps across the Ohio. But even if the Indians had been inclined to let Kentucky alone during this winter, the barbarous murder of their great chief Cornstalk and his son at Point Pleasant blotted out every chance for a quiet interim; it whipped them to a fury of revenge, and all through the winter they never ceased their raids.

On December 12th Colonel Bowman, back again in Kentucky, wrote to Hand at Fort Pitt:

"They have left us almost without horses enough to supply the stations, so we are obliged to get all our provisions out of the wood. Our corn the Indians have burned all they could find the past summer, as it was in the cribs at different plantations. At this time we have not more than two months bread—near 200 women and children, not able to send them to the Inhabitants."

Kenton spent the fall and winter of 1777–1778 at the weakest station as usual—this time it was Logan's. Had he been at Boonesborough he would have undoubtedly been out with the party of salt boilers captured by the Indians that winter.

Boone left his station early in January with thirty of his men to make salt at the Lower Blue Licks and to hunt and cure game. They were to spend some time in camp and they took with them several large kettles together with meal, fodder, and axes. While some of the men scouted and others hunted, the rest stayed in camp, cutting wood for the fires that must be kept burning day and night under the kettles, keeping them filled with water from the salt springs, and taking turns standing guard.[1] So cold was the weather,

---

[1]"Sept. 1. [1786.] Arrived at Main Licking . . . and stopped at Col. Lyons who lives here and boils salt at the Big Blue lick which is close by the river side in a great bend of the river . . . there are only four or five cabins here which people occupy to boil salt—at present there are about 100 kettles boiling but the spring is large enough to afford water to boil 1000 kettles or more I suppose. The water issuing from the spring is very blue; that and the boiling of the kettles has a very particular effluvia arising from it which smells like the salt marshes on the sea shore, but stronger—they have their kettles fixed in kind of furnaces in a place underneath to keep fire in it, and 8 kettles in each furnace, two

so slow the process of salt making and so scarce the game that nearly a month passed before two men were sent back to the station with salt and meat.

The pack horses went off on February 7th, and that day Boone departed with two other men, they to scout and he to get in game for the camp. He killed a buffalo, packed his horse with all he could tie on its back, and in the late afternoon with the snow falling thick took his way back to camp. Four Indians, stragglers from Black Fish's party then in Kentucky, discovered him, took him to their camp a few miles away, and, on the next day, to the salt-boiling camp on the Blue Licks. There Boone persuaded his twenty-six remaining men to surrender peaceably under promise of good treatment, a pledge which the Indians kept not at all strangely, considering that white prisoners could be sold for a good price at Detroit. They hurried their catch across the Ohio to the Miami Chillicothe where Black Fish, having taken a fancy to Boone, renamed him "Turtle" and adopted him as his son. Sixteen others were adopted by other warriors and the remaining ten were taken to Detroit and sold for twenty pounds each. Black Fish took Boone along and rather magnificently refused one hundred pounds from Hamilton for him. But Boone

---

and two—Col. Lyon says it will take about four men to supply 100 kettles with water and fire and about as many more to keep them in wood if it is pretty convenient; himself boils 32 kettles and makes from 3 to 3½ bushels of salt in the 24 hours; they boil night and day except Sunday and he sells this salt for 3 to 4 dollars a bushel—upon a Calculation it takes about 120 Gallons of this water to make a Gallon of Salt —his kettles hold 10 to 12 Gallons of water each. The Salt when made is very white and fine and better they say to preserve meat than the imported, owing to the quality of Nitre in it." Diary of Major Erkuries Beatty, May 15, 1786, to June 5, 1787.

had the gift of a horse from Hamilton and trinkets as well with which to purchase favors from the Indians. He remained with them until the middle of June; then, learning they were planning a great foray into Kentucky, he mounted his gift horse at a good moment and four days later arrived at Boonesborough to greet them there.

When Kenton at Logan's heard of Boone's capture he grew impatient for word from Clark, and there came a day when he too was suddenly gone, no one knew where. Clark says that he was careful to keep from the four men he selected as spies for the Illinois scout any part of his purpose; but Kenton's knowledge of Kentucky's desperate situation, his trust in Clark's foresight, and his own intelligence gave him a fair idea that something weightier than five hundred pounds of powder lay behind Clark's second mission to Virginia and his long delay there. He therefore made a trip of his own to Fort Pitt to find out what was brewing in that region.

There he prepared himself for Clark's campaign as he had prepared himself for Dunmore's; he took a second oath of allegiance—this time to the United States. Asked later by Girty how he got over the matter of his first sworn allegiance to the British crown, he replied, "I got out of it this way: I took the oath to be true so long as I remained the king's subject; when I took up arms I didn't consider myself any longer a Britisher."

He may have seen Girty at this time; his son William is "pretty confident that Kenton was at Pittsburg when Girty fled to the Indians." Clark arrived at Fort Pitt shortly after the flight, and if Kenton went on to meet him the chances are that he did, either at Fort Pitt or elsewhere, for his persistence in trailing an object was proverbial. Certainly Kenton knew of Clark's plans before Clark arrived in Kentucky, for he met him by appointment at Limestone.

There is some interesting "Clark material" in two dictations Kenton made regarding this period, one of them his Manuscript Statement, the other a paper known as the "Sanders letter." In the first he says flatly, "Col. Bowman came out with a command. George Rogers Clark refused to serve under him." In the second he implies the same thing and makes the clearest of statements on all of his services under Clark.

> He states [wrote Samuel H. Sanders,[1]] that in 1777, George R. Clark undertook the command of the Kentuckians as a Major, and I as a spy. In the fall of the same year, Col. Bowman came out, commanding Clark, as he did us, at Harrodsburgh; upon which said Clark left Kentucky, and went to Virginia and got a commission from the Legislature. He sent to me and John Haggin to meet him at Limestone, and we got Capt. Montgomery and his men to go and join him at the Falls of Ohio, where we acted as spy and pilots through the Falls of Ohio river to Mississippi; and took Roseblock, commandant of the Indians, French and Tories at that post. That Col. Clark sent me on to Bowman as express to inform him of his success in the capture of that post in 1778. Then Bowman got us [Kenton, Alexander Montgomery, and George Clark—not George Rogers Clark] to come out as a check, and to view the Chillicothe station of Indians, where I bore the name of Simon Butler; and that Alexander Montgomery was killed—and I was taken prisoner by the

[1]Samuel H. Sanders, from "Logan county, 18th March, 1834," wrote to Robert H. Ware of Columbus, Ohio, a letter dictated by Simon Kenton, in which Kenton answered queries propounded for the purpose of adjusting some of his claims against the government for services rendered. A transcript of this letter is in the Draper MSS.—8S5-7.

Indians; That in 1779 I made my escape from Detroit, and went back to the Falls of Ohio, and recommended him to go to Detroit and capture it; but that he declined the advice after one consultation. That Col. Clark met me at Vincennes after my return from Detroit, from whence I returned to Kentucky in 1779; and in 1780 I with the Kentuckians joined Col. Clark on the Mississippi, and that when I had thus rejoined the Kentuckians, my old associates, I resumed my own name. That though I acted as Captain in 1779, it was not till 1780 that I raised a company, and in 1782 as a Captain, and spy and piloted, I came to Big Miami in the regiment of Col. Clark, in which service I continued till the end of the war. That Samuel Stroude and Wm. Bickley of Mason co., Ky., now living, can prove those services.

Clark had met with his difficulties in Virginia—it was December before he saw Governor Henry and made his plea for the command of a force to invade the Illinois. He met with more difficulties in raising his men, but in May, 1778, he left Redstone with "three companies of men and a considerable number of families and private adventurers," out of which to beat up the nucleus of an army to be complemented, as he fully believed, with Virginia troops and the Kentucky militia.

On his way to meet Clark at Limestone, Kenton fell in with John Montgomery and a party of men making salt at Drennon's Lick. Irishman met Irishman over the salt kettles and Montgomery and his men agreed to join the Illinois expedition. So when Clark reached Limestone he made Drennon's Lick the rendezvous for some of the men he hoped to get from Kentucky. "Clark sent across country somewhere about Limestone to Harrodsburg," wrote William Bickley, "with orders to Col. Bowman, who commanded at that Fort, to send on to Louisville all the men who could get horses and such as could not get horses to rendezvous at Drennon's Lick by a given day, where a man would meet the troops and pilot them to the place where Clark wanted them to go. I was of the party that went to Drennon's Lick. . . . Simon Kenton met us and conducted us to the Falls, where we met Clark and went on with him to Kaskaskia."

But the Kentuckians who went either to Drennon's Lick or to Louisville were few. Clark's "mad project" of invading the enemy's country was an extremely unpopular one, and he was bitterly disappointed at their lack of response. When he left Corn Island in June he had with him, instead of the hoped-for five hundred, only one hundred and seventy-five men with whom to conquer the northwest. But Kaskaskia fell without a shot.

Kenton's statements in the Sanders letter and the fact that the most difficult and dangerous enterprises were generally deputed to him give a good deal of backing to the story that he led the detachment which entered the fort. John Reynolds relates it in his *Pioneer History of Illinois*. He says that a Pennsylvanian there conducted Kenton and his small party through a back gate and into the very bed-chamber of the sleeping Governor, Rocheblave. "The first notice Rocheblave had that he was a prisoner was Kenton tapping him on the shoulder to awaken him." Certainly Clark's first choice of men to perform this dangerous and delicate task would be the two he chose to meet him at Limestone and to pilot parties to the Falls and the army to Kaskaskia—Kenton and Haggin. His own account of the taking of Rocheblave is contained in a sentence: "Mr. Rocheblave was secured, but some time elapsed before he could be got out of his room."

Another dangerous mission awaited Kenton immediately after the capture. "The next day," he says in his Manuscript Statement, "Clark started me, Shadrack Bond and Elisha Batty for the purpose of viewing Fort Vincennes. We came, and hid our hats and guns out in the commons, and then at night came back and walked the streets with the Indians and the French, with our blankets around us and tomahawks concealed under our blankets, for three nights. Bond returned and reported to Clark, and he sent on Captain Leonard Helm to Post Vincennes, and they surrendered to him."

Kenton himself did not return to Kaskaskia, his scout at Vincennes finished and his report sent back, he went on alone to Harrodsburg with Clark's messages of victory to Bowman and Governor Henry. Clark's instructions to him were to destroy all papers at any chance that they might fall into the enemy's hands, which means that they were carefully read to him before he left Kaskaskia. Evidently he did destroy them and gave Bowman a verbal account of the victory, which Bowman sent on to Virginia.

At Boonesborough, where he went with his inspiring news, he found Boone returned from captivity and awaiting Black Fish's attack. But the attack was delayed and Boone grew restless. Finally, toward the end of August, when Kenton arrived from Kaskaskia and Vincennes, Boone proposed to him that they make a scouting party of their own into the Indian country, at once to find out what the Indians had in mind and to recover, if possible, some of their stolen horses.

They set out with eighteen men for the Shawanese towns on Paint Creek, stopping a day at the Blue Licks to hunt and secure provisions and then going on to Kenton's old camp on Lawrence, where they built boats and crossed. Within two days after they were not far from Paint-Creek-town.

Kenton was spying ahead of the party. Hearing suddenly a loud laugh from a thicket near by, he drew off and concealed himself. Very shortly after two Indians appeared, mounted back to back on a small pony and talking and laughing in high spirits. When they came within range he fired at the breast of the foremost and both fell, one dead, the other severely wounded. Their pony, alarmed, galloped back into the wood, thus giving evidence of the result of the shot to the rest of the Indian party. Kenton ran up to finish the wounded man, but a rustling in the bushes to one side made him turn to see two Indians taking aim and ready to fire. A quick leap to one side was all that saved him. He fled into the thicket and treed just as a dozen or more savages appeared, but by now Boone and the rest of the party came up and by a concerted fire forced the Indians to retreat.

To go on was useless—the point of their expedition was its secrecy—and realizing this was a war party on its way to join Black Fish's forces, Boone decided to return to Kentucky. Kenton, however, could not find it in his heart to go back without some evidence of victory, and he prevailed upon Alexander Montgomery to stay behind with him and take a chance on recovering some of the horses the Indians had taken during the year.

They advanced cautiously on the village and

waited all day in one of the corn fields, "hid in a brush fence covered with pumpkin vines—so near the Indian cabins that the Indian children came into the corn field and passed within their reach." Asked by one of his grand-nephews many years later if he had any disposition to injure them, he replied, "No! I would not have hurt them for the world!" That night he and Montgomery stole into the field where the horses were pastured, selected four of the best, and returned the second day after to Logan's Station.

In Kenton's later life, when the memory of Indian depredations had faded a little, and when some of his old forays across the Ohio were referred to as "horse-thieving expeditions" merely, he always resented it. "I never in my life," he would say, "captured horses for my own use, but would hand them over to those who had lost their animals by Indian thefts, nor did I ever make reprisals upon any but hostile tribes, who were at war against the white settlers."

Boone and his party returned none too soon, for Black Fish's warriors were already in Kentucky. As he passed the Blue Licks he discovered the main army encamped there, but he slipped safely by and arrived the next day, September 6th, at Boonesborough.

In mid-morning of the 7th the Indians crossed the Kentucky at the point afterward called Black Fish's Ford, a mile and a half above Boonesborough, and soon appeared marching in single file along the ridge south of the fort, nearly four hundred strong. Black Fish, Black Beard, Black Hoof, and Moluntha were there, and Captain Isadore Chene and some French

Canadians represented the British. Before attacking, Chene called on Boone to surrender; Boone asked two days to consider, and at the end of the time refused. Chene then said that if he and eight others would come out sixty yards from the fort and treat there, he would withdraw. Boone consented to this transparently treacherous proposal. He got his men safely back to the fort, but after its thirteen-day siege was raised he was court-martialed on three counts: first, for his assent to this proposal, which was of course but stratagem on the enemy's part to rush the fort; second, for his surrender of the salt makers the winter before; third, for undertaking his Paint Creek expedition at a time when the fort was hourly expecting attack. The hysterical reason assigned for the examination was that he inclined to the British. He went into the court-martial a major and came out a triumphant colonel.

Kenton was not at the siege of Boonesborough, but he commented on it to Judge James.

"The Indians and French," he said, "commenced undermining from the river. Boone had a box fixed with ropes to haul up to the pickets, so that they could see the work; he commenced digging in the block house, and dug out the whole floor to the depth of 4 feet. We could have killed any number of men who could have entered from a mine. Drewyer[1] (and

[1]Pierre Druillard, an Indian trader and interpreter in the employ of the British at Detroit, who a few months later effected Kenton's final escape from the stake.

On the fifth day of the siege the Indians began to undermine the fort. The garrison began a countermine and came to such close quarters that they could hear each others' voices as they worked. The Indians had mined forty of the sixty yards when a succession of rain storms so soaked the earth that their tunnel fell in and they halted.

the Indians also) told me that their plan was broken in on by wet weather and they quit on that account and not because Boone was digging.

"After Boone had treated with them, and it was decided to have amity, the chief said it was usual to shake hands in friendship, but when they made a long peace and a lasting one, they caught by the shoulders and brought their hearts together. Three Indians were as if by accident near each white man, and the design was to capture them forcibly; then Boone gave orders to the nearest basteens to fire into the whole crowd. They did so, and many were killed. He told me it was his pointed orders to the men he had stationed in the basteens, to shoot without one moment's delay, with well directed aim at the enemy; it was wisdom in him to do so; it tended to keep the Indians in negotiation for he expected succor."

But Kenton was not in Kentucky to give it. No sooner had he returned with his parcel of horses than he was sent back to the Indian country from which he was not to return until the following year. In his Manuscript Statement he puts the story of the next nine months concisely enough, as far as it concerned his removal from the Kentucky scene:

"Bowman got me and two more to go to Chillicothe and make discovery—Alex. Montgomery got killed, I got taken, and George Clark escaped, who piloted Bowman there next spring, '79. I did not return any more to Clark till the Summer of 1779."

Chapter VII

HIS CAPTIVITY AND ESCAPE

1778–1779

WHEN Simon Kenton crossed the Ohio on his spying expedition to Chillicothe he entered upon an adventure which for its momentous succession of perils, transitions, and hairbreadth escapes has not its parallel in all the adventurous annals of Western border history. For nearly two months there was literally no moment when his life was not threatened, nor correspondingly a moment when his life was not miraculously "saved." He was, it is true, never off guard; he saved himself when he could; he used all the cunning that Nature had taught him; he ran as it were on his own marvelous instinct —nothing else served him now. But for the most part it was as if the Fates had drawn a cage around him and sat at its corners, wondering with him how much he could endure; playing over him their game of chance, accident and coincidence in the wilderness; watching him curiously when at times he hurled himself into the game of life and death; and then, his brief play ended that fended off death, resuming their own, wondering still how much he could endure. Perhaps it was no more than the endurance of an otherwise helpless man that decided the game.

Kenton was Bowman's spy when he set out for Ohio. For Bowman, fired by Clark's brilliant capture of Kaskaskia, had no longer a mind to sit idle in a Kentucky fort awaiting attack. He too would be aggressor instead of mere defender—a resolve which turned out unfortunately for him, for Clark, for Kentucky, and for the thirteen Colonies. For when he made his expedition into Ohio the following year he was soundly whipped by the Indians; the Kentuckians, turning to him on this lesser campaign, failed Clark on his greater projected one; and Clark, lacking the men he had hoped for, had to give up his plan of attacking Detroit. It was a case of neither man consenting to serve under the other; a case of the smaller man effectively thwarting the other's larger aim.

This spying expedition of Kenton's has often been called merely a "horse-stealing" raid of his own. The phrase always angered him, for it was nothing of the sort. What Bowman wanted and what Kenton went for was information, and that Kenton got. But his recent successful retrieving of stolen horses had fired him too to further aggression, and when he and Clark and Montgomery set out from Logan's Station they carried with them a weight of salt and halters greater than that of provisions. The four horses just salvaged from the Indians were no more than specks in the depleted station yards; if they could bring back more of the property stolen from them through more than a year they would. It was frontier morality.

Kenton always fixed the date of his captivity, as he fixed that of his birth, by its coincidence with another event: "I was captured on the very day my second wife was born." This was September 13, 1778; and this means that he must have set out for Ohio the day following his return from the Paint Creek expedition—on September 7th, the very day on which Black Fish was leading his feathered warriors in portentous single file along the little ridge near Boonesborough.

He and his companions reached Chillicothe on the Miami the 9th of September and made their observations during the night. In the course of their spying they came upon a finely stocked pound of Indian horses, and when they had all the information they needed they returned to the pound. With their salt and soft words they lured and caught seven of the finest, but not quietly enough to avoid arousing the Indian camp, for several of its people ran out and called.

Fully aware they would be pursued, but knowing the pursuit would not begin until daybreak, they put off at their best speed, each riding a horse and leading the others. Impeded by the string of horses, they traveled all night, all the next day, and through the next night, and on the morning of the second day they reached the Ohio at what was later named Logan's Gap.[1] The weather by now was stormy, the wind was high, the river was smothered with whitecaps, driftwood was floating thick, and although they tried repeatedly they could not make their horses take the water. Knowing that the wind often stilled

---

[1]"I passed through this noted Gap this day (September 24, '61)—it is 4½ miles below Aberdeen, and about 3½ miles above Ripley—the road between the two passes through the Gap—and the hills on either side are mostly covered with their thick native trees—while a portion of the Gap is cultivated—a vineyard—and a schoolhouse. On the western side of the Gap runs Eagle Creek—and from the Gap it is about a mile and a half to the mouth of the Creek, near is Charleston's bar.—L. C. D. Draper MSS.—19S128.

at sunset, they went back upon their trail and waylaid it at so advantageous a place that from their ambush they could have easily repulsed a party much larger than theirs. There they hoppled their horses and turned them loose among the river hills to graze, while they lay concealed, waiting for their pursuers and for the evening.

But the wind did not abate and they stayed there all night. The next morning Kenton tried to swim two or three of the horses across but the animals, frightened by the water the day before, utterly refused to cross. Knowing they could delay no longer, they decided to gather up the rest of the horses, move down the river to the falls, and land at Clark's little garrison on Corn Island. Kenton freely admitted later that in this instance they all acted "like fool hardy men"; that when they found they could not get the horses over the river, they each ought to have selected a good horse and escaped. But, used to dangers, they thought little of those now impending.

So they left their covert and scattered, Montgomery and Clark going after the horses while Kenton, realizing they had already risked too much, went back a little on their trail to reconnoitre from the top of a high sharp ridge.

At the moment that he reached it and peered over he saw five Indians coming up from the other side, all mounted. Unseen by them, he said he "raised his rifle, aimed at the foremost one, drew the trigger, the powder burned in the pan without igniting the charge," and he turned and ran for a thicket not far away. As he ran, one of the Indians, Bo-nah by name, jumped from his horse and pursued. The others divided and passed around on each side, and just as he came out of the wood at the foot of the hill he saw a mounted Indian on each side, who saluted him as "Brother, Brother," in a tone he did not fancy. He hesitated a second, then decided to take the lesser risk of going back into the thicket and try to throw off the pursuer on foot, rather than face two on horseback. But by then Bo-nah's hands were on his shoulders, and a swift kick of the knee at the small of his back laid him flat on the ground. Kenton always insisted he would have most certainly outrun the man at his rear, "for no Indian could catch him unless he had his very hands on his shoulders," but headed as he was by the others, he was done for.

The other four sprang from their horses and assisted Bo-nah in tying his hands and feet; they then set him up against a tree and tied him to that. By now Montgomery, hearing the uproar, came up; he fired but missed his aim and fled. Leaving Kenton's captor to guard him, the other Indians set off in pursuit of the runaway. Kenton told his family that Bo-nah stood before him, his rifle but a few feet off his breast, all aimed and ready to fire, and threatening to shoot at the least sign of resistance, that he thought the Indian was really at times pulling on the trigger, and that he expected every moment would be his last. He had one other thing to think of, however, and to listen for—the shot that might kill Montgomery. Not long, and it came—upon which Bo-nah set down his gun as though satisfied that no rescuer would reach his prisoner.

Another space of waiting, which Kenton's imagination could well fill in, and then the Indians returned with Montgomery's scalp. Each then took his flagrant turn in winding its long hair about his fingers and slapping it, still warm and reeking with blood, in Kenton's face, crying, "You steal Indian hoss?" at each slap. They then stretched it to dry on a willow hoop, placed it in front of him, and amused themselves with tormenting him in various ways until some others of their party came up, increasing their number to eight or ten. After these had had their sport with him, most of them went off to gather up their horses.

There was no pursuit of Clark, who at the first sign of attack, being near the river, had thrown in a chunk of wood, and though unable to swim, clung to it until he caught hold of a larger piece of driftwood on which he eventually reached the Kentucky shore. Clark was not built like the ordinary frontiersman; he was "rather inclined to being fat and loggy," and Kenton and Montgomery had rallied him during their flight from Chillicothe on being the likeliest of the three to be overtaken and captured if the Indians came up with them. But he alone of the three got over the river to report to Bowman and to carry back word of Kenton's and Montgomery's capture or death.

The Shawanese were in no state of good temper. They had recently lost one of their captives—Boone—who was giving them plenty of trouble just now at Boonesborough. But they had by the greatest good fortune just secured another equally famous among them for courage and daring, and from the first Kenton was doomed to the stake. There was never any telling when some hot head among them would strike to kill, but barring any such accidental impulse, he was in no danger of death during the next few days.

They had a brave man for a captive and in brave men they delighted; courage prolonged the ritual of torture, and with a good deal of glee they decided on the first punishment for his crime. Meanwhile Bo-nah, his captor, undertook to develop Kenton's moral sense along the simple, native line of Indian morality.

"An Indian [Bo-nah] came to me and held a long conversation with me," said Kenton to Judge James. "'Young man, didn't you know it was wrong to steal Indians' horses?' No, I did not, for you come and steal our horses. Don't you know the Great Spirit don't love people that steal? No—did you ever know it? Yes, 20 years ago. Indians have got no cattle about their doors like white people—the buffalo are our cattle, but you come here and kill them; you have no business to kill Indians' cattle: Did you know that? No, I did not. He then whipped me pretty smartly, and told me it was for stealing Indians' horses."

They camped that night on the Ohio, and here Kenton underwent his first excruciating experience of being "stretched out." They laid him flat on his back, with his arms extended their full length and his wrists tied securely to a pole laid transversely across his breast. A rope passed under his body and around the pole was used to lash his elbows to it likewise. A halter placed about his neck was fastened to a tree near by and stakes were driven in the earth at his feet to which his ankles were tied. He was almost literally unable to move during the long night, and the pain of his bonds made sleep impossible—the pain of his injuries as well, for the Indians had spared him no pain

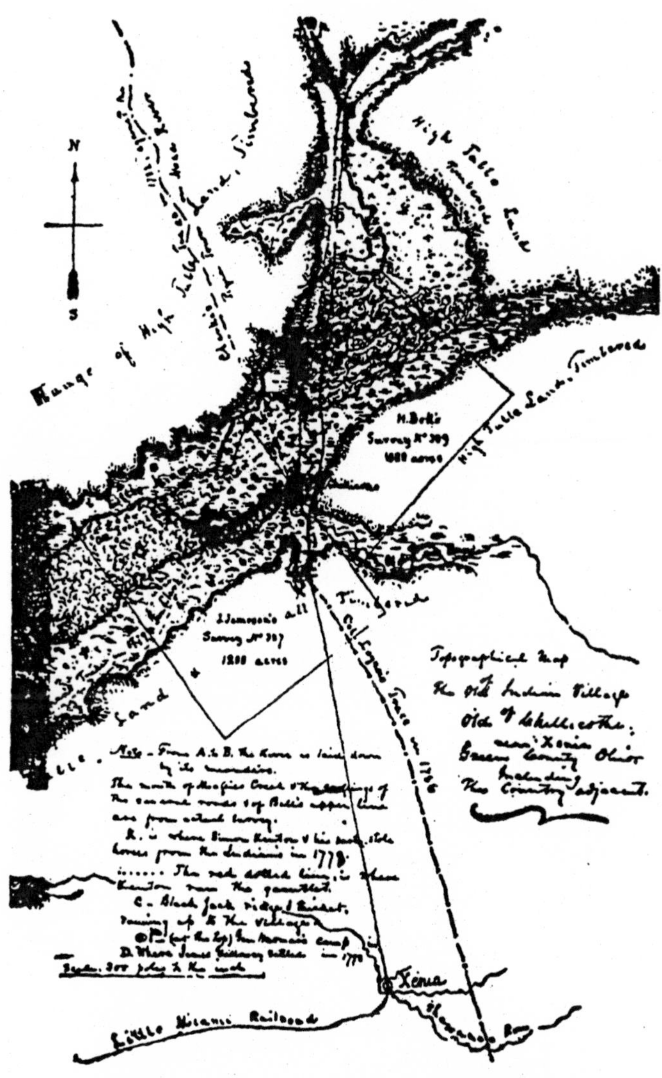

CHILLICOTHE, NEAR XENIA, OHIO

MANUSCRIPT MAP OF THE OLD INDIAN VILLAGE AND ADJOINING REGION WHERE SIMON KENTON CAPTURED INDIAN HORSES AND RAN THE GAUNTLET IN 1778.

REDUCED FACSIMILE FROM THE ORIGINAL BY JAMES GALLOWAY IN THE DRAPER MANUSCRIPTS—8 J299.

of cuffing, beating, and kicking. Their only concern was that no blow should be fatal; in this captive they had a prize and he was not to die too quickly.

Ready to start back the next morning to Chillicothe, they brought up from among their recovered horses a wild, unbroken, three-year-old colt, to which with laughter and difficulty they bound their prisoner. They fastened his hands behind him and his feet under the colt's belly. A halter was passed about his neck and its ends fastened to the colt's neck and rump. Then, all made ready, with Kenton powerless to ward off branches and underbrush from his face and body, they gave the colt a smart blow as they released it, and as it dashed off they roared with mirth at the spectacle. This was Kenton's "Mazeppa ride," famous through all border history. The colt pitched, reared, and rolled to rid itself of its burden; the ragged bushes tore its rider's legs and feet; the tree limbs raked and scourged his face and body. If he dropped forward on the colt's neck to avoid being blinded by branches, his back was lashed by them. Every leap of this ride was a hairbreadth escape, for if he once lost his balance he was finished—the halter would hang him. But Kenton knew horses and he bore a charmed life; gradually the animal grew weary and eventually fell in with the party of its own accord and went on quietly enough. Even with this, his situation was not greatly improved; when one battles with death one hardly thinks of injuries, but when death has withdrawn for a time, the pain of hurts suffered has its way with the body. Kenton told his family that he did not think it possible for him to live until he would reach the first Indian village, so many and so torturing were the wounds he received on the way.

In Asal Owen's old quaint manuscript biography of Kenton he relates, as heard from Kenton himself, the incidents of the second night of his captivity:

> On the second day they halted at nightfall and commenced a war dance around the bloody scalp of Montgomery.
>
> A horrible sight indeed it was. The blood clotted, stiffened and dried all over the hair. They obtained a tall, smooth pole, the scalp was attached to one end and the other end of the pole was set into the earth in the center of a circle 15 feet in diameter. The pole being set erect and perpendicular, the surface of the earth having been made clean and smooth and level, the warriors are ordered into the circle by their chief, as many of them as can stand at arm's length within the circle, a tomahawk in the right hand and a scalping knife in the left. Their chieftain gives the Indian yell, the warriors raise the war-whoop. Thus the war dance begins, the warriors commence twisting and writhing, horrid contortions and distortions of face and body, with grim face and terrific grimaces in succession. Their instruments of music are a drum with one head and a gourd dried and cleaned inside and out and a few gravel pebbles are introduced into the hollow of the gourd; this instrument is used by a warrior to time the tunes of their war songs which is effected by a constant shaking of the gourd and the steps of the warriors in the war dance are all timed by a constant and regular tapping of the drum head by their chieftain. Thus were they engaged whilst our hero was a bound captive pinioned fast to the ground with cords of raw-hide buried in his flesh. In the meantime they requested Mr. Butler to rattle the gourd for them to dance around the scalp of his friend which he indignantly refused to do, so immediately he received a blow with a war club from one of the Indians which broke his arm between the elbow and the shoulder.

It was a ceremony horrible enough. But Owen is mistaken about Kenton's arm being broken at this time. It came much later in his captivity.

For the two succeeding days Kenton was tied as on the first day to the colt's back, but the animal was quieter, had somehow become tamed, and after a few first plunges carried its rider along with the rest of the party.

On the night of the third day's journey from the Ohio they arrived within a mile of Chillicothe, where they again camped out; for their entrance into the village was to be made in full daylight with all pomp and ceremony. They had sent a runner ahead, and having given the customary yell denoting "Captives!" on their arrival at the outskirts, the villagers poured forth to welcome back their victorious warriors and to view the prisoner. Here Kenton was tied to a pole thrust into the ground, with his hands fastened high above his head, and what few rags of garments he still retained from his journey were torn from him while for three or four hours the Indians sang and yelled in their circling dance about him. Plenty of minor torments were his, but good care was taken that he was not disabled; for he must be preserved in good condition for the next day's amusement.

Guided by the slow, distant roll of a drum whose ominous sound grew clearer as they approached the village, Kenton's captors set out with him the next morning. No less ominous than the sound of the drum was the sight of the welcoming host drawn up to greet him. For a quarter of a mile from the council house stretched two parallel lines of Indians—men, women, and boys—standing five or six feet apart and each armed with poles, sticks, thorn branches, hoes, and the like. Kenton said the sweat broke from his pores as he looked down the six-foot lane and realized what his naked body must endure during the race for life to the open door of the council house so far away. He was given a few instructions for running the gauntlet, was told that if he was knocked down during the race it must be run over again, and was assured that if he could enter the council house without being struck by the squaw standing guard there with a hand spike to smite him, he should go free. There was no escape from the test, for behind him were his captors, and two warriors stood at the starting place with knives in their hands, their best runner beside them to give Kenton his first blow and to follow close at his heels.

The signal was given, the first blow was struck, and Kenton sprang forward in the race. He doubled and dodged, knocked an Indian down, and was all but in the council house when he was struck by the squaw at the door and felled. The race must be run again. This time, halfway down the line, he made a flying leap, got outside, and was running like the wind when again near the house of refuge he was knocked down by the Indian drummer's club, upon which all the Indians rushed upon him and beat him and kicked him until he was nearly dead, and another race that day was out of the question.

Then came the farcical ceremony of Indian kindness; he was carefully revived and tended, given food and water to drink, and his garments, such as they were, were restored to him. Meantime, within the council house, the warriors of Chillicothe deliberated over his fate. After hours of oratory the vote was taken and its result announced—Kenton was to die by burning at the stake. Then the question arose as to when and where the ceremony should take place: at once, on the spot, or later at some more central point with due notice given to other villages and after the return of the warriors now in Kentucky. It was finally decided to make the ritual a national rather than a local affair, and to take the prisoner on some forty miles to the larger village of Wappatomika on Mad River.

The next morning, seeing that preparations were being made for a journey, Kenton asked a white renegade in the camp where they were going and how far. He was a little relieved at the chance of forty more miles of life, but when he asked what was to be done with him there the renegade brutally told him his fate.

He was marched a dozen miles under heavy guard when suddenly he heard again the slow roll of a drum in the distance. They were nearing the Indian village of Piqua, to which runners had gone on ahead to prepare the inhabitants to receive him, and here again he saw the gauntlet line stretching before him. This time the race was not so difficult—he was a prisoner under sentence to be burned at another place, and he must be delivered there. But the Indians were adepts in the art of inflicting gentle agonies, and they spared him none of these later on, when, instead of withdrawing to council concerning him, they encircled him and tormented him while they danced and sang.

From Piqua Kenton was carried on to Machachack, twenty-eight miles away; the trail led through the spot that is now Urbana, where Kenton lived for many years and where his ashes now lie. At King's

Creek, three miles north of it, they stopped to drink, and as their prisoner stooped to relieve his thirst, they rolled him mirthfully into the water, used his body as a bridge to cross the stream, and nearly suffocated him in its mire.

It goes without saying that ever since his capture and particularly since sentence had been passed on him, Kenton had been turning over in his mind any chances there might be of escape. At night he was too firmly fastened, by day too closely guarded. But from King's Creek on the idea became an obsession. "Seeing a tree some distance ahead, he would resolve to make the effort upon reaching that point, but on arrival his heart would fail him—and then he would resolve again upon reaching a conspicuous tree within sight he would make a desperate effort to escape and again his heart failed him and thus he did repeatedly."

Until they came to the Machachack Valley, away from the broad Miami, a little back from the rushing Mad River, bordering the little stream known only as Machachack Creek. On one side of the stream the land rose into a little broad plateau; on the other stretched the prairie thick with corn. Forests fringed it, and something in the very pattern of prairie and plateau, woods and water, gave it such a quiet loveliness that Indian and white man alike—when the white men came—succumbed to its wordless invitation to stop and dwell within it. On the broad mound the Indians from Machachack were drawn up to receive him and he was again made to run the gauntlet. At its end he was knocked down and nearly blinded with sand thrown in his eyes, but "after wiping the dirt from his eyes and before rising, he gazed south over the adjoining plain, and it struck him, he said, as the most beautiful he had ever seen."

The march was soon resumed, and Kenton went on as he had gone for miles, wavering between dazed visions of escape and the helplessness of nightmare to make the effort at the "next tree." But when the roll of the drum beating at the Machachack council house fell on his ears, and he realized that within so short a time he would run the gauntlet again, he awoke with the shock and made his quick plan. It was a desperate one—the attempt to escape from a hundred instead of a few—but it flashed before him and he decided to act on it. There was always a chance; if he lost, no more could befall him than the unspeakable death already awaiting him. He had yet to meet his equal in running and leaping; he was lithe like a panther; he could turn and twist like a snake. And he had run the gauntlet often enough to know by now some of its tricks.

He did not this time wait either for the drum signal or the first blow from the runner behind him, but before the Indians realized at all what was happening, he dashed down the line, leaving his pursuer far in his rear. So fleet was his flight that few aimed, much less struck, their blows, and not far down the line, suddenly gathering himself up, he made a great leap over the Indians, landed far outside their ranks, and broke for the woods beyond him. So amazed were the Shawanese at the feat that for a moment they stood inactive, staring in simple astonishment at the fleeing figure, and as Kenton gained the fringe of the forest, a quick glance back filled him with confidence; another second and he would be out of their sight.

He plunged into the thicket and was lost to them. He went on, free at last; for "no Indian could catch him unless he had his very hands on his shoulders." He was free, for though his pursuers were shouting and running, they were far behind.

Then fate struck again. As on the Ohio mounted Indians had cut him off, so here in no time at all he ran straight into an Indian party on horseback making its way to Machachack to greet the famous prisoner there. Blue Jacket, the Shawanese chief who had aided in taking Boone and the salt boilers at the Blue Licks, headed the party and, instantly comprehending that the prisoner was making his escape, gave chase. They soon overtook him, and almost deprived the nation of its prisoner, for one of the men struck him down with a blow from the pipe end of his tomahawk which cut through the scalp to the skull—Kenton bore this indentation, "as large as a dollar," to his last day. Somehow, for those were the days of "tough" men, he recovered enough to be led back toward the village, and long before they reached it they met the pursuing warriors, who beat him with their clubs and fists until he was again reduced to unconsciousness. And as before, fearing they had killed their victim prematurely, they resorted to kindness; laid him carefully down and restored him with water fetched from a spring near by. "It was now that Kenton lost for a time all hope and felt himself forsaken by God and man."

They delayed at Machachack a few days, as much to give their warriors time to return from Kentucky as to give Kenton a chance to recover, and while there Black Fish returned from the Boonesborough siege.

"Black Fish came to me," Kenton said to Judge

James, "and said, 'Young man, did Captain Boone send you here to steal horses?' No he did not; but I stole them because you steal our horses."

He was hopeless, but still defiant. Lying tied in the council house, he was subjected during these days and the ensuing ones at Wappatomike to every sort of torment, insult, and indignity. The women and children, he said, were more prone to torment him than the men. The children amused themselves by touching him lightly with hot charred sticks to see him flinch, by forcing phlegm and nasal mucous into his mouth, by slapping and whipping him. There came a day, when tormented to fury by an Indian boy, he drew up his legs and promptly kicked him into the fire at which he had just set the tormenting stick ablaze. He suffered for this act at the hands of the boy's mother who beat him with blackberry branches till he bled. "The squaws," said his son William, "treated him inhumanly; even, he said, when he was staked down and fastened upon his back, they would unmodestly and insultingly before his face with their excrescences. . . .[1]"

[1]". . . an Indian squaw stept astride of his breast—that was done by way of derision to make little of him because he was not smart enough to avoid the blow [of the pipe tomahawk], which only went to show that he was like a Squaw. In the mean time our female punster deliberately seated herself upon the face of our hero who with the vigor and fierceness of a tiger, he gave his teeth a death-like set somewhere in the reagion of her inexpressibles and held a deathlike grit with his teeth and his mouth was well filled with her sporting flesh. Alass, she began to screach screach and yell like a loon. Now the Indians were convulsed with frantic and savage laughture, loud and sportive yells and howlings; all their mirth was at the expense of the unfortunate squaw—the Indians love fun even at the misfortune of their own friends. Our hero held his holt until he disengaged his mouth and face from her flesh." Narrative of the Reverend Asal Owen. Draper MSS.—7BB63, pp. 33–34.

Attempt at Escape

Kenton's spirit of rebellion against imposition and his resentment of indignities, which was always prompt and unexpected, made the Indians, as a matter of fact, like rather than dislike him. They admired a courage that resented insult even though that resentment might result in direr indignity. He was a man, by the highest of Indian standards, and he carried himself like a man. They could not make a pack horse of him; he would not carry their baggage on the marches, and he instantly threw it off when it was placed on his shoulders.

Only eight miles lay between Machachack and Wappatomika where he was to be burned, and after a few days' delay he was taken there, where again he ran the gauntlet and was again severely hurt. It is likely that in this race he received the second of the pipe tomahawk wounds in his skull, a deep indentation visible to the day of his death.

Yet here again, back on the lovely Mad River, lying captive on the broad plateau where the Indian village stood, gazing at the high, ridge-like hill to the west that dripped with springs, and at the broad, rich black bottoms to the east through which the river meandered like a silver cord, "Kenton said that while doomed to the stake and viewing the fine country around him, the idea flashed in his mind that he would one day own some of that fine country."

This was nothing but the hope that eternally springs from the heart of a dying man, for here at last he was in the stronghold of the Shawanese. Here was the greatest of their council houses, built of split poles and covered with bark, sixteen feet high, seventy-five feet wide, and one hundred and fifty feet long, large enough for the burning of any prisoner within it if the weather outside was bad. To a stake planted inside he was made fast, and his face painted black—certain mark that the sentence of death had been passed and would soon be executed. Word to this effect had evidently gone out, for Indians began to arrive at Wappatomika in large numbers to take part in the ceremony.

One evening while Kenton was sitting at the foot of his stake a party of warriors entered, just returned from a foray in Pennsylvania and bringing with them seven scalps and eight prisoners of whom all but one were children. He paid little attention to them, and had indeed but little time to note them, for he was removed and tied outside while a general council was held within to deliberate concerning the new prisoners and to argue again the definite time for his execution.

He was finally brought back and told to prepare to die—rather to begin to die—within the next few hours. His days of hopeless despair had brought about a comparative resignation, but even at that, "When sentence of death was pronounced on me, with eternity apparently just before me, I felt like it was cutting me off mighty short," he said many times.

With that strange courtesy the Indians often showed a prisoner just before his torture began, he was not tied, but was allowed to stand in the crowded council house, surrounded by savages among whom was not a friend. The war party just returned with scalps and captives had meant nothing to him; their appearance was evidence enough of their savagery, and in his heart was not a ray of hope.

But suddenly he saw a man step out from their ranks and come toward him—of all men in the world his pledged friend, Simon Girty, who with his brother James had come in with the Indians. Hope revived and with it cunning.

For Girty, in the employ of the British and eager to carry back to Detroit any information he could pick up from any source, saw in the blackened and unrecognizable prisoner from Kentucky only one who must be prevailed on to answer questions on the conditions there. As Kenton was brought in Girty went toward him, threw a blanket on the floor, and told him to sit down. When he did not immediately obey Girty jerked him by the arm and half threw him on the blanket; then, sitting down beside him, he began to question him about the number of men in Kentucky. Kenton answered evasively, giving, that is, the number of officers and their ranks from which the number of men might be guessed—an old trick for dressing up the total of a pioneer army often composed chiefly of officers. Girty asked him if he knew one William Stewart. "Perfectly well," Kenton replied, "He is an old and intimate acquaintance." "What is your own name?" Girty asked at last, and Kenton replied through his blackened lips, "Simon Butler!"

Girty sprang up in amazement and horror, dragged his friend to his feet, and forthwith set about redeeming his pledge.

"'He was good to me,' Kenton said; 'when he came up to me when the Ingins had me painted black, I knew him at first; he asked me a good many questions, but I thought it best not to be too forard, and I held back from telling him my name, but when I did tell him, O, he was mighty glad to see me; he flung his arms round me and cried like a child; I never did see one man so glad to see another yet. He made a speech to the Ingins—he knew the Ingin tongue, and knew how to speak—and told them that if ever they meant to do him a favor they must do it now and save my life. Girty afterwards when we were at [I think he said] Detroit together, cried often to me, and told me he was sorry of the part he took against the whites, that he was too hasty. Yes, Girty was good to me.'"[1]

Old border historians have embroidered Girty's famous plea for Kenton's life till its facts have been smothered in fiction; they have given his speech verbatim, as if it had been taken down in shorthand at the moment and on the spot. Kenton gave Thomas the gist of it, and Thomas, like Judge James, was so interested in the natural speech of the old hero that, as he affirms in his report of the visit quoted from above, he exerted himself to quote as exactly as possible.

But there is no doubt that Girty made a good speech in his friend's behalf. It was listened to, according to custom, in silence interrupted only by the usual grunts of approval or disapproval. Then ensued a long series of speeches for and against the request, until finally the objections filtered down to just one, and that one made by the spokesmen for the

---

[1]"A Day's Ramble: A Visit to Simon Kenton, the Old Pioneer," F. W. Thomas: Cincinnati *Mirror*, December 7, 1833.

Girty and Kenton were never at Detroit together. All this took place at and near Wappatomika.

Indians who had come from a distance to be present at the burning, whose chagrin and disappointment, he said, would be great if they were deprived of the spectacle.

Finally silence fell and the war club was raised by the chief at the head of the circle and passed from hand to hand. Those against burning the prisoner handed the club in silence to their neighbors; those for burning him struck it violently on the ground, and as the votes were cast the chief cut notches in a stick he held—on one side the noes, on the other the ayes. The vote went rapidly, for all the old warriors and all the young ones but three "laid down their clubs easily on the ground," and long before it had rounded the circle Kenton knew he was free.

Many an Indian captive has spoken of the lightning speed with which the Indians could pass from enmity to friendship, but few men have come so close to suffering their ultimate cruelty and have found instead kindness. As Kenton was raised by Girty to his feet the warriors gathered about him, each heartily shaking his hand, each calling him "Brother," each expressing admiration of his bravery, his running, his leaping, his cunning, his pride of spirit. And they gave him then a name by which they always called him, Cutta-ho-tha, the Blackened or Condemned man.

"They gave me the English of running the gauntlet," said Kenton to Judge James. "They say when a man comes among a parcel of people that are harsh to him, and they moderate towards him, he will be more attached to them, and I believe it."

But their new kindness did not end with all this.

Asal Owen told Dr. Draper that after Girty succeeded in securing Kenton's liberation, "Kenton was adopted by an old squaw to replace a slain son—hung a kettle over the fire, and when water was warm, she dipped her hands in all over and rubbing them together, and holding up her hands towards the sun, and blowing on her hands, then motioning as if throwing away something, exclaimed *puck-e-ton* which meant literally *throw it away*, but here indicative of throwing away the white man. Next she put some water on his head repeating the *puck-e-ton* and finally stripped and washed him all over and wiped and dressed him in Indian costume and properly painted him—then pronounced him her son, when the chiefs and warriors came and shook him heartily by the hand. 'You was no more white man but an Indian and a brother.'"

It has been often said that Kenton was "adopted" by the Indians, but it was certainly by no chief, else there would not have been a reversal of sentence so soon. This form of "adoption" by some kindly squaw was common among the Indians—the Iroquois called her the "aunt" or the "hostess" of such a captive. It insured him kindly treatment at his adopted wigwam, but it did not insure him the sort of safety that the ceremony of adoption by a chief or a warrior would give.

Girty took his rescued friend to his own quarters that night, where Kenton slept for the first time in a fortnight without anticipations of the stake, burning splinters, and hot hatchets and knives as his lot on the next day or the next. The following morning Girty outfitted him from the stores of a British trading establishment at Wappatomika; he gave him "a pair of maccasins and leggins, a breech-cloth, a hat, a coat, a handkerchief for his neck and another for his head." Kenton was also given a horse and a saddle, and under Girty's guardianship, he lived for twenty days without apprehension and so made a quick recovery from his bruises and wounds. It was too soon to plan his escape—and too dangerous, for the Ohio country was thick now with roving bands of Shawanese. Recapture was almost certain at this time of the year, and Kenton had no mind to risk that.

But he made good use of his time—for Clark and for Kentucky. During these three weeks he went with Girty through all the country round about. He visited Blue Jacket's Town, where Bellefontaine now is; Buckongahela's Town, three miles north of Blue Jacket's; McKee's Town, two miles and a half southeast; Solomon's Town nine miles to the north, and other Indian villages of the region. And everywhere he went he was "making notes" of localities, of streams and forests and prairies, on which he was to draw for fifteen years to come of Indian warfare. It was a hard school in which he learned this "geography" but he stood at the head of his class when he graduated. He was literally an automatically registering "memory" for all that he saw, and he saw, without knowing it, nearly everything.

At the end of almost three weeks of delicious liberty he was with Girty at Solomon's Town, without the slightest suspicion of any overhanging danger. But at Wappatomika there had just arrived from an unfortunate incursion into western Virginia a war party defeated and sullen. Hearing there of Kenton's capture and release, their resentment against this defeat took the form of anger against him, and by persistent argument they succeeded in reopening his supposedly closed case. On the twentieth day, therefore, after his sentence of death had been reversed, a deputation of Indians with Red Pole at their head entered Solomon's Town with a whoop which Girty recognized as the "distress halloo," and he told Kenton they must prepare to go immediately to the council house at Wappatomika. All the people went out at the sound, and when Red Pole saw Girty he shook his hand but refused Kenton's extended one—an ominous sign of hostility. He delivered his message—Girty and Kenton were to go back with him to Wappatomika without delay.

They found the dread council already assembled in the familiar council house. Girty was received courteously enough, but when Kenton offered his hand to those who but a few weeks before had called him "Brother," it was refused successively by all, and finally he gave up in despair, realizing his situation had dropped once more into the dangerous state, and that he was again a prisoner.

Immediately upon their arrival the orators began their speeches, the first to speak being the chief of the defeated raiders, who demanded Kenton's life in payment for those of his slain warriors. Girty spoke again for his friend, and others then spoke in anger, accusing him of assuming too much authority for a man who had been but six months among them; when the vote was taken, the war club thundered on the earth. Girty turned to Kenton, who stood dumbfounded at the swift verdict, and said despairingly, "Well, you must die! I can do nothing more." Yet when the question came up of where the burning should take place, he arose and spoke again, very skillfully. He reminded the council that at that very time large numbers of their people were assembling at Sandusky to receive their annual presents from the British, and suggested that the prisoner should be put to death there, where many more tribes from a distance could witness the solemn ceremony. There was much in this that appealed to the council, and they voted forthwith to carry their prisoner to Sandusky, fifty miles away.

The Indians were in deadly earnest now and five guards started with him without delay, they on horseback and Kenton, with his arms pinioned and a rope about his neck, driven before them on foot. They had not gone three miles from Wappatomika before Girty passed them on his way back to Solomon's Town, telling Kenton, as he went by, that he hoped to be able to do something for him there. Whatever his plan was—if indeed he had any—it failed, and Kenton did not see him again.

As if this captive's cup of anguish were not already full, as if it were not enough for him to be marched through Solomon's Town without seeing his friend and to know by that sign that Girty could in truth do no more, another terrible injury was soon inflicted on his newly healed body. Stopping to drink at Silver Creek a few miles this side of the town, "a small stream scarcely large enough to turn the wheels of a carding machine," Kenton was the first to rise and, quite without conscious intention of any sort, stepped across the little rivulet and sat down on the opposite bank to wait for the others. At this movement without orders one of the Indian guards raised his war club and struck him so violently on the arm that he fractured it. For eleven days, until he reached Detroit, Kenton was to march by day, be stretched out at night, run the gauntlet, and be tied to the stake with this unset arm the source of a physical agony almost too great to endure.

And this terrible day held still more suffering; for after passing through Solomon's Town the party came upon an Indian sitting on a log by the trail while his squaw cut wood near by. Inquiring the cause of the journey and being told, he snatched the squaw ax from his wife and dealt a deadly blow at the prisoner's head. Kenton swerved as best he could to ward it off; the ax missed his head, but struck his shoulder and broke his collar bone. But his guards did not delay; they marched him stolidly on, until they camped for the night.

He went on the next day, so weakened with pain and despair that he made the journey with no more spirit than was required to go step by step; it was no longer a matter of past or of future; he simply existed in the present effort. And yet, not many miles on, his spirits were to soar again on hope. For eighteen miles beyond Solomon's Town, at the spot on the Scioto where the old trail to Sandusky crossed the river, and about six miles below the site where Kenton, Ohio, was to be founded, his guard stopped for the night at the winter hunting lodge of Logan, the Mingo chief. Kenton had not seen him since the days of the Dunmore war, but he knew his reputation for kindness to the white prisoners his people took. It was notoriously known that in the summer of the Dun-

KENTON AND LOGAN

FROM HARPER'S MAGAZINE, FEBRUARY, 1864.

more war, when Logan's fury against the whites was at its height and when the memory of his pregnant sister's body ripped open and raised upon a pole was enough to incite him to any act of vengeance, nevertheless he had cut the bonds of a white prisoner he and his warriors had taken, had saved him from the stake and had him adopted into an Indian family. Kenton knew his case was desperate, but here after all was Logan.

After talking to the guards and learning the facts of Kenton's capture and sentences, Logan approached him and said, "Well, young man, you have been stealing these people's horses and they are very mad at you." "Yes," Kenton replied, "they seem very mad." "Well," Logan said, "don't be disheartened; you are to go to Sandusky—they talk of burning you there; but I am a great chief, and I will send two runners tomorrow to speak good for you."

Then, for the first time since his arm was broken, Kenton received some kindly care. His arm was rudely splintered, he was well fed, and his host talked with him freely during the evening. Next morning, by an invitation to hunt with him and his men, Logan prevailed on the guards to stay over another day, so that the runners he had sent to Sandusky might have time to go and return before Kenton's departure. They returned in fact that evening and sat with Logan for some time, but to Kenton's distress the old chief said nothing to him of the result of their mission. This silence he kept quite likely from caution, for the case was so delicate, the time so short, the outcome so perilous and so dependent on chance that the less anyone knew of his project the better. "Next morning he brought me some bread and meat," Kenton told Judge James, "and told me I must go with these two men [Logan's runners were sent on again with him and his guards] but did not tell me what was to await me on my way."

So it was a cheerless young man who again took the road on the last lap to Sandusky. Girty's plan of rescue had failed two days before; he could only conclude from Logan's silence that his plan too had fallen through. But the preparations ahead were already under way. Long before he reached Sandusky, as he told James, "I began to meet troops of boys painted black and mounted on fine horses (20 or more) who would ride around me and dart off with the most terrific shouts and screams." The Sandusky camp was expecting him and was making a ceremony of the occasion, the like of which he had not yet met with.

Hardly more than halfway from Logan's camp to Sandusky they came to an Indian race path on a low plateaued hill. Here were ranged a number of Indians come far out from their village to view their victim; with them were the group of Indian boys painted black. And on this race track, with no regard for his just-broken arm and shoulder, and as a mere preliminary, he was sure, to the more terrible race for life that awaited him at Sandusky, he was made to run the gauntlet—his ninth. Nearly fifty years later, when he and Major James Galloway were taking the old trail on horseback through the Sandusky plains, Kenton reined in his horse and pointed out the far distant grove in which he had run the gauntlet so many years before. When Galloway expressed his astonishment at his identification of the scene, "Ah," said Kenton, "I had a good many reasons laid on my back to recollect it."

To his great astonishment there were no gauntlet lines drawn up to receive him at Sandusky. But this omission was ominous. His injuries made it no sport for the Indians—another injury might rob them of their festival. He was spared the lesser ordeal, but he was told he would be burned at the stake the next morning.

And again fate intervened. Everything was ready for the burning: the stake was planted; there even hung on it a horn containing water for him to drink during the progress of his torture. When the morning came and the fire was about to be lighted—indeed, according to one account, when the fire was lighted and "just as he felt the flame and began to circle around the stake amid the shouts of the savages"—Kenton raised his eyes in hopelessness to the heavens which were blue and almost cloudless. But suddenly, from a sky so clear as to make the sequel miraculous, there fell "the heaviest rainstorm he had ever experienced, as though a rain cloud had burst over his head. An awe-stricken silence fell upon the noisy throng," at the marvel of "water poured from a cloudless sky." Kenton was silently untied and removed from the ring of drenched faggots to the shadow of the council house whither the Indians retreated to consider again his extraordinary case. So sudden and so heavy was the storm that, quite aware of the charmed life their prisoner had led among them so far, they began to fear the Great Spirit was angry with them and was showing his anger by repeatedly saving the life they had repeatedly tried to destroy. They concluded, however, that as sentence had been solemnly pronounced in a council not their own, their clear duty was to carry it out. And again the date was set—when the sun would have reappeared and the wood would have dried.

But on this third date for his burning there appeared at Sandusky "a great man," dressed in scarlet and gold, and known to all the Indians there as one endowed with authority. He was Pierre Druillard, no more than Indian trader and interpreter for the British at Detroit, but one who handled presents and rum, who could make or mar an Indian at headquarters. It was he to whom Logan had sent his runners with his request for the rescue of Kenton, and in response to Logan's plea he presented himself not in hunting shirt and moccasins but in the fine British uniform that glittered with gold. It would impress the tribes more.

Druillard told the Indians many great matters—took them freely into his and General Hamilton's confidence! He said that a great American general (McIntosh) was coming down from Fort Pitt with a large army to invade the Indian country; that General Hamilton at Detroit, anxious to save their country for them and hearing of their white prisoner from the Middle Ground, had commanded him, his interpreter, to come to them at Sandusky and ask for the loan of this white man; that the information to be got from him about affairs in Kentucky was worth more to them than his burning could be; that after all they had recovered their horses and had had their way up to now with their prisoner; that for the temporary loan of him to the British governor he, Druillard, would pay them the value of one hundred dollars in rum, tobacco, or whatever else they wished; that after the prisoner's examination at Detroit, since he would be no longer worth anything to the British, he would be restored to them, and that they could do with him then what they wished; that they could, if they liked, send some of their men with him and the prisoner, to Detroit, to see that the terms of the contract were honorably carried out.

"Peter Drewyer," Kenton told James, "had been sent from Detroit as a kind of spy to watch McIntosh's army, but not succeeding in learning anything, he prevailed on the Indians to let me go to Detroit to tell the commander the number of troops, etc. It was agreed that I should be brought back to be burnt, though I did not then know it. One of the chiefs accompanied us and waited at Detroit claiming a restoration of me, but finally had to go away disappointed."

The Indians listened sullenly to Druillard, but his appearance at this hour added to the superstitious fears which the cloudburst had aroused. They were not quite sure what manner of man this was they were about to burn—not quite sure what the Great Spirit thought of him or of them. The dress of scarlet and gold impressed them, the rich largess of rum lured them, and in the end they "loaned" their prisoner for a brief time to Hamilton.

Druillard set out with his purchased man promptly enough. He took him on a forty-mile journey to Lower Sandusky and thence by water to Detroit. He reset Kenton's arm on the way, and on the eleventh day after it was broken they reached the British stronghold. There, before he was examined, he received medical aid from Dr. McGregor—Hamilton's physician. The bones were beginning to knit, but they overlapped and the surgeon broke the arm again and set it properly. Kenton said the suffering he endured at its first breaking was nothing to the agony of the second. He was then cleaned and clothed; his long hair had become so matted and tangled with blood and filth that a comb could not be forced through it, and his head was shaven bare.

Hamilton was not at Detroit—he had gone to Vincennes—and Kenton was examined by the commandant in charge, who wanted most of all to know Kentucky's strength. Again Kenton resorted to the old subterfuge of naming all the officers who were or ever had been in Kentucky and of leaving the number of men under them to be imagined. As Vincennes and not Kentucky was then the main interest of the Detroit garrison, he was not subjected to severe questioning and was not put in prison. He was turned over to the commissary to be outfitted with two suits of clothing, was given the privilege of drawing half rations from the British stores, and was put on liberal bounds—he had free range of the town and its vicinity but he was not to cross the Ecorse River a few miles south of Detroit. The Indian chief who had accompanied Druillard and Kenton to Detroit lingered stubbornly on in the hope of recovering his prisoner, but being plainly and repeatedly told by the British that Kenton would not be given up to him, finally went back to his people.

Of his stay at Detroit Kenton says only this in his Manuscript Statement:

"When I got to Detroit in 1778, I found a Capt. Renew [Lernoult] commander at that place, and I was given into his hands as a prisoner. He told me that I was to remain there under his directions. Peter Druyere [Druillard] requested Renew to let him take me with him, and at night we were to return to him to get orders, and we did so; and Capt. Renew told me I was to go to Capt. McGregor—and when I went to him, he told me that I might go and work where I pleased, so that I was there every Sunday morning to answer to my name—and I did so faithfully.

"I continued there from that time until the Spring of 1779 and then I returned to the Falls of the Ohio."

"Frequent councils were held," Kenton told Judge James when talking with him of his life at Detroit. "I asked the com^t^ Renew if I might attend. 'Yes, whenever you please.' At one of them some Indians had returned from an excursion into Penn., bringing many scalps. The com^t^ received them and thanked them in such a way as to show his wish to receive more. He took the tomahawk and pretending to whet it, said, you have dulled it and now it is sharp, go and dull it again. The Indians received many presents and whatever they wished."

How Kenton got into the councils the British held with the Indians is a mystery, for he could not interpret, but get in he did. He was not long in discovering that Hamilton had left Detroit on October 7th—about a month before Druillard brought him in—with an army "to dislodge the rebels from Vincennes." And in the latter part of December he heard with the rest of the garrison that on the 17th of that month Hamilton had recaptured the fort from Clark.

From now on for six months to come his mind was busy revolving plans for escape. His captivity had given him a mass of information regarding Ohio, the Indians and their villages, their temper and their plans, as well as the lay of Detroit with its garrison and fortifications, all of which Clark needed to know, and which Kenton yearned to tell him. Kenton knew well the difference between Clark's and Hamilton's armies at Kaskaskia and Vincennes; he knew enough now of Detroit to feel it could be taken if only his information could inspire enough Kentuckians to join Clark and increase his forces just a little. But while winter held he was helpless.

He had two companions eager to make the attempt at escape with him—Jesse Coffer and Nathaniel Bullock, two of Boone's salt boilers bought by the British the year before—and contriving the details of flight from the fort was simple enough. Supplying themselves with guns and ammunition, clothing and food for the long journey home was the great problem, and one not to be solved immediately. Kenton began to make a little money during the winter by performing odd jobs about town, and soon had enough to pay for a rifle; but rifles unfortunately were not sold to prisoners of war, and the slightest suspicion that he was planning escape would be enough, he knew well, to insure his imprisonment for months if not years—others at Detroit were undergoing this punishment now.

Yet he was not at all hopeless. He had made friends at Detroit as he made friends everywhere all through his life, and what he took for friendly hints had been dropped by several people there: by the doctor, Captain McGregor; by a trader, McKenzie, and by John Edgar, who kept a large trading store which Kenton often frequented and where he picked up many things from the casual talk of transients there. American prisoners, they said, who undertook to escape from Detroit, nearly always made the mistake of going south through the Indian country instead of steering westwardly for a considerable distance and then south through the Wabash country, which was more generally free of the savages. In consequence many runaways were recaptured by the Indians waylaying the usual trails and brought back to Detroit to be sold again. The British did not pay more than twice for one man; they put the recaptured runaways where there was no chance of a second escape.

Kenton listened to everything without appearing to listen and kept his own counsel. But before long he had picked up from the reiterated talk a veritable little guide-book of the Wabash country, its forests and hills and prairies and streams. He had his companions and his route, but he still lacked the essential rifles and ammunition to make escape possible, and he realized that sooner or later he must ask direct aid from some one of these seeming friends. He finally inclined to the most important of them all, John Edgar, who owned "a House which cost him $480 New York Currency also a store of goods worth 3000 pounds and Indian goods worth $2000."

He did not, however, approach Edgar himself; he approached Edgar's wife and with the seeming carelessness of a cat watching a mouse let her know exactly what three men on a secret journey from Detroit to Kentucky would need to make it in safety. He let her know that the three men had money to buy rifles, but that they could not buy them themselves; he let her know that they had no wish to involve any one in the difficulties that would overtake him if it were discovered he had sold firearms to escaped prisoners.

Thus the matter lay for a time without progressing further. But Kenton utilized the interim in developing opportunities for going out from the town with officers on spring shooting parties, both to accustom himself to the routes for quick escape over the river and to accustom them to seeing him there with a gun. Pigeons were thick about four miles from the fort, as were also the wild ducks and geese along the Ecorse. Kenton's markmanship came to interest the British officers for whom at first he merely fetched and carried; he used their guns to display his skill and now and then carried one of his own, until "Kenton with a gun" outside Detroit was not an unfamiliar sight.

There came at last a day in May when, Kenton chancing to be in Edgar's trading house alone, Edgar left him and ascended to his loft; he came down with a large pile of moccasins which he threw on the counter and bade him take from them what he liked. At this the young man's spirits soared; he went carefully through the lot and, with the thought of the four hundred mile journey before him, "said he selected two of the best he could find." No questions were asked, no payment was mentioned—probably no thanks were uttered; "all was done in that mutual confidence inspired by friendship and as though each understood fully the intentions and feelings of the other." "He said he was well satisfied that the secret had been divulged by the Lady, but the Col. kept it."

After that preparations went rapidly on. A quantity of dried deer and buffalo meat was hidden in a hollow tree outside the town, together with salt and parched corn. Kenton, falling in with two Indian traders, filled them with rum and bought their guns for a trifle, which he hid in the woods. There are melodramatic old legends of drunken braves assembled at Detroit whose guns were stacked outside the fort; of Mrs. Edgar secretly taking three of them and passing them over a midnight ladder to the three men who had vaulted over the palisades. All that Kenton told Judge James of the escape from the town pertained only to himself:

"It was on the [3d] June, 1779. Mrs. Edgar had given me a rifle, a pouch of musket balls and a horn full of powder. When I got the gun I went back to the swamp to hide. The officers were shooting after dark and their servants [watching] their course, so I had to be very cautious.

"We set off and travelled 14 nights, lying by all day until we got somewhere near where Fort Wayne now is. We lived on coons and often had as high as three of a night. We then travelled by day."

They traveled as quickly as they could during the first night out, but failed to get beyond the great swamps southwest of Detroit where they were obliged to hide out all through the next day.

On the second night out, Kenton's daughter Sarah told Dr. Draper, "while Cofer and Bullock were walking together, and Kenton was by, Cofer observed to Bullock (Cofer became sick from laying

KENTON'S DELIVERANCE

FROM E. G. CATTERMOLE'S OLD "BORDER" BOOK, "FAMOUS FRONTIERSMEN, PIONEERS AND SCOUTS."

in the water and was unwell the whole route) that he was weary and hungry and would join the first Indians he met. Bullock replied that he would not do so—that he prided himself upom his name and family and would not disgrace them by such conduct. Kenton, hearing the conversation and being close by, Bullock appealed to him—who said as for himself he had been enough with the Indians—that he would sooner die in his tracks than suffer himself again to fall into the hands of such unfeeling wretches. Nothing more was said—there the thing dropped, and everything went along peaceably enough afterwards."

But there are evidences in the old reminiscences of this escape that a serious quarrel occurred between Kenton and Coffer during it. Dr. Draper spent years of desultory correspondence in trying to track it down. It is only surmise that trouble arose between them over the circumstances of Kenton's flight from Virginia eight years before. But Coffer came from Culpeper County, which adjoined Fauquier; and he arrived in Kentucky with a mysterious wound of which he never gave an account. And Kenton, when he arrived at the Falls of the Ohio, began for the first time to make inquiries of newcomers there regarding matters back home. Before the end of the year he had resumed his own name.

There are many old legends of many hairbreadth escapes from the savages on this journey, all very thrilling; but Kenton's uniform statement on this spoils them all: "We didn't seen an Injun on all our journey to the Ohio." Their moccasins wore out, "and then their feet wore out and full of prickly pears"; but these were merely minor woodsman's ills. Luck was with him at last, and in thirty days' time he went through four hundred miles of untracked forest and prairie like a homing bird. On cloudy days "the moss on the north side of trees" guided his course; at night he steered "by the cluster called the seven stars."

He learned later that the Indians outside of Detroit were watching for him—something he never doubted—and that while he was going straight west for the prairie land and the Wabash country before turning south, they, hearing of his escape and supposing he had taken the usual route of runaway prisoners, followed the trail clear to Mad River, but finding no sign of him, philosophically notched another escape on the record stick of his captivity and returned to Detroit.

He heard also, some months after his escape, that with all his care not to involve Edgar in his flight, his good friend had been seized none the less on the 24th of August following it. All of his property was confiscated and he lay in prison for over two years "because," as he stated in his petition for relief to Congress, "I favored the Revolution and had sent intelligence to the United States of the movements of the British forces in Upper Canada and which fact they proved upon me by one of the Messengers (who betrayed me) who caused the communication to the Falls of the Ohio to General George Rogers Clark.[1]" Kenton certified to the truth of this petition

[1]General John Edgar was an interesting figure at Detroit during the first years of the Revolution. He made his escape from the British some time between October and December, 1781. By 1784, in partnership with John Holker of Rouen, and Nicholas Mulburger of Dresden, he, "late merchant of Detroit," took up Indian trade again, selling the

and his certificate was appended to it when it was presented.

Much later, too, he learned from the Indians themselves how they regarded his escape from captivity. He himself, who for seven weeks had seen life and death flash before his eyes in dazing succession, held always a belief in a special providence exerted in his behalf—a belief "so deep," said one of his friends, "as to appear almost superstitious." The Indians used to say, after the peace, when speaking as they often did of his escape from their hands, that "the Great Spirit above took him from them a little by little—then a little farther and finally took him away altogether."

---

merchandise of France and Saxony at Detroit, "Michinackinac," and in the Illinois country. He built later a splendid residence at Kaskaskia, and Kenton visited him and Mrs. Edgar there on his return from a trip to Missouri in 1809.

Mrs. Rachel Edgar "was a blonde with blue eyes and very graceful, amiable, and was a fine dancer . . . very humane and benevolent, remarkably intelligent and interesting in conversation, and was at some period of her life an intimate of General Washington's family," say some of the old memories of her in the Kenton Papers. It is quite evident that Dr. Draper spent much time trying to establish a relationship between her and Shadrack Bond—one of the spies sent with Kenton to Vincennes—which would account for the great interest the Edgars took in Kenton's escape. She was one of the first "ladies" in the Western wilderness, and hers were the first laces that quivered and jewels that flashed at Kaskaskia in the Illinois.

Chapter VIII

ON INDIAN CAMPAIGNS WITH CLARK
1780–1782

WHEN Kenton arrived at the Falls of the Ohio in July, 1779, he at once asked for Clark, being burdened with information for him. But Clark was at Vincennes and Kenton, after but a few days' rest, went back across the river and made his way alone to the post. In his Manuscript Statement he says:

"I immediately sent on to Gen. Clark, giving him my opinion of Detroit, stating to him that Depeyster was at Mackinaw, 300 miles off from Detroit, and that I thought if he could get there, to the Detroit settlement, that Renew [Lernoult] would surrender to him. I met Gen. Clark with one hundred men in the summer of 1779 at Post Vincent, commanded by Col. McGary, and after Clark, hearing my report of Detroit, and deliberating on it, he concluded not to go, and I then returned to Kentucky.[1]

There is no doubt that, with a pilot fresh from the lake region who knew every crook and turn of the British post, Clark would have gone forthwith against

[1]"I did not see Kenton again until July, 1779. I met with him at Vincennes in company with some Kentuckians, who assembled there to proceed on the expedition which Clark contemplated against Detroit, but which was abandoned because of the want of an adequate force." William Bickley's Certificate appended to General Simon Kenton's Pension Statement: Draper MSS.—1BB87-88.

Detroit if he could have in any way mustered enough men to make the expedition. But he could hope for no assistance either from Virginia or Kentucky. Bowman had just returned from his ill-fated campaign against the Indian villages to which he had sent Kenton on his ill-fated scout the fall before; "the first regular enterprise to attack in force the Indians beyond the Ohio ever planned in Kentucky" had ignominiously failed. George Clark, the spy who had escaped when Montgomery was killed and Kenton was captured, "piloted Bowman to the Chillicothe town," says Kenton's Manuscript Statement, "and they whipped him [Bowman] on to the Ohio and killed a great many of his men."

To Judge James, Kenton gossiped a little about the fate of Black Fish, his old enemy, who was mortally wounded in this fight:

"In Bowman's attack on Piqua town [Chillicothe] he was pursued nearly to the Little Miami. Black Fish was not killed, but his thigh was broke and he lived till fall. Abner Chapine, who was captured at Capt. Clark's defeat at the mouth of Licking, told me that he told Black Fish that there were doctors in Gen. Clark's army who could cure him. Black Fish seemed much taken with the proposed relief and thought of releasing Chapine and to agree to pay him on his return in order to be cured. But it is supposed that Nation overruled him."

He gossiped also about Andrew Jackson, whom he first met that fall on the eastern border of Kentucky: "In 1779 Jackson came with Walker and some line cutters. In the fall at Boonesborough. He mated with a rowdy out-breaking set at Danville. He was then certainly twenty odd. Knew him there till '83. Familiar with Roberts' wife.[1]"

On the basis of this statement of Kenton's and its contradiction of Jackson's official birth date—March 15, 1767, which would make him a boy of twelve when Kenton first knew him—Judge James pursued a quest which resulted in an illuminating article on both men, published in the *Historical Magazine*, May, 1859. He quoted Kenton more fully there than in his Notes and gave some details of their taking:

In February, 1833 [this is an error—it should be 1832] I went to visit Simon Kenton, at his house in Logan county, Ohio, where I spent two days in gathering and noting material for the History of Ohio, which I was then about to write. As he talked, I wrote, and generally I secured his precise language, which was very terse and graphic.

Among the Notes I took, and the last one, was the one relating to Gen. Jackson. It was this: "In 1779 Jackson came out to [Kentucky] along with Dr. Walker and some line cutters." They were running the line between North Carolina and Virginia. Jackson had something to do with it as a kind of commissary. "Saw him that fall at Boonesborough. He mated with an outbreaking set at Danville, and was about Crow's Station." "Jackson was certainly twenty-odd years at that time; knew him there till 1783."

Another statement dwelling in my memory, but which I do not find noted, was, that Jackson was one year younger or older than himself—he did not remember which. He never met the General after that until President Monroe was making his tour

---

[1]Rachael Donelson Robards, whom her husband divorced and whom Jackson married.

General Henry Lee was with Kenton in eastern Kentucky at the time he met Jackson and corroborates him fully: "Jackson was with a little party of pack horse men . . . the winter drove them in—went and wintered at Boonesborough—Jackson with the others, and there Kenton saw him. The next spring resumed the survey. It was said he had command of the pack horse men. Then a spare, raw-boned young man." Draper MSS.—9BB60, p. 45.

through the United States. "Word was brought that Colonel Monroe and the gentlemen travelling with him would be at——, near Louisville. I was there with a large company assembled to meet the President; Gen. Jackson was with the President and I was introduced to him. I thought he looked shy at me, but I never said Crow's Station to him once."

Kenton spent the fall around Boonesborough and the winter mostly at Lexington—again with the newest and weakest station in Kentucky. This was the "terrible winter of 1779–1780," when from the middle of November to the last of February Kentucky was shrouded in snow and ice, and when hunting was easy, for starving turkeys, deer, and even buffalo would come so close to the settlements that they could be shot from the cabin doors. Wild turkeys fell frozen from the trees on which they perched, and Kentucky's herds of game were never again so great—thousands of deer and buffalo perished, and all the carefully tended fruit trees of the colonists, brought by boat or on horseback from Virginia and the Carolinas, were destroyed. They must wait yet another period of years for their peaches and apples and quinces and pears.

As in the winter of 1775–1776, Kenton contrived to visit all the settlements and stations old and new between the Kentucky and the Ohio. Lexington had been founded in his absence, Martin's, McAfee's, and Bryan's stations established, and Hinkston's old cabins rebuilt and renamed Ruddell's. But at some time in January, and through March and April, he was constantly in his beloved Limestone region. In early March the Indians began to annoy Boonesborough, and in April Kenton, with Hinkston and a few others, began to build the first rude block house at the mouth of Limestone Creek—a sort of wild inn for shelter, a part of his plan for guarding the newcomers who landed there. But the Indians and the British came in June, and the only record we have of this first beginning of Kenton's Station on the northern border is in Captain Joseph F. Taylor's account of his coming to Kentucky in June, 1784: "There was a fort at Limestone, and the Indians had driven away the people and burned the fort when we got there." It was a premature attempt at settling a dangerous point—it was still a dangerous point when Kenton put up his station near it in the fall of 1784.

He came back from captivity to find Kentucky covered with land jobbers and surveying parties. He heard that a Virginia commission had been appointed for the purpose of drawing up laws for the locating and entering of land. He heard that lands entered in a name other than one's own would lead to trouble later. He was ready to take up land, but he was still Simon Butler.

How he first learned that William Leachman still lived and that he could safely resume his own name is a mystery. One of his nephews says that he heard it at the Falls of the Ohio, in 1779; that he began there to inquire of the emigrants where they were from: "Some answered from Fauquier County, Virginia. Then he asked them if they knew the Kentons and Leachmans in Fauquier: Yes, knew them well—all well, and William Leachman alive." By all the evidence, Kenton made his inquiries cautiously and suspected the good intention of the several men reported to have recognized him. He feared some trap; feared still in spite of contrary report that Leachman was dead and that he had killed him.

His daughter Sarah says that he was first recognized by "a man named Greenwick," who, seeing Kenton enter lands in the name of Simon Butler, called him to one side and told him he must not do that; that in such case, if he were killed, his relatives, who were poor, could not recover the land. "Kenton, startled, but pretending ignorance, said, 'If not Butler, what name?' Upon which the man replied, 'In the name of Simon Kenton, to be sure.'" There is another story of another man who said to him one day, "You are a son of old Mark Kenton of Fauquier county—you need not deny it."

Most of the old sketches and biographies make his brother John his informant, but the whole Kenton connection is curiously ignorant and curiously silent on when or how John Kenton came to Kentucky—there is not in all the records one pertinent date or one illuminating sentence regarding all this except from his son Benjamin, who says that when his father left for Kentucky, standing on a ridge from which he could see Fauquier and its adjoining counties, "he took a last look at them—was determined never to see them again." He probably came out in 1779, for Kenton's daughter Sarah says that soon after the Greenwick incident, her father was at some place where men were enlisting for scout and border service and heard the name of John Kenton called; that he approached the young man who answered to it, discovered that he was truly his brother, and was finally convinced that Leachman lived.

But William Bickley's son gave Dr. Draper an entirely different version of how Kenton came to resume his own name:

"In hard winter of 1779–1780 Kenton wintered at Lexington—William Bickley also. Some emigrants came and brought a letter to Kenton, who up to this time was only known as Butler—and as he could not read, took Bickley with him into the woods, and got him to read it. Stated that Leachman was not dead but alive, and directed to Simon Kenton. Bickley did not know what it meant and Kenton told the whole story—seemed greatly relieved to learn he was not a murderer; and then resumed his name. So W. Bickley often repeated it."

It is not difficult to reconcile all these accounts. Certainly before the end of 1779 Simon Butler became Simon Kenton. For on December 20, 1779, he obtained from the land commissioners a certificate that shows the metamorphosis:

> Simon Kenton this day claimed a settlement and pre-emption to a tract of land lying on the Elkhorn, joining Col. Preston's survey at Cave spring on the south-east side, by improving the same and residing in the country ever since the year 1775. Satisfactory proof being made to the Court, they are of the opinion that the said Butler has a right to a settlement of four hundred acres of land, including the said improvement, and the pre-emption of one thousand acres adjoining, and that a certificate issue accordingly.[1]

It is an ironic circumstance that this first known entry of land made by him was to be the cause of a famous suit with a series of decisions and appeals on "Kenton vs. McConnell" that shook the Kentucky

[1] *Kentucky Reports of the Court of Appeals*, 1794.

courts and many a land title fifteen years later. But it started him on his career as one of the great landholders of Kentucky and Ohio. In the following spring he entered the field of locating land for warrant holders, "3000 acres of land warrants for Edmund Byne, his pay to be one-half" of the land located. In the final division he got one thousand acres on and about his old campsite, on which the town of Washington, Kentucky, was laid out. This article of agreement was made between Edmund Byne and "Simon Kenton, commonly called by the name of Simon Butler"; it was dated April 28, 1780, and it was signed by his mark, "Simon Kenton." He had not yet learned to write his name, but he had taken it back.

Kentucky turned as one man from Bowman to Clark when Bird and his Indians came down from Detroit in June and took Martin's and Ruddell's stations. All the Girtys were with him and McKee joined him on the Miami with six hundred Indians. Bird's first intention was to attack Clark at Louisville. but when McKee's savages learned that the British general carried two cannon with him, they persuaded him to go instead against the Kentucky stations.

One cannon shot disposed of Ruddell's, which surrendered immediately on condition that the three hundred inhabitants should be British, not Indian, prisoners. But the Indians had their way with them and Bird admitted to Ruddell that he was powerless to control his savage allies. Martin's Station was taken, with fifty prisoners surrendered; then the Indians were for going against Bryan's Station and Lexington. But already their success had defeated them; they had three hundred and fifty more mouths to feed; they had taken the horses but slaughtered the cattle; they had not enough meat, and Bird finally prevailed on them to leave. A little more of British wisdom or British control and all of the Kentucky settlements could have been wiped out with one shot each from Bird's cannon. Hinkston was among the captives—he made his escape on the second night and got to Lexington where he gave the first alarm.

"In the Spring [it was in June] of 1780," says Kenton's Manuscript Statement, "the Indians with Captain Bird, a British officer and his men, came into Kentucky, and took Riddle's and Martin's Stations. The Kentuckians then sent on a request to George Rogers Clark desiring him to command us against the Indians. He sent an answer that he would. Charles Gatliffe and myself went on to Riddle's and Martin's Stations, and found them both taken, and a number of people lying about killed and scalped. We then took Captain Bird's trail from there on to the South Fork of Licking, where Falmouth now stands; and when we got there, we found that Captain Bird had built a block-house, and made a stockade fort—and Bird and the Indians had both left there. We returned back to Harrodsburg."

But not without accomplishing something not set down in the records. Clark took a brass cannon with him on this summer's campaign, and Kenton's son William told Dr. Draper that his father once pointed out a white oak at Boston on Mad River, in which a ball from this cannon had lodged, and said it was fired from a brass six-pounder that had been "captured" from Bird's retreating force on Bird's Trace—"thinks Kenton (and Gatliffe) stole the cannon in the night." As these two were the entire pursuing party after Bird and his eight hundred and fifty warriors, it is a fairly drawn conclusion that they did.

Clark was at this time at Fort Jefferson on the Mississippi, defending it from another body of British and Indians who had come down to regain the Illinois and to attack the Spaniards at St. Louis, but when he heard Kentucky's call he left Colonel Montgomery in command and with what men he could spare came on to Harrodsburg, where he found the people eager and willing to go out. "Upon Clark's promise," says Kenton, "we joined into embodying and raising men," but it was late July before the force of one thousand was equipped with provisions and boats for the trip. On this campaign Kenton was for the first time commissioned as captain and commanded a company.

On August 2d the force was landed where Cincinnati now stands and began the march to Old Chillicothe, which they reached four days later. The town was deserted; it had been fired by the Indians themselves, on the preceding day when, forewarned by one of Clark's own men, they took flight; some of the cabins were still smoking. Fifty-two years later, Kenton, talking to Judge James, told the story of the traitor in his own characteristic way. For when talking of old times he would stress the fact of a disgraceful act, but when asked who committed it would say, "I'll not tell ye."

"In 1780," he said, "a man deserted from Clark at Newport. I wanted to follow him and told Clark I would fetch him back 'You shan't go—you will never stop till you find him—let him go.' This man had enlisted as a substitute, and was supposed to have been prevailed on by some one in Kentucky to go and betray. He gave the Piqua towns notice of our approach, and was drowned at the rapids of the Maumee." Then, much later in the talk, he added, "The man who escaped to the Piqua towns piloted Bowman out."

They stayed at Chillicothe that night. "Next morning," says Kenton's Manuscript Statement, "we pursued on to a place called Pickaway Town, and there the Indians embodied and fought us all day, and we whipped them, and for two days afterwards we were busily employed in cutting down their corn. On our return we stopped and cut down all of their corn at Chillicothe, and then returned back to Kentucky, which finished our campaign."

To Judge James he described the towns they burned:

"In 1780," he said, "there was a good wooden fort at Piqua Town on Mad River—hewed logs and stockades well planted—it was built by the British. There was a similar one at Chillicothe at Miami creek; both were burned; when Clark's army reached Macachak the first one was burning, but they added to the fire and cut down the corn. There were fields of corn in every bent of the creek from Boston to Springfield. There was great preparations for crops; and we had no doubt from the condition of it that it had been cultivated by the British soldiers—800 acres at New Boston. The army was three days cutting the corn down—it was not quite ripe enough for eating, but much of it was used. There was a large prairie in Springfield all in corn. The army set out very early from Old Town and reached Piqua (Boston) about nine o'clock—crossed the river, small fire of the Indians, and fought them back to the hills, two miles and returned by night.

"The destruction of corn (at Boston) was a great backwardness to the Indians; they were afraid to go in hunting parties on the frontier for fear of our people falling on them, and they were compelled to live on corn near their towns."

For nearly two years the Indians remembered how Clark's men had battled at the "Pickaway town" and gave Kentucky a long rest. In 1781 Clark, now a brigadier general, made some minor forays, and during the summer Kenton went up the Ohio from Harrodsburg to warn Clark on his way down the river that the Indians were out. How he combined his growing land interests with scouting is shown in one of his depositions (September, 1818) in which, after saying that he "was sent by Col. Trigg to apprize Gen'l Clark who was then expected to be on his way down the Ohio, that there was an Indian army out," he states that on his way he made a location at the forks of Clear Creek by marking with the letter K "the two ash saplins growing from one root." He was learning to write.

In this year also Kenton made the beginnings of a station on Quick's Run near Danville, but it was not completed until two years later. For in 1782 the Indian war broke out again.

The massacre of the "praying Indians" at the Moravian towns occurred in March, and whoever feels that the Indians committed all the savage acts of those days is invited to read the account of this unprovoked massacre of Indians by the whites. "Kenton thinks the Moravian campaign was a shocking affair" wrote Judge James in his Notes on Kenton's talks, "and so thought most of the people of that time." In May Colonel William Crawford led his army against the Sandusky towns and on June 6th suffered a crushing defeat. He was burned on June 11th, and that month a great general council of Indians was held at Wappatomika, which included many tribes—Ottawas, Chippewas, Delawares, Wyandots, Munsees, and Cherokees as well as Kentucky's eternal enemies, the Shawanese. They had just learned of the surrender of Cornwallis which the British had kept carefully from them, and it seemed to them that now or never was the time to strike, before the British had left the land; for it was clear that only time was necessary to make the colonies too strong to resist. Two armies were raised, one to go against northwestern Virginia, the other to descend upon Kentucky. Captain William Caldwell commanded this force, and with him went the famous three—McKee, Elliott, and Girty. James and George Girty were along also.

Three hundred strong they arrived before Bryan's Station on the night of August 15th and the next day attacked. By some miracle the almost defenseless station did not fall, and on the 17th the Indians withdrew. An express had been sent out to Lexington for assistance, which began to arrive just after the Indian retreat. John Todd came with one hundred and eighty-two Kentuckians collected from Lexington, Harrodsburg, and Boonesborough, and Logan sent word that he was raising men and would soon be along. But Todd determined to pursue without waiting for Logan's detachment. He followed on to the Lower Blue Lick, where a battle took place on the morning of August 19th.

Boone says in his alleged autobiography that it lasted fifteen minutes. He scouted for the expedition and saw so much sign of a large Indian army and so many attempts to hide indications of its numbers from the whites that he advised against crossing the river until Logan came up—until at least spies could be sent over to report on the Indian position and strength. The officers were inclined to follow his counsel, but suddenly Major Hugh McGary, a notable "fierce man" of the settlements, dashed into the river, calling on all who were not "cowards" to follow him. That curious shame which such a call can bring to birth in the worst and best of men took possession of his comrades and they all followed across with no plan of battle. It was a disastrous defeat. The Indians had laid a perfect trap and in a few minutes some seventy of the flower of Kentucky's men were killed; a number were wounded and seven were taken prisoners. On the next day Logan reached Bryan's Station with three hundred men and hastened on to the Licks. With him was Kenton, captain of a company. But they arrived too late; all that remained for them to do was to help bury the dead.

We have a description of Kenton as he appeared at this time, aged twenty-seven, given by Joel Collins who, then a boy, saw Logan's division pass through Lexington:

On Clark's Last Campaign

The boys belonging to the station all ran out to see the men as they passed, and Mr. Collins said he well remembered how his youthful fancy was attracted by the appearance of the captain who marched at the head of the first company. He was tall and well proportioned, a countenance pleasing but dignified. There was nothing uncommon in his dress; his hunting shirt hung carelessly but gracefully on his shoulder; his other apparel was in common backwoods style. On inquiry he was told that it was Captain Simon Butler, so well known afterwards under his true name, Simon Kenton.[1]

"From which we see that the name of Butler lingered long after Kenton had taken back his own name. The Indians never called him anything but 'Butler' or 'Cutta-ho-tha.'"

By now Kentucky trusted Clark and his aggressive tactics. "In 1782," says Kenton's Manuscript Statement, "we sent for Clark to come and command us again—he did come. We turned out with him, and he commanded us here to the Big Miami against the same Indians, who had re-embodied, and we whipped them again."

Concerning these "same Indians," Kenton amplified to Judge James: "Phil Waters had been prisoner and got back in 1782 to Cartwright's creek, and I went to see him to get him to pilot Clark; and from talking to him I found that the Indians then on the Big Miami at the towns there were the same that had been at Boston and Old Town in 1780. Logan allowed that Boone and I could pilot him to the country, and then, when we got there, Waters knew every place and could just go from one town to another. . . . There were seven of them, large and small."

Logan, with whom Kenton served, commanded

[1]*Pioneer Biography*, James McBride, 1869. Vol. I, pp. 210–211.

the troops of the interior, and when they left Lexington, the men scattered through the country, to hunt by the way and so provision themselves, and to meet by a certain day at Bird's old encampment in the forks of Licking. They killed a good supply of buffalo and deer, and jerked the meat at night—"each mess with its pack horse kept together." There was one pack horse to each mess of six. The men took from home enough parched corn to last them to the Indians' towns—a handful a day was a ration.

All the county lieutenants provisioned their men likewise, and the united forces finally met across the Ohio, opposite the mouth of Licking where Cincinnati now is. Logan and his men arrived on the morning of the designated day and Clark came up in the evening. On the 4th of November, at the head of more than a thousand men, Clark set out for the Shawanese towns; Kenton, Boone, and Waters piloting. They surprised the towns on the 10th; in a few hours most of them were reduced to ashes and all the property and food the army could not use was destroyed. The army stayed around the towns four days, waiting for the foe to return, and during this time Logan went on with one hundred and fifty horsemen to Loramie's trading store at the head of the Miami and burned the large supplies there.

But the Indians refused a battle, and when Logan came back from his foray Clark began the return march. Their losses had been very few, but they were carrying with them a dying comrade, Captain Victor McCracken, who while fighting beside Kenton in the surprise attack on the Indian towns had received a slight wound in the arm which had gangrened. He

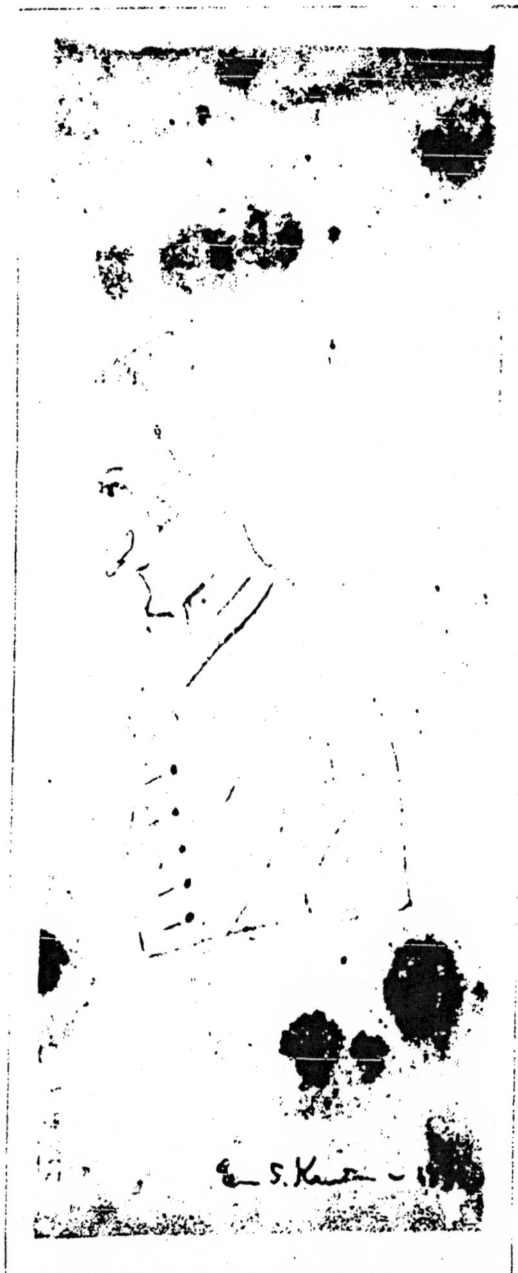

PENCIL SKETCH OF GENERAL SIMON KENTON, DRAWN BY THE REVEREND THOMAS S. HINDE IN 1832

FROM THE PICTURE COLLECTION OF THE STATE HISTORICAL SOCIETY OF WISCONSIN.

died as they were descending the Cincinnati hill and was buried on the Kentucky shore opposite, at the mouth of Licking.

Visions come sometimes to the dying, of all the past—perhaps of all the future. Something of prevision swept through this dying man then—of what the country his comrades had fought for and he was dying for would be when fifty years had passed. Kentucky only seven years before had been an uninhabited wilderness—now its people numbered close to twenty thousand. The Ohio country was still a wilderness uninhabited, but what would seven times seven years bring to both lovely regions—with ten thousand times ten thousand men pouring down the great river to take possession of the land; with settlements giving way to stations and stations to towns and cities—all made possible for future generations of a happy people by the men who were the pioneers! Something of this McCracken said to his friend John Floyd as he died on Cincinnati's hill, and after his comrades had given him to Kentucky's soil Floyd offered a resolution. "The troops were drawn up in a hollow square," said Kenton to Judge James in the February of the "half century year," "and at the request of Clark, all the troops (about 1500) agreed to meet at the same spot (Newport) that day fifty years."

Only a few months after this talk with Judge James, Simon Kenton was to issue his call to the survivors. Clark had died; Boone had died; and of the fifteen hundred men drawn up in that hollow formal square fifty years before less than half a hundred were heard from and only fifteen could plan to attend it.

With this campaign, Kenton's services with Clark were ended. For Clark's work was done. "From my first acquaintance with George Rogers Clark, which was in 1774, I served him at all times faithfully until 1782 in the fall."

Chapter IX

KENTON'S STATION
1783–1789

AFTER Clark's army disbanded Kenton went on to Harrodsburg, and collected there a few families willing to settle with him at his cabin on Quick's Run. They went out that winter and by spring had put up several other cabins, cleared land, and planted corn and flax.

Something akin to the home-making instinct was stirring in Kenton now. He was thinking in home terms old and new. On February 8, 1783, his first son was born, known curiously all his life long by his father's and his mother's first names—Simon Ruth. His mother later married one of Kenton's friends and this child was reared with her other children who always referred to him as their half-brother, but he always bore his father's name. Kenton had an abiding affection for him, and his other children assert that one of the deciding causes for his going on the Thames campaign at the age of fifty-eight was to find out the fate of Simon Ruth Kenton, captured by the British the year before.

Certainly he never "improved" land as he improved it this year. He had an end in view of which he spoke to no one. "He was a man that had very little to say." But toward fall he disappeared from Kentucky, gone no one knew where.

At last he was going "back home." It was no prodigal's return after twelve years—this return of Simon's. He had found the promised land, had made tens of thousands upon tens of thousands of its rich acres his own; he was going back to depopulate Virginia of "the Kentons"; to make the little Bull Run Mountain tract so provincial compared to Kentucky's world-life that his people would follow him there gladly.

He was not recognized when he presented himself at the little home cabin, "no larger than a thimble." There are dramatic old stories of the home-coming scenes, and they vary with the tellers of them. He sought out "the schoolmaster," he sought out "the preacher," he sought out the neighbors to mediate between him and his parents. But the chances are, given Kenton, that he was his own intermediary. There were many changes. His sister Frances had died during his captivity. His brother Benjamin had died during the Revolution. His brother William was the father of six instead of two children. His brother Mark had served in the Revolutionary War, and had seen Major André hung at Yorktown Heights. His sisters Mary and Jane had done their pioneer woman's full duty in marrying and multiplying. The sister he had left a little child was now a mother. Ellen Cummins, the sweetheart of his boyhood days, had died, and his old rival, William Leachman, was a widower. Between these two full reconciliation was made; Kenton offered him land—he offered everybody land—if he would come out to Kentucky. This Leachman eventually did, and there about 1805 he hanged himself.

Old Mark Kenton was feeble and ill, but his prodigal revived him with his tales of Kentucky's wonders. Simon inspired the whole connection and several of the neighboring families to listen, and finally to incline to the idea of migrating en masse to the Middle Ground. His offers of land were prodigious—they made the tiny farms of the Virginia mountain tract dwindle to mere "lots"; and at length all of the family, with the exception of his brother Mark and his sister Mary's family, decided to embark on the great adventure.

The Kenton migration began on the 16th of September, 1783. Their own teams and wagons were loaded and others were hired to convey the large party and their belongings across the mountains to the Monongahela. "Old Mark Kenton," says one of his grandchildren who made this trip to Kentucky, "was in poor health, but he was pleased with the idea of going to Kentucky of which he had heard such a goodly account, and for the better condition of his children and grandchildren. He was anxious to set the example and go there and encourage them to go—said he would go as far as he could."

But Mark Kenton was not to go far. The rough travel across the mountains was too much for him; after some days of riding in the pitching wagons a horse litter was contrived for him—a bed swung from two long poles and these fastened to the collars of two horses, one before and one behind. It was slower traveling now and those in the hired wagons went on ahead to order the family boat to be made. He survived until he reached "the Boat Yard" near the New Store (now Elizabeth), and there almost within sight of the promised land he died on October 16th, in his eighty-third year. They carried his body "about two miles up the river to Yough creek or river" and buried it at its mouth.

At the Boat Yard they sent back the hired teams and waited "for a large boat to be made, at a cost of thirty pounds." It had to be large, much larger than the usual thirty- or forty-foot one which could be purchased for seven to ten pounds. For the Kenton party numbered, according to Elizabeth Arrowsmith's record, "forty-one, viz.:

Mrs. Mark Kenton—negro woman and child: Nancy Kenton and child, in all.............................. 5
William Kenton, wife, 6 children, and a negro girl, in all.... 9
P. C. Kenton, oldest son—then 18..............
Two, Joshua and Mason—grown up—and Jerry and William, younger.............................
Thomas Laws, wife,[1] 4 Owens boys and 3 girls—and 2 of the Laws girls................................. 11
Elijah Berry, wife, 2 children, and a negro man.......... 5
James Whitehouse, wife, and 3 children................. 5
John Metcalf (father of Gov. Metcalf) went to visit Kentucky.. 1
John Griffith, went to visit Kentucky.................. 1
Simon Kenton, and negro woman........................ 2
John McGraw and wife................................ 2

Of these forty-one there were twelve capable of making defense if Indians attacked the party on its journey.

The Kenton boat was one of the first of the "Kentucky flatboats" just then coming into use and, like the hunter's half-faced camp, it has never since been

[1]Thomas Laws's wife was Jane Kenton, who had been previously married to Jeremiah Owens or Owen (variously spelled). The Reverend Asal Owen was her grandson.

improved on for fitness to the conditions that evolved it. It was rectangular and flat-bottomed, drew the minimum of water, and could be easily navigated by no more than four men. At one end were the stock pens, protected from Indian rifles by "sides" built horse-high—they took nineteen horses with them from Fauquier. At the other end was the cabin all sided and roofed and with a fireplace for warmth and for cooking. On the hearth or prowling about the boat was the Berry family cat—first of its kind to be brought to Kentucky. And by the hearth or moving about the boat among his forty people, as quiet as the cat and as alert, was Simon Kenton, captain of the ship and of all his friends and kinsmen on it.

It was a crowded voyage and a long one, but it was pleasant. Indian summer hung over the river and the land. Now and then they halted for wood or for game. When they left Fauquier they had taken along a number of cattle, some of which they killed on the land journey; most of the rest they slaughtered at the Boat Yard and salted down for use on the voyage. They had stocked their boat with corn, flour, and salt, but when they halted for wood. Simon would go ashore with the woodcutters and, leaving them to "work," would return from a hunt with turkeys and deer and, once, with a bear.

They saw no Indians on the way; it was not quite yet the period of river attacks, for this was a pioneer flatboat, and about the first of November they reached Limestone safely, where Kenton was intending to settle. But here came the first break in the perfection of the journey, for going on shore to scout and making his way to his old camp on Lawrence, he saw a dismaying amount of Indian sign. Indians had camped there "since the last rain," for the ashes of their fires were fresh and had not yet been damped down; it had been their headquarters for a great hunt; there they had jerked meat and made merry. Kenton's dream of a station on Lawrence must be put off a while longer, for his force was too small and altogether too inexperienced to maintain such an exposed position.

So the party divided. The McGraws, Philip Kenton, and a few others went on horseback across country with Simon to Salt River; the rest continued down the river to the falls, and then by team to "where Kenton's small group of cabins was . . . four cabins in a four square," says Mrs. Arrowsmith; "a crop of corn had been raised and some flax, and these belonged to Simon Kenton. Cabins not picketed in—some six or eight rods apart, on a fine rise of ground on the west side of Quick's Run. John Kenton resided about half a mile distant. Simon Kenton was there when all of the families and emigrants mentioned in the list arrived—during November—about two months moving—Metcalf and Griffith did not remain long."

But thirty-nine people could not crowd into four cabins, so rough and ready shelters went up, made tighter and warmer as winter came on—and a cold winter this was. Not too much work was put on them, for Kenton's heart was set on a station near Limestone, but logs were piled against the bark-hung frames, and instead of beds of dry leaves, four posts driven into the ground supported a rude framework on which Virginia bedding was placed. For there were women and children of Simon Kenton's blood in Kentucky now; the rude Salt River Station was no longer a lonely backwoodsman's frontier camp. There were household utensils from Virginia for cooking and Negroes to cook the fruits of Simon's hunts; instead of ramrods wrapped with strips of deer or bear or buffalo meat roasting over the fire, kettles hung over it, in which wild meat simmered or hominy boiled day and night. Here Kenton made the first of his "hominy stumps," where corn poured into the bowl-like hollow cut and burned in a rooted tree trunk was pounded up. There was no grist mill yet on this Kentucky frontier, but for luxury days they could pound the corn finely and sift it through the backwoodsman's sieve—deerskin stretched over a willow hoop with holes burned in it with a red hot fork—then mix the meal with water and salt and bake it on oaken slabs set before the fire. Hominy was, however, the good substitute for bread, or parched corn pounded fine and boiled with 'coon or 'possum or rich bear fat. Indian maize has never been sufficiently adored but by the Indians—they have their corn god. Without it this continent could never have been settled so quickly. Most marvelous food plant on the planet; it is an air plant that takes care of itself, matures in one hundred days from seeding time, stands in husk or shock without shattering from the ear, endures any weather, and serenely awaits a dateless harvesting.

Within a few weeks of their arrival Kenton had his Salt River colony well enough established to leave it, and by January he was back at Limestone, locating and surveying more land for himself and for others. The Indians had been more or less quiet since Clark's campaign of 1782, but they were still hovering about northern Kentucky, hunting and thieving in it if not actually striking at it, and any surveying party was liable to attack at any time. They advanced in "military line," therefore; the hunters went in front as spies; the surveyors, chain carriers and markermen followed; after them came the pack horses, and the company cook was the rear guard. Every now and then Kenton's party fell in with lost or frightened travelers and took a day off to guide them on their way. Joseph Taylor's party, which landed at Limestone in June, was such a one. They had come on to Tanner's Station at the Lower Blue Licks for a team to go back after their goods; while they were gone an Indian party swooped down on some campers from Fauquier who, suffering from smallpox, were not allowed in the fort, and killed all but two. "'Twas said the Indians took the pox and it killed hundreds. At Tanner's Station we met Simon Kenton with 13 chain carriers, and were so strong we camped out, and next day went 40 miles to Bryant's station."

This massacre decided Kenton to attempt again to establish a station on Kentucky's northern border. So when this survey was completed he went back to Salt River to gather up a party large enough to support him. William Bickley was of this party; so were the Wallers—Edward and John. Philip Kenton's son says that his father was "one of about sixty men who went from the interior of Kentucky under the auspices of Simon Kenton and built the block house at the mouth of Limestone," and added that

Kenton's Station, near Washington, Ky.

Memo. — The bank is quite bluff from the Station locality, or block-house, to the Kenton spring — some 60 feet above the bed of the creek. to the block-house; & about 35 yards from the Kenton Spring to the block-house. The block-house commanded the spring, an excellent spring; & by long rifle shot also commanded the Indian spring, which was about 110 yards from the block-house.

The Station was about a mile N.W. of Washington, Ky.

The ground descended each way from the Station except the West — & on the East side, quite abruptly.

SITE OF KENTON'S STATION

AND KENTON'S HOME NEAR WASHINGTON, KENTUCKY. 1784—1798. REDUCED FACSIMILE FROM THE ORIGINAL PLAT DRAWN BY LYMAN C. DRAPER (1858) IN THE DRAPER MANUSCRIPTS—7S111 "the very ground on which it stood, his father once told him, had washed away." "And these were the first strokes in those parts."

A cabin was put up near the Limestone block house in which the Wallers, John O'Bannon, and one other, "young men without families," lived for several years. But the block house was "unoccupied—ready for occupation in case of need."

Work began soon after on the block house at Kenton's old campsite—according to a deposition of John Waller's, "in July or August," 1784. By fall it was finished, and it stood as Kentucky's northernmost post, constantly exposed to Indian depredations until the peace of 1795 and the end of the twenty-year war. Strangely enough, it was never attacked, never even raided; why, no man can tell. But it gave Kenton his stronghold from which for ten years to come he could watch the Ohio in two directions, up and across, for emigrants and for Indians; and from this little fortress of loose logs he kept a tireless watch of the northern frontier.

His brother Mark came down the Ohio this summer to visit Kentucky and his people, but soon returned to Virginia, where he died the following year. About October 1st Kenton's "first family" came down from the old home state, and he, forewarned, was at Limestone to meet it. Thomas Dowden had died the year before and his widow with her four children had decided to come to Kentucky to be near her sister, William Kenton's wife. They arrived on a small keel boat and Simon Kenton took them to his station four miles away without an idea that within three years he would make the little fourteen-year-old Martha

Dowden his wife.[1] This was the "one family" Abner Overfield found at Kenton's Station when he landed at Limestone in November. George Berry and his family came out from Virginia in December and settled there along with the Elijah Berrys who came up from Salt River. Bethel Owens arrived "between the 9th and 15th of December, 1784, when there were only three families there." In this month also came William Maddox, William Henry, and Job Masterson and his family. On December 31st William Wood, a Baptist clergyman, with his family, and Benjamin Fry and James Turner with theirs, landed at Limestone on their way to the falls, for the river was freezing over and the floating ice made further travel in their three small boats too dangerous. They found but one cabin there, "Ed Waller's, just below the mouth of Limestone creek." A son of William Wood's, Judge Christopher Wood, gave Dr. Draper some vivid recollections of his early days at Kenton's Station, when he was a boy of twelve:

> At Limestone Mr. Wood and party landed about noon, Dec. 31, 1784, and next day Simon, William and John Kenton—and Thos. Kenton, son of Wm. Kenton, and others, came, and Simon Kenton, as chief man, urged Wm. Wood and party to join his settlement, and would sell them as good and as cheap

[1]Four daughters of Thomas Cleland, a Presbyterian clergyman, and Jane his wife were closely connected with the Kenton family. Mary Cleland was married to William Kenton, Simon's eldest brother. Sarah Cleland was married to Thomas Dowden; his daughter Martha was Simon Kenton's first wife. Elizabeth Cleland was married to Stephen Jarboe, a Frenchman; her daughter Elizabeth was Simon Kenton's second wife. Susannah Cleland was married to William McGinness who lived at Kenton's Station and was killed near there. Philip Cleland, a son of Thomas and Jane Cleland, also settled in Kentucky and from him descended a long line of Presbyterian clergymen. A number of the sons of these sisters were among Kenton's noted spies.

as could be got in Kentucky—and upon looking about Wood and Turner and Fry were pleased, and thought they could not do better, and bought some 400 acres of Kenton and laid out Washington: This was a purchase, not a gift. Kenton did give the use of a 5-acre out-lot at Kenton's Station to all who would settle there, to use as long as they would wish to live on or cultivate it—and to revert to Kenton when abandoned.

. . . Then first of January Kenton had but a single cabin—some 20 feet square—but no roof on it: This was soon put on, with the help of Wood's party, and Chr. Wood helped to roof this first cabin roofed in Mason county—for Waller's was not then covered, and young Wood helped to roof that soon after also. The Wallers and O'Bannon mostly made their home at Kenton's Station, and had their cabin at mouth of Limestone for their own convenience, and the accommodation of emigrants landing there. . . .

During 1785 a large addition of settlers was made at Kenton's Station, and some 16 or 18 cabins erected, and fully 20 families altogether. The cabins were erected in a hollow square, adjoining each other—except two cabins, between which was a space of some 30 feet which was picketed. No gate—entered the cabin doors, and these of nights barred with a stout hand spike—doors of slabs nearly 3 inches thick: One story cabins: Corners were block-houses, higher than the other cabins, and jutting over a foot for defense. The enclose within the station was about 8 rods by four—longest way of the station along the creek. Some 4 or 5 rods below the station and on the hill side, a very large fine spring burst out, from which a supply of water was obtained—this spring had rivulets running a few rods into the creek.

To this spring Kenton crept one night during a severe attack of fever whose orthodox treatment in those days refused the patient water. He stood this as long as eyes were on him; then in the night he crawled down the hill and sat a long time beside his spring, drinking his fill. "It did him no harm; he soon recovered."

Thanks to its advantageous location and to its

stalwart group of fighters, Kenton's Station filled up rapidly during 1785. Arthur Fox was there in the spring, co-founder with Wood of the town of Washington that lay to the south. Kenton sold them the land on which the town was laid out, but he kept a fourteen-hundred-acre tract intact which he let out in five-acre parcels—"allowed any one that chose to sit down on this." He made frequent trips to Limestone to encourage passing parties to settle with him, as he had induced the Wood party to stay; his offer of free land lured them, and these as they came assisted in building cabins at his station until at last "there were twenty odd on each side enclosed."

George Mefford came this spring and stayed several years. Jeremiah Washburn arrived with his eleven-year-old son Cornelius who, trained by Kenton, developed into one of the most spectacular figures along the border. Joshua Baker arrived and "the Edwards boys," with their sister Jane and her husband William Rains—another of Simon's nephews. The William McGinnesses came out, and so rapidly did the station develop that a wagon road was opened to it before the end of the year.

After all, Kenton's Station, if not Kenton himself, founded Washington. If his station had not stood to the north, there would have been no town there for a number of years. The town site was a canebrake, gradually cleared away as the cabins were built, but for a long time its present Main Street was no more than a rude wagon road through the cane, connected by narrow, winding paths leading to the primitive homes set deep in little clearings in the cane forest. It is a sad little town to-day but it was a flourishing one during its first quarter century of existence. At the end of its first five years it boasted one hundred and nineteen cabins—a remarkable record then for the West. Limestone also became a town—but called Maysville—in 1787, laid out on one hundred acres, "the property of John May and Simon Canton." And Mayslick, eight miles from Washington, on the buffalo road to the Blue Licks, began to be settled. A log meeting house was built there; there was "meeting" at Kenton's Station and at Limestone, and William Wood became itinerant preacher of the little settlements on the northern border. The Reverend Robert Finley and his family came to Washington in 1788, and years later his son James wrote in his *Autobiography* of what Simon Kenton, "that truly great adventurer," meant then to the place and its people: "He was truly the master spirit of the time in that region of the country. He was looked upon by all as the great defender of the inhabitants, always on the qui vive, and ready to fly at a moment's warning to the place of danger for the protection of the scattered families in the wilderness." Finley is another of the many who looked upon him as a man raised up by Providence for a special purpose and whose miraculous deliverances from the greatest perils were confirmation of the belief that he was in truth a child of Providence. "He was regarded as the prince of pioneers of this region of the country," he said, and he was the "teacher and captain" of all the young boys in those parts.

On purchased land the settlers began to erect better cabins, still of logs but neater and more permanent. They were one story high with one room, one door, and at first no windows, since through windows Indians might enter. The door, closed and barred at night, was not opened in the morning until the "first duty" had been performed—"to ascend by a ladder which always stood leaning behind the door to the left, and look out through the cracks for the Indians, lest they might have planted themselves near the door, to rush in when the strong cross bar should be removed and the heavy latch raised from its resting place." At first only a part of the floor was laid, for the "puncheons"—wide slabs of wood three or four inches thick—took time to hew by hand. The chimney was built of "cats and clay"—bits of small poles mixed with mud and the down of cat-tails which made a surprisingly fireproof construction; often when the Indians fired a cabin and burned it to the ground the chimney of wood and mud stood high above the ruins. As slowly as the cabin floor was laid the cabin itself was "chinked"—the cracks between the logs filled in with slabs of wood large and small and then "daubed" with wet clay hurled by the strongest arm among the cabin dwellers, to make the new home wind and water tight.

And while all this was going on, patches of cane-land were being cleared for corn, gourds and pumpkins, potatoes, turnips, cabbages, and beans. The forest gave berries and nuts and "winter grapes"—the wild fox that needed several frosts to sweeten them.

In the mornings at Kenton's Station, once the morning duty had been performed and the doors flung safely open, the fires were lighted on the various hearths and flame and smoke went soaring up the cat-and-clay chimneys. In the rear the back log rested; on flat stones in front the hickory forelog. While the water was heating for the simple herb teas, and the meat—"game Buffalo plenty, deer also and turkies very fine"—was roasting or frying over the coals, the johnny cake was baking before them. For dinner, in the spring, "early greens" were picked from the woods; in the summer, vegetables from the secret garden in the center of the corn patch; in autumn and winter, potatoes and turnips and pumpkins from their "holes." At night, without fail, the iron hominy or mush pot bubbled above the fire, and sometimes from Indian meal mixed with a little flour and maple sugar or honey "wonders," or doughnuts, were mixed and fried in the fat of wild game. But wheat flour was rare; it was coming down the river now, but it sold at Limestone for ten dollars a barrel.

A grist mill was contrived at Limestone the year after Kenton's Station was built—a strange machine of wood, stone, and buffalo hide in which the folk from Kenton's could have their corn ground into meal by carrying it four miles. Kenton soon tried his luck with a water mill put up just below the forks of Lawrence, but, says Judge Wood, "it proved a failure, as it would not work, built by old Tommy Lucas. Corneal Washburn, hearing the creaking of the mill, when Lucas was trying to make it go, crept up with his gun, and got behind a tree, and shot at the water wheel, said he thought it 'was some sort of wild animal.'" Kenton did not give up the project, indeed, he added to it, for the December Court of 1792 has on its records: "Leave granted Simon Kenton to build a grist and sawmill on Lawrence's creek."

Indians Prowl About the Station

Shortly after Kenton established his station Pierre Druillard appeared. "Peter Drewyer," said Kenton to James, "became unfortunate and came to Kentucky and lived with me 14 years. He got to drinking."

He lived first at the station, later at Kenton's home, and finally at the tavern in Washington, Kenton always paying the bills he ran up. A son was born to him at Kenton's Station—Simon Kenton Druillard. Kenton gave him land which he never improved, but he brought his family there and for a time lived with them. Kenton's children say that he practically supported Druillard during all these years of idleness and intemperance and always treated him with the utmost kindness and respect; "would always have him sit at his right hand at table, and give him the best he had and wait upon him first." He gave him a horse to use on his trips between Kentucky and the Sandusky towns and dressed him "in broadcloth." Druillard's son George spent much time at Kenton's Station—he who later went with Lewis and Clark to the Pacific coast—and when he removed to Missouri some time after the final peace, he "had a parting frolic at Kenton's and started off."

With the spring of 1786 the Indians, with no regard whatever for the Fort Finney treaty so lately signed, came over the Ohio to steal and to kill. They took nearly all the horses at the Limestone and Licking settlements; by summer they had made off with nearly five hundred. In May they killed Lot Masters and Hezekiah Wood on their way to Kenton's Station for Parson Wood's preaching. When they were missed Kenton raised a party and pursued the Indian trail, thinking they had been taken; it was several days before their scalped bodies were discovered in the woods.

Very soon after this John Kinsaulla, a Pennsylvania Dutchman living at Kenton's Station, out one evening hunting cows after dark, was seized by Black Snake and four of his warriors. Going on with him toward the station, they came within hearing distance of "Old Man Taylor's cabin," which had been built for him outside the fort, near the spring. As he was crippled with rheumatism, preaching was often held at his house, the male worshipers carrying with them their knives and rifles, and services were going on there that night. General Whiteman relates that Black Snake, hearing the sound of William Wood's voice, inquired if the white people were praying. Kinsaulla said they were. "Well—go hear," said Black Snake, and took his party so near that they could peer through the cracks of the logs. After a space, "We goes," Black Snake said, "no hurt white people praying—Great Spirit would be angry." And forthwith proceeding to Helm's Station a few miles away, he stole several horses and took them and Kinsaulla across the Ohio.

This capture was soon followed by another—George Clark's son Robert was taken with a Negro boy from his father's fields. And others followed these.

It was just at this time that Kenton began to raise "on his own hook" his own company of spies, scouts, and minute men, most of whose deeds do not appear in the records of Kentucky. For eight years to come, from the first of April to November of each year, "Kenton's boys" held themselves ready to start anywhere at any time on no notice at all. No records were kept, no muster rolls, no honor list, and no pay roll. Nicholas Washburn was one of these boys and some brief notes taken from him put the case as clearly as it is put anywhere.

He "stated that in May, 1786, while living in what is now Mason County, Ky., he volunteered under Capt. Simon Kenton as a minute man during the continuance of the Indian war and John Masterson was Lieutenant of the company. He was engaged with his company in various operations against the Indians on the western frontier for eight years in succession as often as it was necessary to repel invasion by the savages. . . . During 5 years of his service he acted as Spy under the orders and instructions of Captain Kenton from the first of April to November of each year—that being the usual period for Indian depredations."

This service was quite distinct from that of spies or rangers called into special service by the county lieutenants for which pay and rations were given. It was Kenton's own unique contribution to Kentucky's defense. It was not provided for in the regulations and no particular attempt was made to bring it to the notice of persons in authority. All it meant was that when word was sent Kenton of horses or people taken, he and his "boys" tucked some parched corn and jerk into their hunting shirts, laid hold of their guns, mounted their horses, and picked up the trail. The expeditions often ended in failure, but they never failed to start. There was not an organization like it in all of Kentucky, and the whole of its history will never be told. It was in the day's work for eight years of days—that was all. For it did not end with

November if the Indians lingered late in Kentucky. Nor even then; they still lurked across the river.

But it was work that suited him. He cared little for posts of outward responsibility; those posts meant dependence on others. Briefly, it rounded down to this: he trusted few reports but his own; he preferred to be the pilot of a general's army than to be general and subject to the reports of pilots other than himself. He felt safer, and others—generals and private soldiers alike—felt safer when "Kenton piloted." He *was* the general; for so trusted was he that by his reports the army largely marched, halted, advanced, and attacked. He was a good soldier when he had to be, but military red tape irked him and delays in acting on reports that called above all for quick action exasperated him. Here on the border, with men enough to support him of his own choosing, his own spy and scout, ranger and pilot, and his own commander, he was five men in one.

The result of the continued Indian raids was Logan's campaign of 1786. Logan had meditated this for some time, and all through the late summer boats, ammunition, and provisions had been collected and an army of about seven hundred men had been raised, armed, and equipped as usual at their own expense. "Perhaps fifty head of fat cattle were taken to supply the men," says Henry Lee in his notes. "Each man would take in his wallet perhaps a gallon of parched corn meal mixed with maple sugar, which furnished a very agreeable beverage—with water—peculiarly fitted for quenching thirst—and perhaps a little bacon—sometimes straggle off and kill a deer."

On Logan's Campaign

The forces held rendezvous at Limestone, where the women in all the stations round about stayed up all night parching corn and baking johnny cake for their men. The crossing consumed a night and a day—September 29th and 30th. They landed at Eagle Creek and marched through Logan's Gap—so called henceforth, the very spot where Kenton had been taken eight years before; and their route to the Shawanese towns was his old one; it took them six days to accomplish it.

On the early morning of October 5th a deserter left the camp a few miles this side of Chillicothe and warned the Indians at Machachack, saying the whites would arrive in two days. He was tomahawked on the spot, and Logan, apprised of the desertion, hastened his march and arrived at Machachack about noon of the next day. This town he attacked with half his force, the rest being detailed to go to Moluntha's Town, half a mile off across the creek. Kenton and his company were with this detachment. By the time they came up most of the Indians had fled to the thickets, swamps, and high prairie grass; but Moluntha awaited them in his tent "with his flag flying from the top of a pole 60 feet high." His confidence in the whites was supreme; only the spring before he had sent a runner into Kentucky to warn the people that a party of Cherokees was about to come through and to be on their guard, and Logan knowing this, had in truth ordered his officers to forbid any of their men to kill any among the enemy they might think were prisoners.

Kenton and Boone commanded the advance on Moluntha's Town, and Kenton told Judge James that he himself placed Moluntha and his family under a guard, with orders that no man should go to them until he came; he then went off after the fleeing Indians. But Moluntha was killed—by the same hot head who had lost the battle of the Blue Licks four years before:

"McGary claimed to go in," said Kenton, "and being an officer was admitted, when he killed him. If I had been there when he struck Moluntha, I would have struck him. McGary was an outbreaking man; he was shy of me for he knew I could handle him. I knew Moluntha as soon as I saw him, for I had been prisoner with him in 1778. We burnt the Macachac town, and then the Pickaway town where West Liberty is. Here an Indian was taken and confined in a cabin, with his arms pinioned to the wall. After he had been there a day and a night, a man who was rather a particular acquaintance of mine, went in, tomahawked him. I never could forgive such cruelty after such deliberation. Well, I saw that Indian raise his head as well as he could, and as the brains were coming forth, he put his hands to his breech-clout, and smoothed it and adjusted it as well and as carefully as he could at any time. We went on, burnt Wapatomica, McKee's town, Blue Jacket's town."

In the Machachack cabins, before they were fired, Logan and his men found young Robert Clark's "advertisements"—the names of his parents and sisters written on cards and stuck in the cracks. They had already come on the scalp of a Negro stretched on a tree; they had feared it was that of the Negro captured with him and that Robert too was slain. So on their way back they posted advertisements of their own along the trail, offering any two Indian prisoners they were carrying back for the return of young Robert.

Indian prisoners were a problem always, valuable only as ransom for captured whites. Logan's men took back about forty who were put into stockades at Lexington and Danville and carefully guarded in the hope that through some of them—Moluntha's wife and child had been taken—they might receive some of their own captured friends back.

In spite of Logan's victory, less than two months passed before the Indians were again in Kentucky prowling about Kenton's Station; and coming one December night upon William McGinness's cabin not far away—he had just moved out from the fort—they shot and killed him in his own doorway. Kenton and his men ran over, but the Indians had fled and a snowfall that night made pursuit hopeless by morning. Then it was discovered that the widow had lost not only her husband but her horse. Grief over death was tempered in those days by other misfortunes almost as great; love was not the only measurer of values. When Kinsaulla was taken his wife said sincerely, "I would rather lose a cow than my old John." When a father was slain in Bryan's Station field his son said sincerely, "By Christ, fader's killt and the corn ain't hoed." Death and life were strung on a string together, and there was little time to grieve for the dead head of the house when wife and children must take over his work and bend their backs to the burdens the stolen horses had carried.

And so, in spite of the recent grief, an early morning salute was fired at Kenton's Station on Christmas

Day, and "Kenton and his companions had a cheerful time shooting game"—working, that is, to get in the meat supply for the twenty families already there and two new ones just arrived. They were busy too, this winter, erecting a small stockade in the center of the Washington settlement, so that in case of alarm so sudden that Kenton's Station could not be reached, the inhabitants could retreat to the block house in the town. All through the winter the Indians prowled through the region; they had become so dangerous by spring that all the season's tilling and planting was done under guard.

But before the fields were tilled that year, Simon Kenton's first marriage was celebrated. In his old family Bible the record reads:

> Simon Kenton and Martha Dowden were married February 15, 1787; She died December 13th, 1796—age not known.[1]

This was the first marriage celebrated at Kenton's Station, but it was far from the last. Over and over in the Kenton Papers we find old letters beginning: "My parents were married in Kenton's Station," or, "I was born in Kenton's Station." Parson Wood married, baptized, and buried his people in the perilous years mostly at that little center of life and death on Lawrence Creek.

A few months after his marriage Kenton went out on a scout over the Ohio with Joshua Baker and a few others, to make sure of what the Indians were doing; above all what they were meditating. They came very shortly upon sign of an Indian camp, and

[1]She was born in 1769 or 1770. Her daughter Sarah says she died in her twenty-eighth year.

without going to it saw clearly that it was composed of a large party intent on mischief and sending out spies to the Kentucky settlements to return with information and horses. So they quickly returned and Kenton sent out warning that danger was near. This scout was the origin of Todd's expedition.

In May or June more than two hundred men rendezvoused at Limestone, as usual self-equipped and provisioned, and there elected their officers, also as usual, before starting off. Kenton of course was pilot; Colonel Robert Todd was chosen commander; Hinkston was elected second in command, and Colonel William Russell the third. Kenton, as captain, commanded the Limestone volunteers—his own picked brood.

The camp whose sign Kenton had found lay far up Paint Creek, but before reaching it they came upon a smaller one where they saw an Indian standing. He was shot down and two others taken and forced to tell where the large camp lay. In this small camp they found a "large number of halters or tugs made of raw elk or buffalo hides," which clearly indicated a horse-thieving expedition.

Kenton, without asking permission of Todd, took his own company and set off for the large camp; he so outdistanced the rest of the party that they camped for the night without overtaking him. During the night he sent back a messenger to Hinkston—not Todd—saying he had found the camp but, owing to sign of a large body of Indians, was afraid to attack it until reinforced. Hinkston was about to go on, but Todd forbade it until the whole number was ready to move; they contrived to come up with Kenton at break of day and surrounded the camp, but found only a few squaws and children there with one Indian, all the others having gone hunting. The man escaped; the women and children were taken. "In the camp a large quantity of jerked bear and deer meat were found together with a considerable quantity of bear's oil in deer-skin bags—four or five gallons in each—the skins stripped off whole, with a fastening at the neck and four legs for a bottom." What they could use they took; all the rest was destroyed. They prolonged their trip by scouting for other camps. but found none and finally returned with their prisoners.

To the great relief of the Kentuckians, an Indian embassy shortly afterward reached Washington to propose an exchange of captives and, terms being arranged, the "Limestone treaty" was carried out a few weeks later. Black Snake, Wolf, Captain Johnny, Captain Billy, Blue Jacket, and other Shawanese chiefs with about sixty warriors, all painted in ceremonial style, appeared on the Ohio opposite Limestone, where Aberdeen now is. Logan, Kenton, Boone, Todd, Patterson, and others went over to meet them, and there the prisoners were exchanged. Mrs. Mary Sharp and her child, taken the year before near McAfee's Station, were delivered up. John Kinsaulla was returned—he brought back "a caret of tobacco," a gift from Captain Johnny to his wife. Robert Clark was given up—he told a marvelous story of his adoption by a squaw who had hidden him during Logan's campaign lest he might be killed in revenge for Moluntha's murder.

The Indians also brought back horses which they

offered to surrender, but Kenton and Boone declined to receive them. Trouble began, however, when Mrs. McGinness's mare was recognized, for Luther Calvin swore "he would have the mare if he had to scalp every Indian there to effect it." Kenton and Boone acted quickly; they bought the mare from the Indians at the price of a keg of whiskey, and in full view of both shores swam it over the river and delivered it up to the widow.

A dance and barbecue followed; the Kentuckians had slaughtered a beef and provided plenty of game for their guests. But the festivities took place across the Ohio and the Indians were made to stack their guns before the feast and the dance. When all was over the Indians departed in high good humor. They had got what they wanted—their people back. With that the treaty was voided, and they began immediately to make their usual raids on Kentucky.

This year and the next were years of "false alarms," and many a fruitless expedition was made. It was said of Kenton that he would call out his men at the hoot of an owl. But this was caution and none of them resented it.

Such a false alarm occurred toward the end of 1788. With John Cleves Symmes's great purchase from Congress of two million acres of Ohio land, a little string of settlements began to spring up across the river. One of these was the stockade fort of Columbia at the mouth of the Little Miami, erected in the utmost haste so that the work would be done before the Indians could know anything of it. On the day it was finished the workers celebrated and fired guns of rejoicing frequently. Some of Kenton's minute men were out hunting and heard the firing. They went back and reported. Kenton called out his boys, tumbled them into some old boats, and went down the river sixty miles to "the relief of Columbia." So quick had been the report of supposed trouble and Kenton's response that within forty-eight hours after the guns of rejoicing had been shot off he was there with sixty men to give the aid he had feared they needed.

Another incident illustrating his constant caution may as well be tōld here. About this same time—in 1789—he was out guarding a party of twelve or thirteen surveyors along Licking. At night he was careful in selecting the camp; he doubled and redoubled on his trail—"marched half a mile down a creek bottom, then crossed the stream and up the same distance—the creek only separating the two trails on either side—then left a sentinel and retired back near by and camped."

Spencer Records and Tobias Woods were out hunting buffalo in this same region and came upon the surveyors' trail, looking—as Kenton intended it should look—like the sign of an Indian marauding party, some mounted and some on foot. Never doubting they were following such a trail, they crept along in the dusk and when they heard a horse neigh they were convinced an Indian camp was near by. They stopped to tighten their moccasins and leggins that they might run the better, threw their hats onto the trail, and soon came to the place where Kenton's party had first crossed the stream. They followed this up the half mile to the next crossing sign, and there Kenton's sentinel, seeing them without hats and in

Indian dress, took them for savages and ran back to report. The two hunters treed, supposing the Indians would soon appear, but when they heard Kenton's rallying shout to the panic-stricken surveyors, "Stand your ground and not a man run!" they hallooed that they were friends and went over. From the fact that Kenton offered them a dollar a day to join up, it would seem that it was his own surveying party he was guarding—another indication that where the Indians were concerned Kenton trusted no one so much as himself.

"Movers" were frequent now along the wagon road leading from Limestone to the Blue Licks, for the great flatboats called arks were coming down the Ohio, laden not only with families but furniture and household treasures. The Limestone waters were thick with boats—they came in sometimes at the rate of thirty a day—and the shore was thronged with Kentuckians, come from the interior to meet their friends or the friends of their friends and relatives. Men from Washington and Kenton's Station were there with teams and pack horses to take the travelers and their goods to the interior. This meant that many an emigrant family made their first camp in the wilderness almost within hearing of the station and, without knowing it, were under guard.

In the spring of 1789 Thomas Kelsey of Kenton's Station and one other engaged to move a newly arrived family to Lexington by packing on horseback, and spent their first night within seven miles of Kenton's. Their fires were in full blast and all were seated around it, "comforting as well as possible," when three Indians fired on them, killing one of the men and wounding Kelsey severely. His companion ran to Kenton's Station for aid. Kenton came out and held the ground until morning, then raised a party, trailed the Indians to Cabin Creek, and killed them as they were crossing the Ohio.

In the Kelsey letters on this incident, one of the sons-in-law wrote that when Kelsey recovered from this wound he went to Lexington to tend a water mill near there, and added this anecdote on Kenton enraged:

> While there my wife says she saw Simon Kenton. She thinks the mill was owned by him; there was a great man came into the neighborhood with a mighty land warrant and was for laying it in a great scope of country including Kenton's Domain—which raised his ire, he took hold of the great man and no one ever got such a caning—that man run and tried to hide himself, but Kenton would follow up and caned him over the face and eyes and beat the fellow within an inch of his life, but that settled the land warrant, my wife says that she saw the man afterwards—he was as bloody as a butcher.

Lewis Wetzel, in full flight from the law, arrived at Kenton's Station this year. He had just made his escape from the Marietta jail, where he had been imprisoned for shooting an Indian in time of peace—no crime, this, to a Wetzel. At Washington he found old friends in the Arrowsmiths and plenty of sympathy from Kenton's boys, who knew, all of them, all his exploits. When soldiers followed him down, decoyed him aboard a boat, and took him on to Fort Washington, his rescue was made a county affair. A party of two hundred men was immediately raised under Lee and they went after him, determined to have him at all costs. Kenton and his troop were

IMLAY'S MAP OF KENTUCKY, SHOWING COUNTIES IN 1793 AND THE LEADING ROADS.

along, and they finally returned with him to Limestone, where he remained for some time and went out on several of Kenton's expeditions.

Four years of work! At their end Simon Kenton, through his station, his trained boys, and his own ceaseless vigilance, had transformed the face of Kentucky's northernmost frontier from an unsettled wilderness to a county. Petitioner himself of Virginia for a division from Bourbon, her Assembly had marked and passed the petition as "reasonable." His region was no longer Bourbon but Mason, with its own court, its own county lieutenant, its own militia, its own half dozen chartered towns, its own dozen stations—for fortified possession of Mason County, first taken by Kenton, was never relinquished; station after station went up around his. The long battle was not yet won; the next five years were to be a continuous engagement in the final struggle, but the outcome was assured. With the Limestone port made safe, emigrants' boats packed its shores—Fort Washington was built from their timbers. From twenty thousand people in Kentucky, their number had leaped in these four years to more than seventy thousand. And the marvel of this tidal emigration from the East had only begun.

Best of all, in face of Mason County's new military machinery, Kenton was still a man on his own hook, careless of fame, careful only to keep pure a peculiar power. His reports of Indian sign told to others could raise armies now with commanders for him to pilot—all this was good when he needed armies. But his reports kept to himself made him commander and pilot alike of a force of trained men and boys he could raise by a single roar from his station; they would follow blindly if that was his pleasure, in full faith that he was about to do "something clever" again. Cornelius and Nicholas Washburn, Christopher Wood, and Benjamin Whiteman were among these boys he had trained; John and Archibald Dowden, Thomas McGinness, Philip Kenton, and a host of his other nephews and kinsmen. On these he could rely for instant action, and instant action in Indian warfare was more often than not all that saved the day. So, more often than not, their commander ignored "the military" and acted on his own.

The little block house stood on its hill, open to all and known of all who passed in and out of Kentucky. It was no secret fort; it was a literal magnet for collecting information on which not only Kentucky and Virginia, but the central government itself, acted. And yet, for all its fame in history, it might have been a little secret center set up in some Kentucky cave, never seen or known of men. Its commander operated outside of the "regulations," and this is why most of his services were never written into the records of his time; why they lingered only in the memory of the people he served.

Chapter X

HIS INDIAN CAMPAIGNS
1790–1793

KENTON'S own particular private defense along the Ohio was dealt a devastating blow by the United States government in the spring of 1790. For orders came to Henry Lee, Mason County lieutenant, that if it became necessary to call out parties to resist attacks on Kentucky, "you will issue the most positive orders that no such party shall under any pretence whatever enter the Territory either of the United States or of any Indian tribe."

This was absentee government of the most drastic kind, exerted of course to prevent Kentucky vengeance from interfering with the new settlements in the Ohio country, but leaving the Kentuckians powerless to make any reprisals on Indian horse pounds, Indian crops, or Indian villages. They could no longer pursue across the Ohio after horses or captives; worst of all, they could no longer scout there for advance sign that an Indian party was on its way to the settlements.

Kenton, outraged, replied at once with a border patrol, its beat extending from the mouth of Licking River to the Big Sandy—one hundred and fifty miles. For several months—until August—he and his boys kept it going; then the government provided for "county scouts" at "5/6 per diem" to act during periods of danger. Mason County was allowed six, of whom Kenton had full control. Two went up the river from Limestone, two went down, and two branched off into the interior, all crossing and recrossing each others' trails at agreed points and periods.

The prohibition laid upon excursions over the river did not prevent one being made early in April, after Black Snake and his warriors had capped a series of Kentucky plunders, captures, and murders by taking John May's boat on the Ohio shore. A party under Lee, with Kenton along, went over but returned with no greater victory than four Indians killed.

And it did not prevent Kenton's rescue of James Livingston in the early fall. In some ways this rescue is the finest example we have of his quick foresight, his sure guesses born of a faculty which made him unique in his time. His men recognized it and trusted it; these old reminiscences show it in the turn of a phrase. "But Simon Kenton came up"—and all was well. "But Kenton advised"—and the plan was changed. "But Kenton had seen"—and his was the vision.

Livingston was captured while on his way from Lexington to Limestone with wagons of supplies destined for the troops at Fort Washington. Indians were waylaying the road and about sixteen miles from Kenton's Station they attacked his party, killed his two companions, and took him captive. They cut up the harness and wagon spokes, scattered the sugar, and knocked in the heads of the whiskey barrels, first taking the precaution to fill Livingston's bottle, which they gave him to carry.

Word of his capture interrupted the first wedding ever celebrated at Mayslick—but all the guests had come armed. They mounted their horses and dashed off, but arrived at the scene they found only the wrecked wagons and stores and the bodies of the slain.[1]

Kenton raised a party—"a pretty smart one"—next morning and pursued. "They took off through the wilderness from Kenton's Station," says Benjamin Whiteman, who was along, "steering where they knew full well they would find the Indian trail; as they did, and then followed it to the Ohio river, crossing the Ohio that day; and the next day on the waters of Bullskin and perhaps half a day's travel from the Ohio, where the Indians had halted for refreshment, they first discovered Kenton's party, and ran off."

They ran off in haste, for they left blankets and other plunder behind. And before they had gone far they divided into three equal companies, each taking a different course. With one of them—but which one?—was the prisoner. For reasons never to be known, Kenton, after scouting a bit along the three trails, came back and chose the middle one. He led two miles along that one when again the trail split—

---

[1] "In or near the year 1791 my aunt, Lydia Shotwell, was married. A number of my father's acquaintances in and around Washington were invited. They came armed, and while assembled in the house, a report was brought that the Indians, about five miles up the road towards Lexington, had attacked a wagon. All the armed men mounted their horses and galloped off in a style so picturesque that I shall never forget it." *Pioneer Life in Kentucky*, Daniel Drake; p. 24.

this time into two forks. He went up and down the trails—and chose the right-hand one. This led them along until dusk, when they camped for the night. At daylight they took up the pursuit and soon heard the Indians hallooing, as was their custom upon breaking camp. "We then felt certain," said Spencer Records, who was along, "of overtaking them and soon came to their camp from which they had steered a north course. We followed them about two miles in that direction, when coming to a large tract of fallen timber that crossed their course, they turned short to the right in order to go around it or find a passage through it. The road for some distance had been brushy, which prevented us from seeing them sooner; but near the fallen timber the woods were open. When we came to the turn they had made, we discovered them about sixty yards distant. There were four of them, with one horse laden with skins on which an Indian was riding. Two walked next to him, the prisoner behind, and one brought up the rear."

The Indians had stripped their captive and given him an Indian calico shirt, so that he looked like his captors. On his back he carried the whiskey bottle wrapped in his coat. Suddenly aware that they were caught up with, the Indians began to run, and Livingston with them. The whites fired; one shot caught an Indian; another went through Livingston's coat, "cutting 16 holes in it and breaking his bottle in many pieces." Livingston said later that he thought his captors were running from other Indians, not believing it possible that a pursuing party could come up in such a short time with a choice to make between so many trails. But at the shot he turned and gave the best countersign he could think of, calling out, "Wagon, my wagon!" Whereupon they ran up and took him.

They returned with the horse, the skins, the gun of the wounded Indian, and the blankets retrieved from the first camp they arrived at. The horse went to Livingston as it was his; the rest of the plunder was divided up among them after their custom.

This rescue remains one of the great technical and intuitive feats of Kenton's life. He had five trails to chose from and he chose right each time. It was a superb exhibition of reading the trail, but it was more than that, for the reading sprang from a native faculty for "guessing" raised during these hours to its greatest power.

One wonders if Kenton once thought of the mandate against such excursions into the Ohio country while he was making this one. True, the curse had been lifted a little the April before when Scott and his Kentucky volunteers combined with Harmar and his regulars at Fort Washington for a military scout along the Ohio. Kenton went out on this expedition as captain, and there is a good deal of evidence—although the military records do not show it—that after his Bullskin foray he went out again with Harmar on his October expedition against the Miami Indians and conducted himself with his usual spirit. For two years later Colonel John Hardin—who bore the brunt of the disastrous October battles—"went one hundred and fifty miles out of his way to see Kenton and learn what he could from him about the Indians, their towns, and how to demean himself, on his fatal mission to the Indians." Kenton's old friends were prone to concede his probable presence on most of the campaigns when Dr. Draper interviewed them, even when memory failed them on details. "Don't remember," they would say, "but very probably concerned, as he was mixed up with everything then."

Kenton had a little surcease from border defense during the winter of 1790–1791, for the Indians remained in Ohio. There was a gay Christmas at his station, for his second child, John, was born there on December 11th—his first, a daughter called Nancy after the sister he tenderly loved, was then a little over two years old. Good cheer was added by the fine preparations then well under way for a new station across the river not far above Limestone. For Nathaniel Massie, with whom Kenton had been exploring the Ohio lands during the past three years, had served general notice to Kentucky that he was about to settle Manchester opposite the lower of the Three Islands, and that to each of the first twenty-five families joining him he would give a lot and one hundred acres of land. About thirty families went over, some of these from Kenton's Station.

Then, to protect this new settlement as well as the Kentucky border, General Scott ordered out "one Ensign, one Sergeant and sixteen privates" to range from above the Three Islands along thirty-five miles down the river—"It will be necessary to procure and find at least one ax for every Six Men and Kettles in the proportion directed by law." So this company of militia—the privates' pay three dollars a month—took temporary charge of the border. But they were all Kenton's "boys" and reported to him more often than to the county commander.

With the spring of 1791 the Indian attacks on boats grew more frequent and disastrous. Strong's boat, filled with returning soldiers who had served out their enlistment under Harmar and accompanied by a party of traders who walked along the shore, was attacked on March 19th; several on board were killed and all but one of the party on shore were massacred.

Five days later Plasket's boat was attacked at the mouth of the Scioto and Greathouse's boats were taken there. The Plasket boat (usually called "Hubbell's boat" because Captain Hubbell was on it) got by to Limestone with only a few killed, but the Greathouse party was taken ashore and brutally murdered. Early in April a party of some three hundred men under Alexander Orr left Limestone and went up on the Kentucky side until they found the bodies of Strong's massacred men, which they buried,[1] and on the other side of the river they came upon the bodies of the Greathouse party, some of them presenting the appearance of having been whipped to death.

What Kenton saw there Judge Wood, also an eye witness, described to Dr. Draper. It is not pleasant reading but it will show in what temper Kenton and

---

[1] "16 white men buried by Simon Kenton near the river, 8 miles above the mouth of the Scioto, on the Kentucky side, Indians dug up." Verbal statement of John McCoy to John Shane: Draper MSS.—13CC217.

This is a very good example of how Kenton dominated the expeditions he went on whether he commanded them or not. Orr commanded this one, but in the popular parlance it was Kenton who buried the dead.

his thirty men set out a few days later on his famous Snag Creek expedition:

> Found three dead Indians about one half mile above the Scioto on the Indian shore, there found the Indian pirogue—fully 50 feet long—in which a barrel could be rolled from one end to the other. . . . In the canoe Orr's party found fully a barrel of blood. Near the canoe found the three dead Indians thrown into the hole of an uprooted tree and a few clumps thrown over them; and though they smelled badly, old Joe Lemon went and scalped them. The canoe was well roughed up with bullets.
>
> A little below the mouth of the Scioto a few miles found Greathouse's boat—lay on Indian shore—presenting a melancholy appearance. It was several days—9 or 10—since the massacre—weather warm—the dead all mangled and eaten by a dozen large hogs taken down and several sheep also killed and eaten up—and the human and animal remains all mingled together, something terrible. Luther Calvin went in, bad as the stench was, and shoveled out the remains and the filth into the river. Pirogue was cleaned and taken down—the Greathouse boat left. On shore were found Greathouse's remains and those of a female, a rod apart, both naked; and each lay at the foot of a sapling, and their entrails wound round the sapling; had been cut and entrails fastened to the saplings and evidently dragged or driven round the small tree until all entrails were wound out. No recollection about finding whip. Bodies swollen and a horrible sight. These buried in the sand.

Before Kenton left on Orr's expedition he had despatched Cornelius Washburn along the river to Point Pleasant to warn all boats landing or setting out from there that the Indians were waylaying at the Scioto. Before he returned a large Indian party took advantage of Orr's expedition to cross the Ohio farther down and scatter through Kentucky. He had hardly reached his station before two of his scouts—Washburn and Whiteman—came in with the report of four Indian canoes hidden in driftwood and willows at the mouth of Snag Creek. The horrible sights he had looked upon in the last few days incited him to make a little expedition of his own which would result in something more than burying the dead.

He immediately raised a party of thirty men and boys whom he knew through and through; Whiteman, Washburn, and Wood were among them, and John Mefford, Fielding Figgans, Jacob Wetzel, Alexander McIntire, Joe Lemon, Charles Fallenash, and Jacob Boone. They went from his station to Limestone, piled into a forty-foot boat, and went down about twenty-two miles to Bear Creek on the northern shore. There they hid the boat and went down a little farther on foot; then Kenton left two spies on the bank to watch and report and retreated some forty rods across the bottom to the undergrowth of a hill where he and his men camped.

For forty-eight hours they lay in ambush without sighting an Indian. On the second night the men grew impatient, but Kenton insisted on waiting.

About noon of the second day the shore spies ran back with word that three Indians with seven horses were at Snag Creek raising a canoe, and Kenton sent six men back with them to take care of the matter. The Indians crossed slowly, swimming their horses. As they neared the shore one seemed to have discovered something, for he turned sharply; on the instant the men on shore fired and killed two. The third, "who had on a white shirt," was badly wounded, but some of the killers went out and despatched him without mercy while others caught the horses. So furious was the temper of the men at the horrors the Indians had wrought on the Greathouse party that Jacob Boone, says his daughter, offered White-

JAMES WEIR'S NOVEL

THE COVER DESIGN FOR THE FIRST EDITION, 1852.

man a round price for the privilege of skinning the first of the Indians killed, to make from his skin parchment and razor strops, "but Kenton would not allow it." They pitched two of the Indians into the river, but recognizing the third as one taken on Harmar's campaign and set free, they dragged him ashore, and after hiding the canoe, "Kenton's party cut off the fellow's head, stuck it upon a pole 20 feet high at the camp, and there left it."

On the next day three Indians appeared with five horses, raised a canoe, and started over—when within range they were shot by the same party of eight. "The appearance of their shot pouches, with a small piece of jerk in each, nibbled and sucked, showed that they were on short allowance"—that they had lingered, that is, in Kentucky and had shot most of their ammunition there. One of this party sought for quarter by crying, "Poor white prisoner—don't shoot!" but Kenton's men were pitiless.

They lay in ambush all through the next day with no Indians sighted. Their rations were running low and, the day being rainy and the air heavy, Kenton allowed several to go two miles back and hunt. They returned with packs of meat, and after night fell and their smoke would not betray them, he and his men went behind one of the river hills where their fire could not be seen and cooked their supper.

About ten o'clock that night they heard halloos from the Kentucky shore; another party and, from the volume of sound, a larger one was about to embark and was signaling the others over the river. Had it been daylight or even a clear night Kenton would probably have lured them over with an answering cry. As it was, only dead silence answered them, and finally they too became silent.

The night, says Judge Wood, was "very foggy; two sentinels were walking along the bank—walk and meet—then turn back and walk off—and while backs were together, an Indian slyly landed in a canoe and darted off without being seen, though his canoe was quickly discovered—came over to spy—having seen the fire of Kenton's camp from the opposite river hill; viewed, and then got upon the high hill above Kenton's camp—made loud Indian talk, the others over the Ohio answered, and the fellow disappeared."

With the dawn Kenton and his men crossed over to Snag Creek, but the Indians had scattered, leaving their horses and a little plunder, mostly knives and tomahawks. Altogether thirty-two horses were retaken and six Indians killed.

Stopping only at Fox's Station for provisions, they went on to Washington in triumph, only to learn there of Timothy Downing's capture the day before the expedition started and to have the white shirt they brought—its many bullet holes a silent tribute to Kenton's sharpshooters—identified by his wife as his.

Kenton learned too of another capture: Israel Donalson, late schoolmaster of Limestone, had been taken near Massie's Fort the day after Downing was seized. It was too late to pursue after him, for nearly a week had gone by, but Kenton called for a volunteer to go to Lexington for additional men to take on a scout up the river. Seventeen-year-old Nathaniel Tomlinson, one of his boys, offered himself as express. "I started from Washington on foot at eight o'clock in the morning and reached Lexington—60 miles—by eight in the evening." He returned with what men could be spared, and with these and others to the number of about fifty, Kenton went up on foot on the Kentucky side above the Three Islands, scouting for stragglers from the Indian party which had taken Donalson, but finding none.

Kenton was concerned about Donalson's fate, for he was new to the country, but he had faith in Downing as "a real backwoodsman," and repeatedly told Downing's wife that her husband would surely find his way back. His faith was rewarded ten days later when Downing came in with a story that delighted him; word of the Snag Creek expedition had traveled fast through the Indian country. When Donalson came back, his story carried Downing's on until the three became one.

Downing had been taken on the Lexington road by a party of the same Indians Kenton was then making ready to waylay. They stripped him of his shirt and gave it to one of his captors, plundered his loads of "linnens," then put him and his horses in charge of an old Indian chief and his son while they went off to gather up more horses to take to Snag Creek.

Downing's guards made a leisurely way to the Ohio, camping out several nights on the way. For some reason they crossed the river below Snag Creek out of range of Kenton's ambuscade, even then lying in wait. For when they reached the other side they heard the firing of Kenton's first attack. The old chief listened with satisfaction: "Me warriors taking boat white man," he said. They went up toward the Chillicothe towns and after several days came on the sign of someone making for the villages (evidently the Indian spy who discovered Kenton's camp), about which Downing said they talked earnestly. Their apprehension worried him and he made up his mind to risk everything in an attempt at escape.

That night they camped at Rattlesnake Fork on Paint Creek, not many miles, as it turned out, from the main Indian camp toward which Donalson was journeying. The evening was rainy and Downing was untied that he might bring in water and wood. Then the Indians said, "Must tie," but Downing begged that he might eat first and they unsuspiciously consented. At a moment when the old Indian was squatting before a kettle of food and the young one was drawing his shirt over his head to dry it, Downing leaped up, seized a squaw ax, and dealt the old chief a crushing blow. He then brought the ax down on the young man's chest and made off on one of his horses in the darkness and rain. In his confusion he went far astray and came out on the Ohio near the dreaded Scioto. He hailed a passing boat, but the travelers, already warned by Kenton's scout and believing him a decoy, refused to stop. But he raced along with the boat and was finally taken aboard.

As for Donalson, his story began where Downing's left off. He had hardly arrived at the main camp before he met with John Ward, brother of James, Charles, and William, who had been captured when a child and had grown up with the Indians. He asked, says Donalson in his Narrative, "if I knew the Wards that lived near Washington, Ky. I told him I did and wanted him to leave the Indians and go to his brothers and take me with him. . . . He and I had a great deal of chat and disagreed about almost everything."

On the second day after his arrival an Indian came up toward the camp and was met outside it, "when they formed a circle and he spoke, I thought, near an hour, and so profound was the silence that had they been on a board floor I thought the fall of a pin might have been heard. I rightly judged the disaster, for the day before I was taken, I was at Limestone, and was solicited to join a party that was going down to the mouth of Snag creek, where some Indian canoes were discovered hid in the willows. The party went on . . . and they succeeded in killing nearly the whole party." The newcomer was of course the Indian spy who had detected Kenton's ambuscade and warned his brothers from the hilltop.

Later on the wounded chief's son came into the camp. "I saw the son of the chief that Downing killed at the Shawanoe camp—he had wounded him badly." This second ill tidings caused great consternation; "they calculated on being pursued and they were right," says Donalson, but he and his captors left the camp that evening and that night he made his escape.[1]

[1]In Donalson's narrative, written forty-nine years after his captivity, and in all of his letters to Dr. Draper, he insists that he was captured April 22, 1791. But he also dates his capture as the day after Downing was taken, and says also that the day before he was captured he was in Limestone where Kenton's Snag Creek expedition was making up. Kenton's muster roll fixes the date of his expedition—April 10, 1791. Downing's captivity is usually given as lasting from three to six weeks; it was less, for on his information regarding the main Shawanese camp Kenton made his Paint Creek expedition of April 28th. Everything in Donalson's story coincides with Kenton's movements and Downing's story except the date he gives of his capture; if it is put back to April 10th all falls into place.

No sooner had Downing told his story than Kenton set about raising a party of sixty men—Alexander McIntire and Christopher Wood his spies and Downing his pilot—to retrace Downing's trail. They came on strange things at the old chief's last camp, but they did not pause; they pushed on toward the main camp and at night lay within two miles of it.

Next morning the spies on ahead "found," says Judge Wood, "a large number of trees peeled for bark for the camp, and found the camp on the edge of a large prairie, with an unusually large fine spring. It was a frosty morning, and the smoke or fog rose from the large spring which the spies took for the smoke of the camp, and also heard a dog bark. Not doubting but the Indians were there, the spies, as ordered, ran up to the camp to commence the attack, while the men were surrounding the camp—and the spies called out, 'You black rascals, show yourselves.' But all had gone several days. The camp was composed of three or four very large bark camps well enclosed, and from the representation of horses marked on the inside of the bark camps, they must have had 50 or 60 horses."

He adds that they learned subsequently—from Donalson—that the Indians were about one hundred strong and could easily have defeated Kenton's party, "for many were out who were old or who knew nothing of Indian fighting, and only came out to get credited for a tour of duty." And Whiteman says also that "Kenton's brilliant success at Snag creek induced many to join the expedition who had never stepped forward before. . . . At least a fourth raw and inexperienced men."

The Indians had left little plunder. Bear's oil which they could not carry they had poured out on the ground. There were only "great quantities of onions, which we tore up and threw in great heaps into the fire and ate as soon as they wilted." Most of the plunder they took back the whites garnered at the burial camp of the old chief. For his people had paused in their flight to give him a sepulcher.

On a slab floor, under a pen of elm logs built up in the form of a cone, they had laid his body, dressed in "2 shirts & Downing's linnen on and 2 blankets," says Judge Wood, "a double coverlid wrapped around him—new leggins and moccasins on—and a paint bag on his breast, and by his side a butcher knife, looking glass, comb, scissors, awl and patch leather laid by his right hand, and a pipe tomahawk at his feet. One Thomas Evans got the coverlet, smelled badly and was made to keep far in the rear, and at night washed and smoked it to purify it, and then went with the others. Kenton carried home a blue capeau taken from the old Indian. Downing got his linnen, and the other articles were scattered among the men. The dead was rolled out and left."

Kenton's next expedition across the Ohio was not on his own but in one derisively known as "Edwards' Blackberry Campaign"; Kenton's scout on this trip gave it its title. It seems to have begun as it certainly ended, in dissension.

The taking of horses had kept up without ceasing and when word came in July of a great horse-thieving camp near the head waters of Mad River, some three hundred Kentuckians gathered at Washington and Limestone and went over. "We expect to camp in the neighborhood of Limestone," wrote Colonel John Edwards to Lee, "on Saturday evening [July 19]. I hope, sir, you will have your men ready to cross early in the morning before us. . . . I have ordered twenty days' provisions . . . pray, sir, be satisfied with regard to good pilots, that we may not miss our object. . . . My friendship to Captain S. Kenton and hope he will do something clever."

Kenton piloted and commanded the advance company. But Edwards went along timidly and without spirit; the campaign was doomed to defeat. "Finally," says Captain James Ward, who was in Kenton's company, "Col. Edwards says they are too weak, and he suspected they were near the Sandusky plains, and perhaps another Crawford defeat awaited them. Finally the feeling pervaded all, save Kenton's company, who went on alone several miles and found Indian sign so plenty in blackberry bushes, and being weak, rejoined Edwards's party and soon after commenced the return march. . . . It was afterwards ascertained that where Kenton turned was within three miles of the town against which they were destined. Had Kenton been commander, the result would have been different."

When Dr. Draper first interviewed General Whiteman—in 1846—on this campaign he got little for his pains. "Gen. Whiteman," he says, "was out in Kenton's company, but will tell nothing about it, so disgruntled was he at the time with the abortive result. All the Gen. would tell was this;—that Col. Edwards was an improper selection—cowardly. It was expected that Kenton would have commanded, and there was much ill feeling when Edwards was appointed. Had Kenton been the leader, the result would have been different."

Six years later Whiteman told Dr. Draper that dissension began at King's Creek. Kenton and his advance company saw from a grove of timber a number of Indians across the creek. They went after them and encircled the tall grass plat where the enemy had hidden. A shot was fired and Edwards and his men soon came up. Kenton proposed that all the men should form in line and scour the prairie, but Edwards objected and ordered his men forward.

Kenton and his men found the camp—its approximate position, that is—from the myriad blackberry vines plucked clean of their fruit for drying; but. being too small a force to advance farther unsupported, he went back to report, never dreaming that the order to advance would not be given. Edwards not only flatly refused to go on; but he ordered an immediate retreat.

Kenton himself had this to say to Judge James: "I accompanied Edwards of Bourbon, who was but a homespun commander—we did nothing. I came upon an Indian concealed in the grass. He raised his gun and one of the three with me shot at him, and the ball grazing the back of his neck, he fell. I sprang at him, and Col.——riding by, and handing me a tomahawk, I killed him. This weighs heavy on me at times, and it is the only thing in my campaigns I much regret, for he was in my power and I need not have done it. He was a young King, and had just been promoted. After him and fromt his circumstance, King's creek took its name."

Kenton's anger unleashed was a terrible force.

He knew it and feared it and fought it. One of his nephews who nursed him through a dangerous illness years later says that during the hours in which his uncle believed he was dying, his mind went back to this same deed done when "enraged." He was a terror when his temper was up. He once drew his gun on a man who had laughed at him as he went sprawling one day to the ground, but the fall had knocked the powder from the pan and the weapon was not discharged. Kenton was contrite and penitent over the action done on the flash in a moment of anger. He was not afraid of deeds done in cold anger; they satisfied an extraordinary sense of justice. But there were times in his life when time dropped out, and later he could only draw off and look back in horror at what he had done when "enraged."

His wrath, hot or cold, was nothing to invite. Shortly before the Blackberry Campaign he was carrying important messages from Scott in Kentucky to Harmar at Fort Washington. Upon reaching the mouth of Licking he found Kennedy the ferryman not at all inclined to take him over the river, for the weather was cold and the ice was running. He offered the man a reasonable fee which was refused; finally he offered five dollars and paid in advance. He did a large share of the work on the trip and his indignation grew with every stroke of his oar. As they neared the shore and he gave the final thrust which grounded the boat, he brought his paddle up and dealt Kennedy such a smashing blow on the head as to knock him into the river. Kenton said he never looked back, lest what he saw might delay him; he sprang on shore and hastened on, and he did not until some time afterward learn that the ferryman had survived his cold dousing.

With St. Clair's defeat on November 4th of this year, the Indians—who had never ceased their maraudings since Harmar's alleged "victory" the year before—overran Kentucky. It was open hunting season through the winter—for game, horses, and white men. During this month Fielding Figgans, one of Kenton's border men, came into Washington hatless, horseless, and gunless, with word of an Indian attack ten miles out. He and three others had been hunting and were on their way home with bear and deer meat. They had camped for the night and next morning were about to start in to Washington when they were fired on by a party of Indians under the warrior whom the whites called Captain John.

Kenton raised a party and went out. John McDonald, his future biographer, then a boy of fifteen, made his first "excursion" under him then—made it by disobeying his father and Kenton and following after on his father's horse and with his father's gun. Once again it was but a story of burying the dead who had been scalped and brutally mutilated. Kenton followed the trail to the Ohio in the small hope of recovering the horses, but the Indians had crossed hours before. Years later Captain John told Judge Wood that he and his party had smelled the smoke of the hunters' fire, had crept up, and, finding a bear's carcass hung up near by, had cut off chunks of meat and fed them to the hunters' dogs to quiet them; then they merely surrounded the camp and waited for morning.

And once again, with the spring of 1792, scouting over the river was forbidden the Kentuckians. St. Clair had resigned his command of the Western army; Mad Anthony Wayne had taken his place, and an Indian peace was talked of. The prohibition against Simon Kenton's form of Indian warfare left Fort Washington April 2d; on the 3d or 4th thirty-six horses were taken from near his station, and if his Little Miami expedition of April 7th–13th was legal at all, it was by no more than the wink of an eye. It was, however, "ordered" by the county lieutenant of Mason, and Kenton's muster roll shows it.

Twenty-nine men were in the party of paid rangers and several others—eight or ten in number—went along without pay. Kenton's objective was a large Shawanese camp which his scouts had reported as lying on the East Fork of the Little Miami. They followed the Indian trail to the mouth of Lee's Creek, made rafts, and crossed the Ohio the first night. They pursued all the next day over wet ground and in the rain, and by the second morning ten or twelve of the men rebelled on the ground that the party was too small to accomplish anything, and going off from camp under the pretence of getting water, returned home.

The others continued the pursuit till about noon, Kenton advancing very cautiously, for he was satisfied the camp lay not far off. Suddenly a belled horse was heard in the distance, and Kenton, Whiteman, Fielding Figgans, and Josiah Davis went forward while the others halted to lay useless baggage and clothing aside. Coats, blankets, hats, and provisions were tumbled together on the ground, leaving their owners stripped and free for the anticipated fight.

Figgans and Davis were going in front under orders to reconnoiter merely and under no circumstances to fire. Suddenly they saw the belled horse with an Indian astride riding straight toward them, and Figgans, who had gone on duty with two bullets in his mouth and two in his gun, on some impulse shot and killed the rider. Kenton instantly dashed forward, asking why he had not obeyed orders. Figgans showed him the dead Indian, but Kenton was not appeased and told him to consider himself under arrest—evidently for some court-martial proceeding—to which Figgans replied, "Arrest and be damned." There was much excited talk on this, Figgans charging that if the spies had acted on orders they were "nothing but bait for Indians."

The horse, recognized as one stolen from Kentucky, was captured; the dead Indian was rolled into some brush, and the party proceeded on his back trail, realizing that the shot had not been heard.

But trouble, which had begun that morning with the desertion of a fourth of their numbers, continued. Again Kenton halted his men and sent McIntire, Washburn, and Whiteman ahead to find the camp. They returned saying that by the evidence of the large number of peeled trees and horse tracks it was too large a camp to attack in the daytime. Though they did not know it then, it was filled with chiefs and warriors. Black Snake, Black Hoof, Chi-ux-ko, and the young Tecumseh were there. This is the first known engagement in which Tecumseh faced the whites.

Kenton therefore went into council, Indian fashion, with his men. Everyone was called on for an opinion and there was great division: some were for returning, some for attacking at various hours and in various ways, others for erecting a breastwork of cut saplings and waiting for an attack, others for taking the horses only and getting off.

But it was finally concluded to attack at dawn the next day, and Kenton ordered his men back to where they had discarded their clothes and provisions, so that they might make small fires in hollow places to dry themselves and their guns.

He himself did not go; he went out on a scout of his own to the Indian camp and viewed its position. "Tecumseh," he told Judge James, "was stationed on an island of wood, surrounded by a low prairie and swamp," on the Little Miami, near where Williamsburg now is. In the rear of the camp beyond and above the marsh was a gradual half-mile rise to a bluff, which he determined to utilize. There was no other Indian camp near by.

When all had returned back to the little meeting place it was reported that the Indians were under cover this rainy day, and apparently awaiting the return of the solitary Indian lying dead on the trail, for they would at times go to the edge of the camp, give a loud halloo, and then go back, laughing immoderately as if believing him lost. But when night fell, the camp drum sounded until near midnight, as if to guide the lost hunter back to his home.

Jacob Wetzel, chancing to be at Limestone when this party was raised and volunteering to go on it, was chosen as night spy with Samuel Frazee. Able to see more at closer range in the light of the campfires, he reported the camp a very large one, with tents of bark and a large marquee, taken in St. Clair's defeat and set up for young Tecumseh to occupy. And again the advisability of retreat was discussed. Wetzel was the one who turned the tide of depression; like a true Wetzelian, he said that if no other would go he would go alone and kill at least one. Wood and Whiteman and others spoke up, and it was finally resolved to attack.

From the beginning of the trip, Luther Calvin had been mourning the loss of two horses and Whiteman and Washburn proposed to ease his soreness by creeping up on the Indian pound they had discovered and taking his two out of it. Kenton assented, if they could recognize the horses and get them off without noise. This they did, and Calvin's son James and one other were stationed with all the horses while the others divided into three parties, Kenton commanding one, McIntire another, and Calvin the third. Again strict orders were given that no man was to fire before the signal, and "Boone" was given as the watchword. Then the detachments moved along the low ridge to make their attack simultaneously from right, left, and center.

Unfortunately Kenton's center division had not reached its place and completed the semicircle before the bark of a camp dog aroused an Indian, who sprang up and advanced a little toward the fire. The temptation was too much; Calvin heard the tick of his men's rifles in rapid succession as they cocked them, and, desirous of saving their fire, himself fired and shot the Indian dead. It was signal enough, and firing began all along the broken line. The Indians yelled and began to return the shots.

Kenton told Judge James that the fight lasted about three and a half hours, but that it was only sporadic fighting for it began long before daylight, thanks to Calvin's premature fire. There was some hand-to-hand work and the Indians were quick to catch the watchword which the men used to recognize each other in the darkness; "Ch-Boone, Ch-Boone," came as often from an Indian's lips as "Boone" from a white man's.

About dawn Samuel Barr, who had come to Kenton's Station just six months before and who was making his first Indian expedition on this one, inadvertently exposed himself from behind a tree and was shot down. Whiteman was just behind him, and Kenton always attributed the immediate cause of the retreat to him; for, shocked at Barr's death and hearing at the same time a splashing in the creek across which the squaws and children were then escaping, he called out, "Barr killed—Indians across the creek." Upon which, as if it were a command to retreat, the flight began. It was each man for himself and his horse, but many horses bore strange masters that night—each mounted the first one he came to and started for home.

On the retreat they went in pairs and avoided making sign that could be read by any pursuing party. But the morning after the attack eleven of the fugitives got together—Whiteman and Washburn among them. On that day Washburn shot a three-hundred-pound bear and thirteen men supped on its meat. For, knowing that Wetzel and his companion were just behind them, they left a piece cooked for them which was found. Kenton and Joe

Lemon came in together, the last of the party, and Washington and Limestone were much alarmed; in the rain and fog they had gone far out of their way and reached the Ohio above Manchester, from where they had had to descend some fifteen miles to Limestone.

McIntire never came back. When Kenton got in and found him still missing he made up another party to go in search of him. They found nothing of McIntire, and recovered none of their clothing and blankets thrown off at their little camp; but going on to the Indian camp, they discovered cheering traces of unsuspected disaster wrought—signs of Indians carrying off many wounded; they learned later that seventeen had been seriously hurt.

Kenton had scouted for himself on this expedition and had laid his plans carefully. He had calculated that at a surprise attack the Indians would escape over the creek, leaving their guns and property and horses to be seized, but the premature signal upset everything. He had lost two men, had recovered only two horses, and the disregard of his orders laid the foundation for charge and countercharge that did not die down for many a day. Most of the stories of this engagement speak of Indian reinforcements coming up from across the East Fork, but Kenton always insisted that he had reconnoitered himself and *knew* there was no camp on the other side. Almost the only thing at which Washington laughed without malice during the next few days was Luther Calvin's involuntary lapse from warrior to land locator when, creeping up in the night on his hands and knees to his appointed place, "he grabbed up a handful of light rich bottom soil and whispered to those near him, 'This is mighty good land.'"

McClung's story of this affair in his *Sketches of Western Adventure*, evidently obtained from Captain Ward, says nothing at all about an Indian camp on the other side of the fork; his account, so jocular in tone and so plainly indicating that pure panic seized Kenton's men, greatly mortified the valiant Kentuckians who had survived the rout. General Whiteman in particular thought it "well calculated to dampen the ardor of every patriot." They were all engaged in saving their skins, not only in the flight but after their return. Kenton's arrest of Figgans for firing against orders brought upon him the charge of sending out scouts as "bait"; and he was blamed indirectly for the "reinforcements" coming across the creek. On both counts he was guiltless, and the "bait" charge was laughed at. Spying was always dangerous work, but, says Judge Wood, one of his spies on this very expedition, "Kenton was always tender and careful of his men's lives—very cautious of running unnecessary risks." As for the second charge, he was too well aware of his inferior and the enemy's superior forces to run the risk of any second camp near by; after three spying parties had gone out and come in, he went out by himself and made his own scout. In such a crisis he never trusted any report but his own. But "reinforcements" was a better excuse for flight than panic at the sound of splashing water.[1]

[1] "Last week the Indians stole a number of horses from the neighborhood of Limestone; they were pursued by twenty-six men under Captains Kenton and McIntire who came up with them about 40 miles up the Little Miami, and attacked them in the night in their encampment:

McIntire's loss grieved Kenton greatly. "Red-headed Aleck," one of the finest of woodsmen, extraordinarily small, extraordinarily strong, was one of his most trusted men. He had been ill and depressed on the journey; he had had a "dream"—one of those strangely foreshadowing visions to which the frontiersmen were often subject (Kenton had them; Donalson had one the night before his capture). He had been wounded during the fight; and when he reached their little camp after the flight, he refused to leave it.

Much later Coo-na-haw told the whites how McIntire died. He had shot a deer for food, and the Indians, hearing the shot, captured him while he was cooking it and took him back to camp where he stayed while it was breaking up. He might not have been killed but for the fact that on the last day an Indian, wounded in the privates, was "making a great groaning"; McIntire laughed at him, and the wounded man flew at him in a rage and tomahawked him. This Coo-na-haw related after the peace.

The Indians returned the fire unluckily, by which it is supposed they had discovered our men previous to the attack; after a smart fire our men thought proper to retreat, and in the dark got separated. Six only had got home when the last accounts left Limestone." *Kentucky Gazette*, April 14, 1792.

"The party of men from near Limestone under Captains Kenton and McIntire, who went in pursuit of the Indians (as mentioned in our last) we are informed, have all returned except two, one of whom it said to be killed, and the missing one said to be wounded.

"They came on the Indian encampment undiscovered in the night and poured on them a well directed fire, by which it is thought not less than 15 or 20 fell; they were encamped on the bank of the Little Miami, on the East side; another party encamped on the West side (which our men knew nothing of) crossed and began to reinforce the camp, upon the discovery of which our men thought prudent to retreat. The Indians had a markee and tent pitched—trophies of their late success.

"We learn further that Captain Kenton has raised another party and is again gone in pursuit of them." *Kentucky Gazette*, April 21, 1792.

Time was to pass also before Charles Ward learned that he and his brother John had fought against each other in this skirmish—the same John Ward Israel Donalson had met in the Shawanese camp the year before. He, his Indian wife, and their several children were in this camp that night. A pretty legend grew up that Captain Ward, standing near the camp a few moments before the firing began, saw an Indian girl whose "peculiarly light complexion" attracted his notice and whose likeness to his brother made him wonder and spare her; but a modicum of common-sense applied to this little story is enough to destroy it.

Later still they heard from a Mrs. Gardner, prisoner in the Shawanese towns at the time, that when the Indians returned from this encounter, "they were surly and had nothing to say—no whooping as when victorious, and when questioned about their troubles, would snap off such questions summarily." But she said that twenty-six never came back.

Kenton faced the young Tecumseh again a year later on his last Scioto scout. Morgan's Station had been taken, and horses from Strode's Station, and Kenton raised a party and pursued. It had an embarrassment of officers—there were seven captains—Kenton, Ward, Baker, Cassidy, Davis, Massie, and one other. Thirty-three men comprised the party and they chose three, Kenton, Ward, and Baker, to command the usual three detachments if they should come upon a camp and attack it.

From Manchester, where they had picked up Massie and his men, they had followed the warpath up the Scioto, and on the afternoon of the third day out they fell in with a fresh trail from down Paint Creek which they followed on until dusk. Then, near Reeves Crossing, they halted. Very soon they heard voices and laughter, and, being evidently very near an Indian camp, they dismounted and sent their horses back some distance where they were tied in the woods. Kenton, going forward with Cassidy and Baker to spy, found that the Indians were camped on the banks of a creek, that there were three fires, and that there was no evidence of any suspicion that a pursuing party was near.

He noted that the opposite bank of the creek had a high, abrupt, rocky bank not easy of ascent, so that if he succeeded in surrounding the camp the Indians would have scant chance of escape across the stream.[1] Then, with the memory of his Little Miami expedition fresh in his mind, he laid his plans.

From all the old accounts Joshua Baker appears to have been in a mood to insure him every consideration from the start. He was one of the three commanders chosen; he was given his choice of ten men and probably of position. He was to bear off around the camp and take post below it. Kenton and Ward divided the rest of the men between them; Kenton to attack from the rear, and Ward to move with his men shortly after Kenton and complete the semicircle.

A little before dawn, therefore, Baker moved down

[1]Tradition has placed the site of this battle a few hundred yards below the old Reeves Crossing of Paint Creek. But Dr. Draper, interested in the contradictions between the appearance of the cited place and the descriptions of its "high hill," succeeded finally in locating it about three-quarters of a mile below the Crossing, just across from Little Copperas Mountain. *See* Draper MSS.—4BB113–119.

along the creek with his group, to take up his position on the far side of the camp. By some misunderstanding, as he said later, he did not go around it, but placed himself on the near side, the one Ward was to attack. Yet he sent word back to Kenton and Ward, as agreed on, that he had reached his proper place. For this attack, as for the one the year before, Kenton's orders had been positive that no gun should be fired until it was light enough to take aim and not then until the proper signal was given.

When Baker's runner reached the waiting men, Kenton's party began to move, but suddenly one of the Indians' dogs barked, and then to his intense wrath Kenton heard Baker's party fire. All was lost in that moment. Kenton and Ward ran for their places—and ran straight into Baker's party, which should have been far on the other side. It was not yet dawn, and the Indians, free to run in two directions, scattered and treed. There was firing on both sides, during which Jacob Jones in Baker's party was killed and, on the Indian side, Captain Ward's brother John was mortally wounded.

Kenton kept his men together and at daylight made a demonstration of surrounding the camp, upon which the Indians, having achieved their own military victory, fled. For during the interim, while the treed Indians kept the whites engaged, Tecumseh had the inspiration to send a party back up the creek to where the whites had left their horses, and when his men had returned with a good haul he gave the order to retreat.

The plunder in the camp was considerable; besides the blankets, always good loot, the most valuable booty was a quantity of powder and musket balls which, as they surmised and afterward learned, was to have been used against the Kentuckians in a raid just then being planned. This Kenton's foray stopped. It was learned too that there was a large Shawanese camp hardly five miles from the one they had attacked.

Then a hasty retreat commenced, which, given rain and no horses for a number of the men, was no happy journey. Expecting pursuit, which did not however happen, they traveled almost forty miles that day and camped at night within seven miles of Manchester.

Kenton's wrath against Baker was not quenched through a year. All the records left by the men who took part in this expedition unite in saying Baker blundered. But Kentucky courtesy had its rise in those earliest days. Now and then someone was healthily cursed out but not often.[1] He lost the pursuit of the Morgan Station raiders to Kenton; this fresh trail followed along Paint Creek was only a side issue; but

[1]There is no reference to blundering in the first printed "history" of this expedition. The *Kentucky Gazette* implies that the alarm was "an act of God."

"Capt. Kenton, with about thirty-five men, who went up the Ohio in order to intercept the Indians who took Morgan's Station, fell in with the trail of a party of Indians on the waters of Paint Creek, coming into the settlement. He followed them, and at night observing he was near them, sent forward some spies to discover their fires. Unluckily the spies fell in with their camp, and before they discovered it, the Indians were alarmed by a dog, which flew out at the spies, upon which the Indians fired on them. The spies returned the fire. Upon hearing the firing the whole of the party came up, and the Indians retreated, leaving their baggage, amongst which was a quantity of powder, lead and blankets. Kenton had one man killed. It is supposed two Indians were killed and carried off, from some discoveries that were made next morning." *Kentucky Gazette*, April 20, 1793.

with Tecumseh's quiet taking of their horses, further pursuit was impossible.

Kenton told Judge James that on this second fight with Tecumseh they "drove him, burnt his camp and all his skins and furs." But there is no reference in any of the other accounts to the burning of this camp. It could hardly have occurred, for the camp was drenched with rain. Kenton may have had the first Tecumseh battle in mind, of the year before, when they revisited the spot, roasted onions in fires they built, and without doubt destroyed whatever they did not wish to carry back. He added:

"John Ward was killed on Paint Creek; he had been clever to me. His daughter [Su-tow-nee] told me her father would friend me. I did not then know his brother." But he was soon to know Colonel William Ward of Greenbriar County, Virginia, a veritable figure of a gentleman in pioneer Ohio and in Kenton's imagination.

Good news reached Kentucky in the summer from Fort Washington. Mad Anthony Wayne was taking up the work St. Clair had dropped the year before and was planning the campaign which as it turned out was to free Kentucky forever from the Indians. Good news reached Fort Washington from Kenton's Station. With Scott's mustering of a thousand Kentucky volunteers to meet Wayne's requisition for men, Kenton proposed to raise a volunteer company of spies—his condition being that he should select them. Wayne not only accepted the offer, but he made Kenton a major at the head of his hundred volunteers, and appointed him also the advance pilot of his army. Never were courage, knowledge, dare-deviltry and "luck" more embodied than in Kenton's unit. The boys he had trained were with him, sifted out to the finest degree of fitness; he took with him as well nine friendly Indians.

Kenton shared in the officers' councils and informal meetings on the campaign, a trusted member of the official body. When Judge James talked with him in 1832 he asked him what he thought of St. Clair:

"Well, he was a minister-looking man. He was well dis-siplined too; but dear me, he had no briar-look—no keenness in him." Of Wayne he said that in the councils he was always joking, and added:

"Wayne and Scott never gave me any orders in scouting—how long to stay out or how far to go, but to make my own time."

This little band of spies rendered perhaps more real service than any other body of equal number in Wayne's army. They brought in prisoners by the score and killed as many as they took. Without rivals in the army, they aimed in each excursion to outdo their own former exploits. They were "lucky" men; they had come off unscathed from so many desperate conflicts that fear was transformed into confidence.

And yet Kenton never lost his high sense of caution. When the season was far advanced, when Fort Greenville was built, and when Wayne announced that he would erect Fort Recovery on the site where St. Clair was defeated, Kenton grew restless. He had no interest in the mere building of forts; he felt the time spent in building might be much better employed in attacking, and Wayne, seeing him and another "wild man"—McMahon of the regulars—

depressed with inaction, gave them permission to go out toward the lakes and told them to keep going until they found something to fight. So with three hundred men they set out and near the mouth of the Auglaize found sign enough of many trails, all seeming to trend toward a common center. McMahon was all bravely for fighting; but Kenton, indifferent to the laugh that would greet them on a battleless return and with all his instinct to caution in full play, said flatly that he did not like the look of things and believed it foolhardy and hazardous to go farther with their small number of men. He also said that if McMahon insisted on fighting he would join him on one condition, that if flight became necessary he would order his men to retreat and that they, being mounted, must and would leave McMahon's marching men far in the rear.

McMahon slept on this and next morning agreed to turn back. They came into Fort Greenville without firing a shot for other than wild meat and the men there had their laugh. But Wayne congratulated them for good soldiers who mixed caution with courage.

Kenton was not out with Wayne in 1794 and so missed the final battle of the twenty-year Indian war at the Fallen Timbers. He had suffered a severe illness in camp during the winter and when he was able to travel took his discharge and went home. When the Board of Officers met early in the year to appoint, Kenton was put in charge of a company of spies and Joshua Baker was appointed his lieutenant. But Kenton declined the honor. "He wouldn't serve," says Colonel Sudduth in his narrative. "Baker was then appointed Captain and I his Lieutenant."

Kenton's one condition of service had been that he should choose his own men. In his absence military red tape had got wound about his little picked company. Other men had come in, and he was given as one of his officers the man who the year before had laid his Paint Creek expedition in ruins. "He wouldn't serve"; he stayed at home and attended to his own affairs. Wayne's campaign of 1793 was his last campaign until the Ohio days.

Chapter XI

LAST YEARS IN KENTUCKY
1794–1798

IN A "fine brick house" set within sight of his old station and on the edge of a thousand-acre farm, Simon Kenton settled down to pass his last Kentucky years in luxurious comfort. His home had been long in the building—the first brick house to go up in Mason County—but it was finished at last, its bricks the symbol of permanent settlement, and when his work at his station was done he moved his growing family into it. To his children Nancy and John, Simon Junior had been added, born February 8, 1793; two years later, on May 18th, his daughter Sarah was born.

He was head of his clan. His brothers William and John had brought their families to his county. His mother left her daughter Nancy's home on Scott River and came up to make her home with her son Simon.

He had his slaves and his horses and his tenant farmers. He kept open house and spread a bountiful table. He owned more acres than he or any man could count.

His corn cribs groaned with their plenteous ears, and he shared his corn liberally with the poor and needy as well as with travelers and newcomers. He was magnificent in his refusal to take any payment:

"Have you money to pay for it? Then go and buy of those who have to sell: mine is not for sale but for use and to bestow without money and without price upon the needy and newcomers. There are my cribs filled with plenty—go and shell as much as you need."

He did nothing himself about farming his fine lands; his tenants did that and at harvest time put his share in his cribs. But when their provisions gave out, "they would without asking permission, use up as much of Kenton's as they might wish, and he was too indulgent ever to say anything about it. By such management he never made farming profitable."

As with his corn, so with all else he owned; it was shared as a matter of course with neighbors and strangers. His lands about Washington were still free to any newcomer who might wish to settle there and raise crops rent free. His trading store at Washington, stocked with guns, ammunition, axes, hoes, blankets, provisions, clothing of all sorts, shoes, and the like, gave unlimited credit to customers; on this store of goods his many friends drew as they required and paid or not as they chose; whoever in town needed—or wished—to live on him so had little difficulty in evading pay day; there was small profit at the end of any year. Druillard was still one of his steady pensioners. About this time "Col. William Ward from Greenbriar Co., Va.," says Kenton's son William, "settled in Mason County, lived on Kenton there—kept store for him in Mason, and went with him to Ohio."

Packet boats were going regularly every week up the river from Cincinnati to Pittsburgh—it took one month to make the round trip. Mail was coming down the river regularly from Wheeling. Zane's great Trace cut from Wheeling to Limestone at last united the East and the West. The river seemed covered with boats—keel boats, flatboats, "arks," and canoes. Not only travelers scantily provisioned filled them now, but goods and merchandise of every sort—flour, bacon, sugar, iron, potter's ware, glass, cabinet work, all the produce and manufactures of the East were being sent down the Ohio to Kentucky.

Kenton became so largely engaged in trade and business of all kinds that he called in Israel Donalson, the first school teacher of Limestone, to act as a sort of secretary in handling his business papers, deeds, and

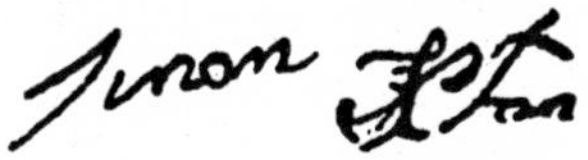

SIMON KENTON'S FIRST KNOWN SIGNATURE, AUGUST 18, 1785. FROM THE ORIGINAL IN THE DRAPER MANUSCRIPTS,—3BB33

so on. Donalson says that Kenton did a great deal of business "or part did it," and that he had "a most extraordinary system" of his own which was a maze of confusion to others but clarity itself to him.

"I was sworn in (and gave him security)," Donalson wrote to Dr. Draper, "as surveyor in Mason county on purpose to do his business; he was a man of noble character: entirely illiterate he had by practise learned to make a kind of hyroglyfficks that would read Simon Kenton, but had an extraordinary memory: he once called on me to file his papers; when I went to his house he had two drawers of an old fashioned file full of papers and would come and stand by me, and when I picked up a paper, before opening would tell me what it was."

Donalson did what he could in organizing Kenton's enormous affairs and his many projected schemes, but "could never get him ready to embark; the consequence was he suffered greatly."

The man's memory for visual details was extraordinary. Although he could not read any paper, he could select any one he wanted out of any number in a packet, by its shape or some peculiarity in its appearance, and give its gist before it was read to him for the refreshing of his mind on some detail. Colonel Charles A. Marshall wrote to Dr. Draper at length on this:

> Gen'l Kenton's faculty of mastering the Physical geography of any region over which he passed and his recollection of its topography was something Phenomenal; for Instance. Virginia in settling her domain, had no system, such as the Gen'l Government so admirably maintains with her public lands. She issued her warrants as they were termed to the settler or speculator; those warrants were put in the hands of a surveyor or other person known as a locator, who laid off the quantity of land named in the warrant, by metes or bounds, with fixed corners and marked lines. Patents were then issued to grantees by metes and bounds as described in the surveys. In consequence of this system—or rather want of system—the fine lands of Kentucky were literally shingled over with patents, leading to interminable litigation. Gen'l Kenton, although illiterate, was much employed as a locator, and his interest by a fixed rate generally layed off at time of location, would have made any man more provident or prudent than Kenton immensely rich. In the litigation of the period, Kenton's testimony was frequently in demand in the land suits. On such occasions I have been told by the old County surveyor of fifty or sixty years ago, that Gen'l Kenton, when accompanying him for the purpose of establishing some beginning corner, generally near some noted spring, creek,

branch or other permanent land mark, would make him read over the patent containing the field notes of the survey—as he read he could see the countenance of the old man light until the full train of association had been established, and then would lead the surveyor to the natural land mark—spring, creek or branch—stop—give one of his quick glances around—"Yes, yes, I am right, but no marked corners—read again the trees."[1] Another pause, again, "Yes, yes," as if speaking to himself, "dig here, you ought to find the roots of an oak, or ash or maybe a walnut as the post might be. Of course Kenton's testimony on such occasions was decisive, as in no instance, so the surveyor informed me, was he known to be mistaken. In my life I have known instances of extraordinary memories—never perhaps so wonderful as always possessed by the illiterate and uneducated as was Kenton.

In Dr. Draper's Notes is another instance of Kenton's phenomenal power of registering in his memory the lay of skyline and land. He had come over from Ohio to Louisville (about 1819) to enter 3,000 acres in land warrants. A large map of the military lands was shown him: "To him it was merely 'a fine map,' seemed all ignorant of its uses even when the water courses were pointed out to him—finally he was desired to point out where he would make his entries—he placed his broad open hand covering ten times as much as warrants called for, and said, 'I'll take it here.'" The land-office men then asked him to describe from certain natural boundaries what location he wanted, and at once he began to plat it out so clearly

[1]In one of Kenton's old deeds of sale—for three hundred and twenty acres near his station to William Wood and Arthur Fox, October 31, 1785—the trees "read" as follows:

"Beginning at a Hackberry & Small Hickory on the west side of s'd fork, thence south 213½ p. to a Hackberry, thence East 240 poles to a Sugar tree White Ash and Cherry, thence North 213½ poles to a Sugar tree Mulberry and hiciory, thence West 240 poles crossing the said fork to the Beginning."

that he soon made his entries. He spent the rest of the day in "describing the country" across the river and aided others, come there to enter land, in choosing their locations wisely.

As we have seen, there is nothing in the meager accounts of Simon Kenton's youth which show any natural trend toward his later career as scout, pilot, spy, and Indian fighter. Perhaps this is because these pursuits by which he is best known were after all not his native ones. His native instinct was for the earth, the lay of its lands and its waters, and land was his dominant passion.

"Kenton was land-crazy," said his friends.

It was a curious craze. It was not an avaricious one—he never seemed to care for riches. And he did not care greatly for the land's development, although he liked it to be settled with newcomers who were free to do what they wished with it. He himself simply loved it; land in vast areas was his own personal, passionate hobby. No one will ever know how many hundreds of thousands of acres in Kentucky, Ohio, Indiana, Missouri, and Florida passed through his hands from 1780 on—he could never resist the lure of entering some fine large tract and calling it his own. Joseph Vance, one of Kentucky's early governors and one of "Kenton's boys," who in his youth "looked upon Kenton as his *beau ideal* of a great man," told Dr. Draper that land was Kenton's ruling passion, and that when he last saw him, in 1835, only a few months before his death, "though a mere wreck of a man, old and broken down and could hardly walk, yet talked of going west to buy government land."

His love for the earth shows even in his formal pension statement, where adjectives except when applied to services rendered do not abound. The adjectives describing his exploits are few; but he speaks irresistibly of "the fine country on the Ohio," "the fine territory which now constitutes the state of Kentucky," the "fertile Territory Northwest of the Ohio," and of spending "the best energies of his life in rescuing from barbarism so fine a country." As he lay almost dead at Machachack after the gauntlet race there, he "gazed south over the adjoining plain" which seemed even then to him "the most beautiful he had ever seen." And at Wappatomika, doomed to the stake, the thought nevertheless flashed into his mind that some day he would own some of that "fine country."

Kenton's wealth in Kentucky and Ohio lands was enormous—its total is now incalculable. Men who owned a hundred thousand acres were called capital landholders; Kenton was one nearly four times over. From the time he had claimed settlement and preemption rights to fourteen hundred acres on Elkhorn in 1779, he never ceased to take up land and more land. His Kentucky entries range from one hundred and fifty-two and a half to fifteen thousand acres all through Mason, Fayette, Lincoln, and Bourbon counties. When he left Kentucky in 1798 he assigned to his brother John in trust more than one hundred and forty-five thousand acres with which to meet his engagements; and this was only the residuum of his Kentucky holdings, for he sold a great deal before his departure. To this must be added the quarter million of acres he owned in the Symmes purchase of

Ohio land. His son's claim, therefore, that in 1798 he owned "several hundred thousand acres obtained chiefly by locating upon shares for others, also by purchasing warrants and making entries," is not extravagant.

Two little tracts of land Kenton owned in Indiana should not be omitted from this general total, even though they add but one hundred and eight acres to his "several hundred thousand." When Clark was planning his Illinois campaign in 1778, Jefferson proposed that some of the conquered land should be set aside and given to the soldiers and officers aiding in its conquest—no less than three hundred acres to each private soldier and to the officers land in proportion to the commissions they held. "Clark's Grant" of one hundred and fifty thousand acres in what is now Indiana was set aside and apportioned out by lot. Unfortunately Jefferson's proposed quantity of land was cut to one hundred and eight acres for common soldiers, and when the drawing was over it had somehow happened that more than one hundred and twenty-three thousand acres went to sixty-four officers, and a little more than twenty-five thousand acres were divided among two hundred and thirty-six privates. Kenton was always scornful of this little grant; always claimed that as "express man, Spye, Pilot," he was entitled to more for extra service; he never had it surveyed and finally gave it away.

Curiously enough, his misfortunes in land began with his first land certificate in 1779. As Colonel Marshall wrote Dr. Draper, from the loose land laws by which the land commissioners granted certificates of settlement and preëmption rights, "the fine lands of Kentucky were literally shingled over with patents, leading to interminable litigation." Anyone giving proof of a year's residence or the raising of a crop of corn prior to 1778 could get such a certificate and make an entry; this guaranteed title if no other previous entry was valid. All shapes and sizes of areas were patented and all manner of irregular strips lay between. The same piece of land could be patented over and over again, and some of the land cases which packed the dockets of the early Kentucky courts have not been settled to this day.

Such a double claim arose over Kenton's first entry of land on Elkhorn. The famous case of Kenton *vs.* McConnell, based on this disputed title, first came before the Kentucky courts in August, 1788, and was in the courts for more than ten years before it was finally and for all time decided in Kenton's favor. It was a famous case because it decided not only his title but that of hundreds of others of the earliest settlers to land they had claimed. It stayed in the Kentucky Court of Appeals for five years, from 1793 on. The court's first decision against Kenton involved all but the dissenting judge in a scandal of high order. A year later the decision was reversed in his favor. The case was appealed by McConnell twice after that, but each time the decree in Kenton's favor stood "confirmed and unaltered." Had it been otherwise, the possessions of almost every Kentucky pioneer would have been endangered, for any decision of the early Virginia commissioners could have been questioned, and by the fine splitting of legal hairs in which this case abounded, home after home could have been taken away from the men who held Kentucky during the first three years of its settlement.

The case of Kenton *vs.* McConnell settled many fine questions of law but the benefit went to others; Kenton had long since disposed of this holding. The personal issue between the two men stretched through the years; twice Kenton was imprisoned on account of it. When his battles with the Indians ended, his battles in the courts of the white men began: he understood Indian warfare better and fared better in it.

A white man's battle over land occurred in Ohio during a land-hunting trip of 1795, which seriously involved one of Kenton's nephews, William Owen. Kenton, Owen, and William Ward were out on the upper Scioto and met there one Robert Miller also out with a party; for there was a report that Congress, following the old tactics of the mother state, Virginia, would grant settlement and preëmption rights to fourteen hundred acres in Ohio for "tomahawk improvements." Miller had already made his easy settlement on land which Owen coveted. Owen promptly took off Miller's horses and hid them, in the hope that their owner might think Indians were too near and abandon the place. But Miller thought otherwise, and when he charged Owen with stealing the horses, a quick quarrel arose, guns were raised, and Miller was killed. It was regarded as an unjustifiable deed, but Owen, tried at Marietta for murder the following fall, was acquitted. Simon Kenton was there as a witness for his nephew, and there Judge Jacob Burnet, sitting with this court, first met him; the following year he visited him; it was the beginning of a life-long friendship.

"He was then possessed of a large estate," Judge Burnet wrote, "and a more generous, kind-hearted man did not inhabit the Earth. His door was always open. 'Neither stranger nor friend ever found it shut and the latch string pulled in.' Travelers of every grade were received with kindness, treated with hospitality, and pressed to stay."

Kenton's home was filled then with newly arrived relatives. Stephen Jarboe had come out from Maryland with his wife and children. Mrs. Jarboe was the last of the "Cleland sisters" to come to Kentucky, and her first home there was with her niece, Kenton's wife.

But the large, generous, happy Kentucky days were drawing to a close. In December, 1796, disaster and tragedy overtook the "fine brick house" and its inhabitants. On a day when the place was almost deserted and Mrs. Kenton lay sleeping in a downstairs room, a brand from an unwatched fire in the chamber above her rolled from the hearth, burned slowly through the floor, and fell flaming on her bed. The house was partially destroyed and she suffered such burns and shock as to result in premature childbirth and her death.

The Jarboes stayed on to care for the home and the four motherless children, and fifteen months later, on March 27, 1798, Simon Kenton married their daughter Elizabeth. Like her cousin "Patsey," she was much Kenton's junior, having been born on the day he was captured by the Indians. Black-haired, blue-eyed, with many of her French father's characteristics, she was in all ways the very opposite of her silent husband, "all life and animation and action. She was the smartest of pioneer women." Granddaughter of a Presbyterian clergyman and daughter of a clever mother, she had had all the opportunities of education open to girls of that day. To her insistence is due the existence of Kenton's Manuscript Statement and his "Recollections of Gen. George Rogers Clark," which she took down from his dictation. A number of her letters, written to her children in her old age, lie among the Kenton Papers; they are brave and cheerful on the surface, but their underlying tone shows that the life of a pioneer's wife blossomed into few flowers. The handwriting is clear but the spelling is quaint—no quainter however than George Rogers Clark's, or even George Washington's.

In this courtship Kenton proved himself more adroit than in his first one. Here too he encountered a rival, but instead of calling Reuben Clark out he sent him away on a mission which removed him for some months from Kentucky; by the time he returned Parson William Wood had pronounced Simon Kenton and Elizabeth Jarboe man and wife.

And then, leaving the four children in the Jarboes' care, Simon and Elizabeth made a honeymoon trip to—of all places—Missouri. They went the only way, on pack horses and rafts, camping by the way to see the country. Boone, far more restive than Kenton under the restraints of civilization in the "crowded country," was soon to seek "more elbow room" in the wilds of Missouri, whence the game had retreated and where man had not yet come to spoil Nature's largess; where once again he could throw his wood into his fire as he cut it. Kenton went seeking not more elbow room but more land—as if the areas of Kentucky and Ohio were already exhausted!

Contrary to all his biographers, he did not remove to Ohio on account of poverty or because "all his lands had been lost to him by better titles." As a matter of fact, "his locations were so special," says his son William, "that they have become proverbial in that particular in the courts of Kentucky. His immense land dealings had given him a thirst for the land trade, and probably to some extent for acquisition—though he never seems to have been avaricious—and as all the good lands of Kentucky had been entered and much also of an inferior quality in the mountain regions, he concluded to go to Ohio, as presenting a new field for land speculations. He was able to take with him considerable means to Ohio, and left with his brother property sufficient to have paid his debts several times over."

Then too a break had come; his wife had died, his house had burned, and his major work for twenty years—watching the Ohio for Indian raiders—was finished. So upon his return from Missouri, he wound up his Kentucky affairs, and leaving huge holdings behind him as well as huge debts, went over the river to huger holdings there, taking with him the saving knowledge that when all of Ohio's lands should have been entered, Missouri's lands would remain. In the late fall following his second marriage he went with his wife to Cincinnati, where they remained until the birth of their first child, Matilda, on January 23, 1799.

But before he left Kentucky, he had lighted the fuse of another "Kenton migration," this time not down but across the river. His brother William's family were thinking it over, and the Arrowsmiths likewise. The Jarboes and the Owens, the Dowdens and the Berrys were lured by the prospect. Colonel William Ward was going; Benjamin Whiteman decided to go. To one of his nieces who demurred, wondering why her uncle wanted to leave Kentucky when life was growing comfortable there, and seeing no good reason for it, "Why," said he, "if my wife couldn't *see* her interest better than that, I would cover her eyes with sand."

So, twenty-eight years after he first came to the country of the cane-lands, one of perhaps a dozen white men in its wilderness, he turned his back upon near a quarter million citizens of a civilized and settled state, and went out again upon the northernmost frontier. Boone's work was finished; for twenty years to come he would trap and hunt and dream in a Missouri wilderness, content with no more than that. And Clark's work was done; for twenty years he would sit on Mulberry Hill, dreaming bitter, idle dreams, an old, old man before his time. Of the three men, Kenton had the staying power. His work too was done—in Kentucky. But across the river lay Ohio. The border line had shifted; it called him, and he followed it in his middle years to live his second youth.

Chapter XII

EARLY DAYS IN OHIO
1799–1813

COVERED wagons were soon to roll through Ohio along Kenton's Trace, but Kenton's first detachment of Ohio pioneers made their April way as best they could through a roadless wilderness. From the depths of saddlebags flung in front of mounted mothers, children's faces peered at the fathers who walked alongside. In front of his riding and marching people went "the prince of pioneers," flanked on either side by the "Dowden boys," John and Archibald, whom he had trained and whom he could trust to scan the trail for Indian sign as persistently as he himself. For he was on his way again to take possession of Indian hunting grounds.

It was a beautiful spot—the place Kenton had chosen for his first Ohio home: a rolling hill in the midst of a great prairie, skirted by groves of wild cherry, wild plum, and wild crab, and graced with a gushing spring so fine that it became a well-known and general camping ground for wagons and movers coming later to Ohio. Here on his thousand-acre tract, four miles north of where Springfield was to be laid out, on the 5th of April, 1799, he brought his people safely: his own family, two mothers-in-law, for the Dowdens and the Jarboes joined him, his nephew William Owen and his family, the Berry family,

William Ward and his family, and half a score of Negroes. And here they were busy through the summer erecting fourteen cabins and making the beginnings of a block house. The building must be better done here than in Kentucky, for they had left the Southland for a colder region; half-faced camps would not serve them when the Ohio winter came.

Kenton's party were not to settle here without trouble. Asal Owen, then a boy of seven years, says that while the cabins were building, a company of Indians camped only a few hundred yards from his father's cabin (William Owen built about a quarter of a mile from Kenton's home) "on a beautiful night in June when the broadfaced moon was pouring her mellow rays of light upon our dusky ball the earth." Kenton had dropped over for a visit and an inspection of the camp. He found Joseph Whittlesey and one Felix, another Indian trader, there; they fell into a discussion of Indian character and "The General observed . . . that an education obtained in the school of Indian warfare was well calculated to teach white men the native disposition and character of the aboriginal, and that he was a regular graduate from the school of torture which was a fair picture of the disposition and true character of the Indian race and that the lessons which his cruel preceptors had taught him were engraven upon his memory, his mind, and in particular his body, and at the same time . . . he called my father to him and placed two of his fingers into an indentation in and on the scull engraven with the bowl of a pipe-tomahawk."

After these reminiscences, satisfied that all was well with the Owens, Kenton went back to his own cabin. But soon afterward a "tall stout square built Cherokee Indian" (probably Billy George, who loomed large in later years) came into Owen's cabin from the drunken camp. Whittlesey began to jest with him about "swapping squaws," which rather ominously came to include Owen and his wife. When midnight came the Cherokee refused to go and his intention was clear. Whittlesey, regretting his ill-timed jest, took his arm to lead him away, but quick as a flash the Indian stabbed him. Owen threw him across the bed on which his three children were sleeping and called for help; it was a hard fight before the Indian was bound to a tree outside with a guard set over him. He escaped during the night, but was captured and whipped and in the morning marched down to the old chief, Wolf, for punishment.

There followed then a bit of common-sense Indian justice. When Wolf had heard all, he said simply: "You whip him—whip him enough? Then let him go —he a bad Indian—did wrong to stab Whittlesey—but you whip him enough. If Whittlesey die, then you, Owen, kill him—or I will."

Kenton, always keeping an eye on his brood, came down the next morning as usual. He walked in with, "How are you, Jinney?" Then, seeing the shamble-like cabin, wrecked and spattered with the bloody struggle of the night before, he was down at the camp before the Indian court of justice had ended.

Word came from Cincinnati in midsummer that a body of Indians was collecting near Detroit to work mischief on the frontier. Kenton promptly left cabin building to the rest of his party and set out on a trip of discovery to "ottoway town." Nothing is known of this private expedition but what appeared in the *Western Spy* of August 27,1799—a long letter from Kenton's old enemy, Black Snake, and six other chiefs, beginning "Brothers," and going on to say that, "being the last to make peace at Greenville with our father General Wayne," they would be the last to break it, and regretting that "you have received a false alarm by some bad person." Following it was this note:

> The above is a copy of a letter received in answer to one sent by us to search the truth of the report respecting the attack from the Indians. The public will draw what conclusions and security they see proper from it. We are this day going to meet some of the chiefs; any of the information we may receive shall be communicated in some channel.
>
> (Signed) SIMEON KENTON
> WILLIAM WARD

No concerted attack was made by the Indians, but individually they gave trouble all through the winter, and Kenton kept a strong hand ready for these. He still continued to "raise parties." One day a "bad Indian," One Eye, entered the cabin of a Mrs. Dement when she was alone and demanded food; she refused it, whereat he seized her by the hair and dragged her about till she was senseless; then went down to her spring house and helped himself. Kenton heard of the attack that night; the next morning with fifteen men, he started for One Eye's camp. There they tied the Indian up and whipped him round robin fashion, each of the party giving him a certain number of blows so that no one might be blamed for the punishment, and to each one he was made to say "*Ni yaw way*—thank you." One Eye was not deceived however; he always held Kenton to have been the leader in this punitive visit, and a number of times during the winter lurked about his cabin for two or three days, saying that "when the bushes got green" he would kill Cutta-ho-tha. Five years later, when on a mission to the Indians at Stony Creek, Kenton met him there, and noticing that One Eye was following him, drew out his knife (for his gun, like those of the rest of the Indians and whites, had been left behind for the council) and taking far aim at a tree trunk, let it fly. He walked up to the tree trunk, drew the knife out, and looked straight at the Indian who a few moments later came up to him, saying, "Me friend."

That same winter Kenton's youngest child, then a year old, was stolen from her cradle by a drunken Indian who walked into the cabin, entirely naked, when Mrs. Kenton was alone, and demanded whiskey. Refused it, he caught up the little Matilda from her bed and made for the Indian camp not far off. It was a friendly camp and Mrs. Kenton ran toward it; she was met on her way by the chief man bringing back her baby, and the punishment of the baby stealer was left to his own people.

Old Indian friends of Kenton were in these hunting camps settled so near him and his people. Bonah, squat, large, and heavy, who had captured Kenton in 1778, claimed him for his prisoner, guarded him, whipped him, and after all cared for him, lingered for years about this locality. He visited Kenton often, always for presents, and often ate at his table. Kenton once asked him why he should continue to give him presents when he (Bo-nah) had been "so harsh on him." Bo-nah was silent a moment; then he unexpectedly replied: "Because I didn't kill you."

One day Bo-nah was at Kenton's house when Colonel Ward and several others were present. At dinner Bo-nah turned to Ward, saying with his characteristic pantomine: "I and Cutta-ho-tha are now on better terms than we were the day I made him extend his arms and tied him, when Cutta-ho-tha cried—now I am sitting at his table in friendship." At this Kenton's quick wrath flamed; he was carving a great deer haunch, and springing to his feet, knife in hand, he lunged across the table at Bo-nah. Ward and the others interfered and the Indian, a little alarmed at the miscarriage of his humor, tried to make peace; but Kenton's anger endured for a long time. Yet when asked why he didn't kill Bo-nah and make a good riddance, he answered indignantly: "No! it is peace, suh! What Bo-nah did was an act of war."

Coo-na-haw, otherwise old John Coon, calmly settled down on Kenton's farm with his squaw, his son William Moses, and his two daughters Katy and Betsy and lived there for years; a little son Abraham died early and was buried on Kenton's place. Coo-na-haw was a full-blooded white man, captured when a boy of three and reared by the savages. He used to say he was "an Indian, but a white Indian." When John Dowden came up from Kentucky to visit his mother the second summer after the migration, he found Coo-na-haw already settled at Kenton's, and recognized him as the Indian who had nearly shot him on Paint Creek in 1793. Coon told him then, as he had told Kenton, that in the Little Miami skirmish of 1792 it was the splashing of the Indian children and squaws making off through the stream which made the whites believe that reinforcements were coming up. It was he who related also the manner of McIntire's death.

Old Chi-ux-ko was also a permanent dweller on Kenton's pastures. Many other Indians camped down on Kenton from time to time, but these two and their families followed him from Springfield to Lagonda and then to Urbana. It made living easy. They had no objection to supplying themselves with game, but planting and tending corn was another matter; and they helped themselves freely from the grain in Kenton's cribs. Chi-ux-ko was "a very witty, playful, jovial Indian and would keep a whole company in laughter by his drolleries." He was by now in full middle age, no chief, merely a warrior, though one of distinction, and very active and athletic. He too, like Coon, had opposed Kenton on the Little Miami, and he had been out against Wayne: "We caught Wayne's waggons lagging behind," he told Kenton, "and we ran up and cut spokes fast." An "honest Indian," than which in those days there was no higher praise for even a white man, Kenton often trusted him with what Chi-ux-ko called "books" which he carried to other settlements and forts in time of alarm. He had a squaw and two sons, Spy Buck and Cornstalk, and from these little Indians and John Coldwater's son Pa-mo-tee, who lived with his father on Owen's farm, "the small boys learned to talk considerable" of Shawanese. In fact, in this picturesque colony where their father operated as master of slaves and patron of Indians, all of Kenton's children picked up bits of the Indian tongue which linger in their latest reminiscences.

Something of the Old World dignity of a clan's chief attaches to Simon Kenton in these early Ohio days. He was rich head of a family and all its branches, with slaves and retainers, and the living had the simple dignity of the tribesman's life, close to the earth and all in the open except when rain and cold drove them to shelter as primitive as ever existed. on Asia's plains. He was patron of the arts as well as of the Indians, for there was a school in the Kenton colony as early as 1801 when the William Kentons and the Arrowsmiths came, and he sent the Indian children to school with his own. Spy Buck took more of the white man's learning than any of the others, and Kenton encouraged him to go as long as he would; he was interested in watching "an Indian learn to read." He took Spy Buck back with him once to Kentucky, as an example of what education could do for a savage; unfortunately the lure of drink caught him and his education went none too far.

As chieftain of his clan Kenton defended not only his blood kin and friends, but his red retainers as well. During a period of Indian alarm some of Kenton's neighbors at Lagonda became so infuriated at the whole red race that, gathered at his cabin one night, they declared they were going down to the two Indian camps on his land and wipe out the devils he harbored. Kenton listened long enough, then suddenly took down his gun and promised them all that the massacre of these friendly Indians would take place after his own death and would certainly be preceded by the sure taking off of a few white men present. All of Kenton's memorialists agree in saying that although he was a man who never had very much to say, what he said was "impressive." Assuredly he impressed his neighbors that night with his remarkable faculty for combining "good enemy and good friend" in one body, and with his extraordinary ability to pass with the swiftness of light from one to the other when occasion arose. Coon and Chi-ux-ko slept that night untroubled.

Two years in Ohio—and Kenton's great land holdings there dissolved over night. John Cleves Symmes could not meet the payments for his two million acres and Congress canceled the purchase; Kenton's land went like mist.

But Springfield had been laid out—Elizabeth Kenton had named it, "on account of the many delightful and valuable springs within and around the place located for the town"—and Kenton was full of new plans for new ventures. That fall he sent Chi-ux-ko out to cut Kenton's Trace from Lagonda creek near Springfield to Newmarket, lying almost opposite his old Limestone on the Ohio. It was slow work, making a road through the wilderness, but, first blazing the trail and cutting through the worst tangles on the route, it was widened a little on the return trip. Travel must do the rest.

Kenton worked with the party on its slow way to the river; there he left them and went on to Kentucky with young Spy Buck to get supplies and materials for the saw and grist mill he purposed to put up on Lagonda, and for the trading store he was to establish there. His saws were brought down from Pittsburgh; his millstones were cut at Laurel Hill in Pennsylvania, hauled twenty-five miles to Redstone Old Fort on the Monongahela, there put on a flat boat and sent down the Ohio. "From there they were waggoned to the mill site, a distance of over 100 miles. All millers who ever used them said they were the best corn stones they ever saw." Kenton's millstones were on the first wagon that ever passed over his trace. William Kenton's son Thomas went over it in May, 1802. His covered wagon, one of the first to creak and sway in the West, was the second wagon to pass over the trace.

But Kenton did not go back to Ohio with his millstones. He was caught in a tangle of land troubles in Kentucky; he sold his brick house to Samuel Tebbs, and then he came down with an illness so serious that his wife left her infant daughter Elizabeth (born December 6, 1801) and came down to Washington to take care of him. His millstones had been lying for months on Lagonda Creek before he got back there and began to put up three cabins all at once, as was his impetuous custom.

His mill building was interrupted however by an attempt to put through a great land deal "on his own hook." And now began his mysterious departures from home which continued until his old legs would carry him no farther than the nearest neighbors. "Uncle Simon used to go out in the woods alone," writes one of the Owen grand-nephews "and be gone for months at a time. He never said 'Good bye' nor how do you do when he returned, but would walk in and hang up his gun and sit quietly by the fire. After several days he would begin to laugh in a quiet way to himself; then mother knew that Uncle Simon was getting ready to tell his adventures. They never questioned him until he was ready to open out on the subject. He always talked through the nose, and would begin like this, 'Well with-thee, Betsey,' which was my mother's name. I am afraid you cannot convey the peculiar sound by the way I write it, but he would invariably commence with that 'Well with-thee, Betsy.'"

This departure in 1802 was—and still is—shrouded in a tolerable amount of mystery. He took a French trader and interpreter—Felix—with him and went to the "Wabash Indians." There, says his son William, he made an "Indian treaty with Tecumseh for near all the land between the Miami and the Wabash on his own hook—treaty prohibited by Congress." His son recollected seeing the treaty, "written by one Abey Clark," which gave Kenton most of the land lying between the Miami and the Wabash, "near half of Ohio and some of Indiana," in return for "considerable goods and provisions paid to the Indians and promise to pay more money or goods as long as grass grows and water runs and other stipulations similar to other Indian treaties."

This was patterned of course on Henderson's Watauga treaty with the Southern Indians for the Kentucky lands which he began to settle in 1775—a treaty which Virginia had promptly declared invalid. Nevertheless Henderson had been allowed a portion of his claim; but not so Kenton. His son remembered that some "Kentucky lawyers" came to his father, trying to get something out of it to satisfy a certain debt, and that, remembering that "Henderson was allowed a portion of his claim" an attempt was made "to gather up the remaining scraps." But there was no money to press the case—and no great land company behind the treaty maker—and no friends at court. Then too Ohio became a state this year and would see to it that no single citizen owned "near half of Ohio and some of Indiana" by any private treaty with Tecumseh and his chiefs.

However, with a new air castle to live in, Kenton strolled back to his family one day in time for the birth of another child, his daughter Mary, born March 3, 1803. That spring he began the erection of his mill, a high, eighteen-foot square log cabin, but it was not finished that year or the next. His millstones, cut with such care in Pennsylvania and transported so many miles at such pains, lay on Lagonda four or five winters before they began to grind Ohio corn. For Kenton had a hundred other things on his mind; he was away on numerous land trips with Ward; he vibrated between Kentucky and Ohio on "business"; and any Indian trouble found him in the center of it.

He *was* the center of the famous "Billy George affair" in the summer of 1804 when the whites took justice into their own hands and administered it with cold order even though without law. Billy George was a Cherokee alien dwelling in the Shawanese land, and was notoriously known as a "bad Indian." From his solitary camp at the head of Lagonda he made solitary expeditions to the homes of settlers old and new whose men were away, demanding food or whiskey or lodging and, if these were refused, brandishing his knife or tomahawk with terrifying gestures and threats. Several mysterious killings of whites had occurred in the neighborhood, and one night Chi-ux-ko brought Kenton warning: Billy

George had been boasting that he had killed two big captains and would be satisfied when he had killed another. Chi-ux-ko was convinced that Kenton was the third "big captain" Billy George had in mind, and insisted on staying with him that night for protection.

Billy George himself appeared at Kenton's the following night, saying briefly that he wished to sleep there. At bedtime Kenton told him to turn in, and when he refused said he must leave the house or he would tie him. Billy George drew his knife, but the watchful Chi-ux-ko appeared and the three men sat up all night together. The next morning, after the Cherokee had gone sullenly off, a neighborhood group meeting was held, and it was decided in cold blood that he should be killed. Some legally inclined mind among them suggested drawing up a warrant for his arrest to read to him first, in the sure conviction that he would resist it. Archibald Dowden, Robert Renick, and Jesse Bracken headed the small party that set out from Kenton's a day or two later. Kenton himself was ill at the time; there is small doubt that otherwise he would not have been out of it. Arrived at Billy's camp, they found him away and, a deer hanging by, they cooked and ate some of it while they waited. When he came back, full of sullen suspicion at their presence, they read him the warrant with two men secreted, and when he drew his tomahawk to fling it these two fired together and killed him.

Dowden and Renick were both tried for murder at the first court ever held at Springfield. Kenton went to the trial, himself a "bad man"; "loading his rifle before he left home, threatening to shoot any person who would make it a crime for ridding society of so dangerous a person as Billy George—whether judge or juror." Had the prisoners been convicted he and others had determined to hold up the court and the spectators while the men made their escape on horses standing ready with provisions and guns. Everybody in the neighborhood—and quite likely the honorable court—knew all about these arrangements. But justice in the early days rather settled itself. No one really believed that either of the so-called murderers would hang or even be imprisoned for the killing, and neither was—they were both acquitted.

New Madrid is perhaps the most romantic spot in all Missouri. Here—had George Morgan's plans for his great purchase in the Spanish Grant gone through—would have been a palace for the Spanish king, "as long as grass grows and water runs." Here along the Mississippi, and extending for miles north and south, would have been a great Old World boulevard with plazas and parks, and the virgin forest kept inviolate forever except for carefully planned châteaux, and their surrounding gardens. But the government interfered with Morgan's purchase from the Spaniards by its own Louisiana purchase, and a few years later Nature interfered with a remarkable earthquake which startled the world and made the name of New Madrid known all around it. The earthquake centered there; beginning in December, 1811, it lasted five months, and sent out tremors that were felt from New Orleans to Detroit, and from South Carolina to southern California. The Mississippi "ran backward" and tore out new banks for itself. It washed away the boulevard and palace lands, and, incidentally, most of Simon Kenton's purchases.

For Kenton—General Kenton now—went out again to Missouri in 1805. The Symmes purchase had collapsed; his Indian treaty had collapsed; and although he owned much Ohio land, it was in small parcels, not in great, magnificent tracts. In April he resigned the brigadier generalship of the Ohio militia to which he had been elected six months before and rather uncharacteristically took military Ohio into his confidence regarding his reasons:

> Sir [he wrote his general, John Gano, on April 18th], Having taken a Resolution of making a tour through the late acquired lands of the United States, in consequence of which think proper to resign up my commission of Brigadier of the militia, and you hereby requested to regard this as full notice of the same, given under my hand.
>
> (Signed) SIMON KENTON.[1]

For the second time Kenton crossed the Mississippi, taking with him his son John, then a boy of fifteen. He went first to New Madrid, where he made large purchases, and then worked up the Mississippi and along the Missouri to the village of St. Charles, a small town on the north bank, whose single street rambled along the river for about a mile, not at all crowded with its hundred small wooden houses. But its "historic background" had already been thinly

[1]The *Western Spy*, October 3, 1804, gave notice of the coming election of a brigadier general, the first of its kind held since the state of Ohio was organized November 29, 1802. In its issue of November 8th it said:

"In October, 1804, Simon Kenton was duly elected Brigadier General of the 3rd brigade of the first division of Ohio militia—so certified by Major General John S. Gano.—This election was held at the court house in Dayton by the commissioned officers of that brigade on 16th October."

painted in; William Clark, George Roger's brother, had passed that way with Lewis the year before on his way to the Pacific. George Druillard, old Pierre's son, was with him; Kenton had given George his "parting frolic" before he left Kentucky for Missouri and the long Western trail. And back of St. Charles lived Daniel Boone, whom Kenton had not seen since the Kentucky days.

Boone was out chopping wood when Kenton approached the cabin, as Kenton very well knew from the fresh-cut armful beside it and the sound of the ax in the forest. He gathered the sticks in his arms and knocked at the door, and when Mrs. Boone opened it, he walked across the floor and in neighborly fashion laid them by the fireplace. Boone was called in but "took his own time"; and the venison supper was almost ready when he appeared. There followed a week of reunion—"a happy visit." When Kenton left, his son stayed behind; "made his home at William Morrison's," says Boone's son Nathan, "and went some to school one winter, was active and sprightly."

Back again in Ohio, Kenton found more Indian trouble simmering. Tecumseh had gathered his people together early in 1806 and was counciling on the headwaters of Stoney Creek. Other chiefs were counciling at Wappatomika and at Greenville. Reports reached the whites that the "Shawnies nation" was preparing for war, that war belts were passing among them, that some were "painted black," that their tomahawks were painted and feathered, that a war post was planted at Stoney Creek, and that runners were being sent from place to place with word from the various councils.

Captain James McPherson came down from his trading place above Urbana to council a little with Kenton—this was about the 10th of February. They decided the situation was serious enough to warrant their sending out a general warning to the settlers and set promptly about it.

Unlike the huddled settlements put up in Kentucky in the early days, those of Mad River ran in a string of scattered cabins along each side of the stream. Kenton went down the east side and McPherson the west, giving notice of danger and advising the settlers to fort for a few days at the strongest house in their immediate neighborhood. When William Owen's wife heard the news she instantly decided to take her two youngest children back to Kentucky. Within the hour she mounted a horse and, with her two boys tucked in a pair of saddlebags flung in front of her, began her hundred-mile journey over Kenton's Trace to the Ohio. She reached it safely, but it seems a strange choice between dangers.

A number of people gathered that same night at Thomas Kenton's, whose double cabin was "fortified" better than most in his neighborhood. For the ten-foot strip between the two cabins was fenced in at each end, and in one end a gate; the roofs slanted inward and had outside projections over which the Indians could not climb. And there were "juts" in the corners, with portholes from which the defenders could look out and take aim. A well had been dug within the enclosure, and the place was equipped to withstand a several days' siege.

Kenton stayed there that night with his family. "He said the Indians had their war post properly planted and were striking it and exhibiting other great signs of war." But the next morning it was decided to go to Joseph Reynolds's settlement where "there was a great gathering of people," and where there were more cabins to shelter them. All of Reynold's buildings, his cabins, his fodder houses, his stables, were filled with men, women, and children. The rains were excessive just now, but sentinels kept watch day and night for four days.

There was no attack, however, and to end the suspense a mission to Tecumseh was decided on. Kenton, McPherson, and Charles McIlvaine went with Major Thomas Moore to the Indian camp on Stoney Creek—this was on the 16th.

I went to the Council [wrote Thomas Moore to Acting-governor Kirker two days later] accompanied by Capt. McPherson, General Kenton & Mr. McIlvain we arrived at the Indian Town about two o'clock when we attempted to go to the Council the sent a man to tell us not to some there at all (when we was at about 40 yards Distance) but said the would come to us at another place we immediately mounted our horses and started for we considered ourselves very unwelcome guests we had not gone farr before the called to us to Stop and talk we got off our horses again the came to another house we went in with about 18 Indians whare the following Discourse took place viz. we your friends Conceive we have just Reason to be much alarmed from the information we Recieve from our white friends and your Neighbors . . . and we your Brothers . . . wish for Nothing but trew friendship and handed the Chief a fiew Things of white wampum which he Recieved and s'd the Intended know harm and thanked the great Spirit above that we their Brothers Still wished that trew friendship might subsist we then appointed to meet them on the 21st of this Instant in the Settlement then and there to see if we can compromise and all parties be Satisfyed but when we went to take our Leave the allmost all give us their Left hand in a very cool manner Capt. McPherson is a gentleman that has been well

> acquainted with the manners of the Indians for upwards of 15 years and he says that he verily believes their intentions is not good for these Reasons · 1st their not Letting us into their council and 2nd the Number of panted fiethers which he Never Saw the Like amongst them accept in time of war. . . .

With this mission to the Indians the Mad River settlers were relieved of one anxiety, only to fall into another. All their improvements had been made on land within the Symmes purchase. They had reared cabins and forts, stables and grain houses, had cleared acres of land and planted them in corn, but they had no clear titles to their farms. Kenton and Ward proposed to buy up this land on which they would sell preëmption rights, "from 12½ to 100 cents the acre, but usually from 25 to 50 cents," and in 1806 and again in 1808 William Kenton, Simon's brother, traveled "on horseback from this city (Urbana) to the Federal City on business with the Congress of the United States." He went as Kenton's and Ward's representative to get from Congress a revival of the preëmption act on the Mad River lands and so worked with the senators and representatives there that an extension act was put through whereby the settlers, by paying annually for eight years one eighth of the amount due under the Symmes contract, could finally own their homes. Thus nearly all the first settlers along Mad River were enabled to keep what they had worked for so laboriously.

An English traveler, Thomas Ashe, was on Mad River in 1806 and himself caught a little of the primitive dignity of the life there.[1]

---

[1] *Travels in America Performed in 1806*, Thomas Ashe. London, 1808.

> I visited at least one hundred farms, and found the inhabitants in the possession of abundance of every common necessary and even absolute comfort essential to a modest and unassuming life. . . . You who have been always accustomed to the refinements of luxury, will scarcely be able to conceive how these settlers, with no other clothing than coarse homemade apparel, with no other shelter but a log house constructed with the rudest art, and with no food but of the coarsest kind, and destitute of coffee, tea, wine and foreign spirits, can enjoy any happiness; and yet as I observe, to judge from their manners, language and external application, their state may be envied by the wealthy of the most refined natures. . . . They are composed of all nations, and live as yet in a kind of native freedom and independence; in a kind of equality of rank which banishes all distinctions but those of age and merit—for the old control the parochial administration, and the learned govern the legal and ecclesiastical. However, as population increases, and as towns and villages abound, vice, which appears the propensity of man, will erect its power and call for the influence of the general regulation of the State and destroy the innocent and primitive characters which now distinguish the republic of the Mad River. Nothing in truth can be more primitive. Justice is administered with decency, but no forms. In the open air and on Sunday the people gather together in appointed groves, and silently attend to any person endowed with the grace and talent of instruction.

In the late summer of this year (1806) Kenton made another of his mysterious trips. One morning he saddled his horse, flung his old blanket across the pommel, mounted, and rode casually away. At some distance from his home he met one of his children; he told her to tell her mother he was "going away," and his family did not see him again until the spring of 1807. His son, William Miller, was born during his absence (February 12th).

Kenton had nothing whatever to say of his adventures when he returned. He brought back a bundle of North Carolina pear trees which he planted during the first days of silence. "He had had a leg broken during his absence, about which he would give no account to his family or others." Surmises that he might have been concerned in Aaron Burr's conspiracy brought hot denials, but only from words dropped and caught back through the years did his son William succeed in making a skeleton story of what his father was about during these months of absence.

Shortly before he left Kentucky Kenton had gone bail for one Robertson, who disappeared and made him liable for a large sum. Kenton appears to have been imprisoned under the old debtor's law for a brief period in 1797, probably on this matter, particularly if he considered it an "unjust debt." How he finally settled the difficulty is unknown, but he never forgot the man who betrayed him, and when he got his first clue to Robertson's whereabouts he mounted his horse and went clear to Florida after him. "This Robinson [Robertson]" William told Dr. Draper, "had swindled him out of a large amount of money by being his bail, and he wanted satisfaction and suppose he got it . . . was wounded when he came back, never told the particulars, but the neighbors thought that if my father had found Robertson and his confederates in a big swindle . . . that his wound was in the matter of settlement of that claim."

There were new neighbors, the McBeths, on a farm three miles north of Kenton's; their cabin was a sturdy one "arranged with port holes and an iron-strapped door." Across the road from them lived Major Moore, who blacksmithed and did gun repairing for the settlers and the Indians. And Kenton brought out another party from Kentucky that year —the McFarlands and others—who settled in the Mad River valley. When new Indian trouble broke in the fall of 1807 the neighborhood was better prepared to meet it, for the population had doubled in a year.

The British ship-of-war *Leopard* had shot upon the United States frigate *Chesapeake* and both the whites and the Indians knew it. Ohio citizens were passing resolutions of loyalty and forwarding them to their governor, while English agents were moving among the Indians, inciting them to distrust of the Americans and inviting them to cast in their lot with the British. Captain McPherson was spying among the Chippewas. Benjamin Whiteman, who had succeeded to Kenton's post as brigadier general of the militia, reported a large Indian gathering at Yellow Spring and urged a general calling out of the state troops. Governor Kirker wrote an official letter to his "red brothers" on Mad River, expressing the hope that their attitude toward their white brothers was fraternal. From Fort Wayne came the report that the Indians were gathering at Greenville as they had the year before, numbering, on the "most favorable calculation," seven hundred and sixty men. Tecumseh's brother, the Prophet, was busy here, and his influence was great.

Kenton felt the situation was serious enough to warrant a dangerous trip into the enemy camp. So, after consulting with Whiteman, he left about the first of September for Greenville, McPherson, Ward, and James Reed accompanying him. The following report of their observations was sent to the governor and they also signed with Langham and Whiteman the long explanatory letter sent with it:

From a report that a number of forreign Indians were collecting at Greenville, the undersigned were induced to go to that place to endeavor to ascertain the truth of the case—

When we arrived there, which was on tuesday morning last, we found there a trader who is a half-blooded man, being part French and part Indian, who informed us (by the interpretation of Mr. Fisher, who accompanied us and who understood the French and several of the Indian Tongues among which was the Potawatamies) that the Shawnee chiefs were all away from that place, mostly gone to Detroit, and that there was there a number of Potawatamies and other foreign Indians at that place, on which we consulted what steps we should take to obtain the object of our journey—

Previous to our reaching the place, it had been proposed by one of us (Ward) that if from circumstances it appeared doubtful what usage we might receive from them, he would take Alexd'r Dougherty (one of the men with us, and who was related to the Indians) with him, and try the event of their humor, but that was objected to by Kenton, saying that if the other went away then he would certainly go along and run the same risque—

When we got to Greenville and received the above information, as well as what other we could get, Kenton proposed our going to their encampment and endeavor to judge of their number by the size of their camp, but Ward objected, alleging that when their first surprise (which was visible in the faces of those we saw) was over they might (by geting information from some of the Shawnees who we were) think it a good opportunity of destroying so many of those that in future might prove detrimental to their designs, and that the danger was still the greater our not having the responsibility of the Shawnees to depend upon, as their chiefs were not present; in which Opinion we all acquiesced, and concluded to return with the following information, part from the Trader and part from the potawatamie: The trader said he never quitted his house to go to their Camp that he had seen some parties coming in and some few returning, so that he could not tell what number was there previous to a certain time some few days past, but that since that time he had seen, tho in Different parties, as many as one hundred and forty coming in and none returning of which number was twenty-two, of which there was two women of whose language he never before heard, nor was there an Indian at that place who understood them, except by their interpreter who was of the Sauky nation.—The Potawatamies said they were of a nation that was called (as they pronounced it) the Wynapaas, and that they had been three months and a half constantly travelling, coming from their homes.—The trader said they had all rifles and were nearly naked—we saw round one the Potawatamies neck a number of strings of rich looking Wampum, white and black mixed which he said was given him by the Wynapaas; we took him to be a chief by the belt being given to him, tho we could not discern that he had a single shred on him but his blanket.

In talking among themselves, perhaps before they knew they were understood, they supposed we were coming against them, and that the Militia was as plenty behind us as the Masketas, but on shaking hands with them (which we did not do at our first meeting) they concluded we were not Americans. On parting, they all gave us their left hand, resolutely refusing the right.

The reason given by the Indians for coming to Greenville, is to listen to the Prophet.

Signed
Simon Kenton,
James McPherson,
James M. Reed,
Wm. Ward.

On the return of this little embassy it succeeded in arranging a friendly council of the Indians and whites in the Mad River valley, which actually convened at McPherson's home. But the signs of hostility were so alarming that the place of conference was changed to an open space near Kenton's mill at Lagonda. The procession passed through Urbana on its way to the mill, armed to the teeth, "two and two abreast, an Indian and a white man together throughout the whole line of march."

When they reached McBeth's home, halfway on their journey, with Major Moore's gun shop just across the road, all the Indians were made to leave their tomahawks there, carrying only their guns; for it had been agreed that when they arrived at the council grounds, all armed men not taking part in the council should stand in the rear, each on his own side, and that the chiefs and the principal whites, no one of them carrying weapons of any sort whatsoever, should advance to the center and council unarmed in full view of all.

Tecumseh was in no civil mood at this council; he resented the belief of the Mad River inhabitants that his party and not Black Hoof's was responsible for the murder of one Bowyer a few months before, and he had come ready to charge Black Hoof with the crime. He and his party had therefore evaded McBeth's and, coming by a different path, retained their tomahawks. All but Tecumseh surrendered them at the council ground, but as the councilors advanced unarmed to the center, he walked out from his people carrying his pipe tomahawk and declaring that he must smoke his pipe and would keep it. A dangerous moment or two followed, but he finally gave it up to one of his own men who bore it away. "The Indians had been required to leave their tomahawks at McBeth's," Kenton told James. "Tecumseh wanted his pipe to smoke. Pinchard made him a corn cob and presented [it]—gave Pinchard a look and tossed the pipe over his head and did not afterwards deign to see him."

Kenton, Whiteman, McPherson, and Ward were among the councilors and all spoke. One of the old records says that the others were much excited in their talk and manner but that Kenton was composed and calm throughout, an Indian among Indians for stolidity, and that when his time came to speak his words, because of his manner, carried far greater weight. McPherson had known the Indians for sixteen years. Kenton had known them for thirty-six years, had been in too many councils not to know the Indian form of conduct and speech, and he could adapt himself to it readily. Then, too, the man was without fear. He bore himself as if he knew his life was a charmed one.

Tecumseh listened to the whites in silence until one of them referred to President Jefferson as his "great father"; this was a mistake which he instantly corrected. He said that the Sun was his father and the Moon his mother and he acknowledged none other. Later he disclaimed passionately any responsibility for the murder of Bowyer and had prudence enough not to charge Black Hoof and his Indians with its commission. Finally, through many speeches and formal stages of counciling at Kenton's Mill, a certain amity and understanding was arrived at, and again the Indian trouble was pushed away.

For a year or two Kenton busied himself with his mills and store on Lagonda. These had been in operation since 1806, but before he left for Florida on his mysterious trip he employed one James Robinson to take care of them. As usual he had great confidence in his clerk, and as usual it was confidence misplaced. "This man Robinson," says one of his friends, "betrayed his trust and acted the rascal to perfection. He collected as many of the outstanding accounts as he could, which of course included all that were good, and got hold of all the money within his reach, and left for parts unknown." The son of Kenton's old miller wrote Dr. Draper even more tersely about this matter: "He had a store at the mill, and had a man by the name of Robinson tending to it that was a regular rascal; he was defrauding him both in smuggling his goods and taking his money. He finally had to leave when it came to the old General's knowledge that he was defrauding him, and then he wrote back that he saw a storm was coming and if he stayed he would have to come under the lash of a damned fool's tongue and that he preferred to leave. The trouble was that he seen his hide was in danger."

Robinson's departure came in 1808, and Kenton undertook to restore order, and to replenish his stock. He "would buy goods of James McPherson, and had to send for many to the rapids of the Maumee; would get furs and skins of the Indians in trade, and gingseng and cranberries—of the latter a 'bark' contained a bushel and a half, which could be bought for a few trifles." He sent to Kentucky for much of his stock which rolled slowly along Kenton's Trace from Newmarket to Lagonda; but however bountifully his store was fitted out, his returns from it were trifling. As in Kentucky, he gave credit right and left and at Lagonda, as at Washington, there were "several men in the neighborhood who were worthless trifling fellows, and in so far as they possibly could, they obtained a living from Kenton's store, without making any returns for the same."

With his mother's death in November—"a woman of fine appearance and good character" is the only line on her in the Kenton Papers—Simon went back to Kentucky. The results of this trip were unfortunate indeed, for sleeping dogs in the Kentucky courts waked up with John Kenton's reconveyance to him of the residue of Kentucky lands left in John's trust ten years before. A few months more and the law's long arm was to stretch across the Ohio and never let go its hold of him until the debtor's law was erased from the Kentucky statutes.

But before he fell upon the days of his imprisonments he went back to Missouri to review his lands there and to buy more with the proceeds of some recent Kentucky sales—one tract alone he had sold for $36,000. He purchased another "Spanish Grant, upon which he paid $16,000 and obligated himself to pay $8,000 more." Before the balance was due he was offered in exchange for it "several thousand dollars and 1600 acres of choice land near Columbus, Ohio, very valuable," but he declined the offer, never made the remaining payment and subsequently lost it all. What the earthquake left of his first Missouri purchase at New Madrid the commissioners refused to confirm, and the great Missouri tracts went the way of his Kentucky and Ohio "thousands upon thousands of acres."

But all this lay in the future; the present was rosy and the trip was holiday. He went up to St. Charles again to visit Boone and to pick up his son John and take him back home. While there he learned that those good friends of his latter days of captivity at Detroit, General and Mrs. Edgar, were living at Kaskaskia, and on the return journey he and his son "went a day's travel out of their route" to visit them.

Roads led now from all directions to the place where, a generation of years before, he had piloted Clark through a roadless wilderness to Rocheblave's unsuspecting fort; "fine houses" stood on the sites of the first log cabins, and in one of the finest the Edgars lived.

There was great feasting and great talk, and while there Kenton's next venture bloomed—his Missouri "stores." For John Edgar knew the business of frontier trading posts—none better—and while Kenton questioned he invited his young son to listen. John went back the next year with William McCarty, one of Kenton's sons-in-law, to open two stores, one at St. Louis, the other at St. Charles; "the stocks were valued at $18,000" and consisted of everything called for in the trade of those days—corn, whiskey, tobacco, knives, needles, threads, garters, leggins, moccasins, vermilion, kegs, lead, powder, paints, blankets, "white" goods, flour, meal, pork, flints, knife handles, gun screws, scarlet leggins, shirts, "leggins for chiefs," wampum black and white, and the like. "Out of the earliest proceeds they were to liquidate this debt due on the Spanish Grant. But both mismanaged and in the end wasted it all."

With old vivid memories of his captivity and miraculous escapes revived in him by his visit with the Edgars, Simon Kenton made his long way back home to find waiting for him there another unforeseen working of "the power of God." But when he set out with his wife and family for a week at "Voss's camp ground" that fall, he was following no more than the usual neighborhood custom when the camp-meeting season opened.

He had never been an irreligious man; he had

lived too close to Nature and trusted her too much for that. He attended church services in the early days—whether as worshiper or sharpshooter is not material; either attitude was a religious one then. He could appreciate the practical religion of that early preacher who paused in the midst of a sermon to scan more closely the top of a tree and then said, "I want to remark right here that yonder is one of the best forks for a pack saddle I ever saw in the woods. When services are over we will get it." But for ten years he had moved untouched through a continuous revival almost unparalleled in America's religious history. He had seen scores of neighbors quickened by "jerking," until the quickened man was hurled literally of himself yet without his volition to the ground where his movements were like those of a live fish on land; and he had witnessed the manifestations of quickened consciences about him for years without manifesting any of his own.

But this fall he confessed and was shriven. It is almost impossible to avoid connecting his family's story of his conversion—his confession is the high light in it on which he pledged the Reverend Bennet Maxey to the utmost secrecy—with what happened on his mysterious Florida trip two years before. Kenton's temper made him a "wild man" at times, and it is not likely that he took the long road to Florida for the mere purpose of controlling it after he got there. "He wanted satisfaction and presume he got it," said his son laconically. Something occurred on the Florida trip about which his family knew nothing and of which they were always extremely reticent in all their surmises.

His old friends unite in asserting that Kenton was not "much changed" after this experience. But there was not, after all, much scope for outward change. For all his old friends assert that he was always universally and greatly beloved, "always played with children and they liked him"; that his manner, especially to women and children, was "courteous and tender"; "the expression of his countenance mild, his voice low and gentle"; that there was never a taint of wrong-doing attached to him. They say that his habits were "natural"; that he did not indulge in even the temperate use of liquors; that he used tobacco only in snuff; that he was abstemious in all his habitudes of life—simple and unsophisticated in everyday life; "for a man without scholastic culture was remarkably chaste in his behavior and conversation."

Not that he did not use vigorous and forthright words to express like meanings! The Kenton Papers show this plainly, and on this count of "chaste talk" a fine incident is related by Daniel Cowgill, whose letter to Dr. Draper regarding Kenton's death, happened to be the last of the Kenton Papers Dr. Draper received. In it he added of his own accord a "Kenton story" he had never forgotten, and this is it, in his own words, mixed as they are:

> He had a large hickory cane he always used when walking. He hired a stout young man to make rails, and by some means he thought Kenton's girls did not treat him well, and as two of them were going near where he was at work, he sang the hardest song he could in their hearing. They went home and told their father. In a short time this young man came to the house which had but one door and took a seat. The Old General came in and stood in the door. Mr. Hatfield my girls tell me you sang them a

song and now you're going to sing the same song to them and to me. Oh no I can't sing. If you don't I'll cane you. Then he tried and got through. Now you are at liberty, and he went.

Kenton's removal in July, 1810, to Urbana, the little county seat of the new Champaign County, is another nice instance of how a primitive communal sense of justice may take hold of almost any "due process of law" and deflect it.

For nearly a year the shadow of imprisonment had been hanging over him. A Kentucky claimant, hearing of his latest Missouri purchases and fearing he might be about to remove there, had sent lawyers into Ohio to recover a debt which Kenton, holding it to be an unjust claim, refused to pay. Whereupon the old debtor's law was invoked, under which his body could be seized and held until the judgment was cleared. He must go into jail; the Champaign County Jail was at Urbana; and Champaign County, settled mostly so far by his friends, his "boys" grown men, his relatives by blood, and connections by scores of inter-marriages, elected him in the promptest and friendliest way to be his own jailor. One of the outstanding incidents of the first court held in the county was the sheriff's scrawl on the writ of *capias* issued against Simon Kenton and Philip Jarboe for the recovery of this debt: "Found Philip Jarbo and have his body in court; found Simon Kenton, but he refuses to be arrested."

He was not arrested—the court simply smiled. He took his own time to close up his Lagonda and Springfield affairs, which were small enough. His mill and store on Lagonda had gone to ruin; his farm near Springfield had never been cleared; he evidently believed for some years to come that he shared ownership with Ward in the fine new county lands—Urbana was laid out on land to which Ward held the patent—and "old but not discouraged," says his son, he turned his face northward again.

He lived in Urbana at first a free man, in "a house on a small hill where one Lemon lived." Then he took his oath of office and moved into the county jail with his family, where he had "five rooms above and one below," and where he remained for a year or two. Here one of his daughters died; here one of his daughters was born—named Elizabeth after the little dead sister; and here two of his daughters were married.

Being confined for debt did not necessarily mean confinement in a cell. Urbana had "town bounds" through which the prisoner might roam if he were properly bonded. George Fithian, William Fyffe, and Zephaniah Luce were Kenton's bondsmen for his not breaking bounds and Kenton observed his limits with rigid formality. After the rifle-carrying days were ended, he always walked with a long staff, rifle high, which he grasped firmly about a foot from its upper end, and this end was deeply charred, for he constantly used it as a poker for stirring his fire. During his imprisonment he would walk with this staff from end to end of his bounds, "from the alley on Scioto street to High street and from Ward to Reynolds street," as if to pass over; then he would bring himself up with a quick military halt and march back. When his little daughter Elizabeth died, shortly after his imprisonment began, he attended the services in the family room below and went with the small coffin as far as he could without crossing his bounds. But the town cemetery lay beyond, and he stood a long time on the boundary line watching the funeral procession wind its prairie way to the grave.

Such as the prisoners were, he kept them and fed them. For his family, "he would pound enough hominy before day to cook a kettlefull which would last two days. He would purchase of Indians bear's oil in coon skin sacks and use it for shortening and cooking purposes." He traded with the Indians for other things when they made their half yearly camps at Urbana, in the spring bringing deer, bear, and wolf skins, moccasins and maple sugar cakes, in the fall coming back with more pelts and sugar, with honey, cranberries, and other wild fruits. With the remnants of the stock from his store on Lagonda, blankets, handkerchiefs, vermilion, powder, and lead, he bartered with them for what he wanted of what they had.

During Kenton's term as his own jailer, some horse thieves were busy around Urbana, and since he could no longer "pursue" he hired Captain John and several other Indians to go after them. The pursuers returned to "Labana" in triumph with two white men, whom Kenton put in cells to await trial. They were jolly prisoners with a gift of song which they exercised freely. But one day, after a prolonged concert, silence fell, and when their mates called for more song there was no response. While singing the two thieves had made their escape; they were never recaptured.

Kenton lay under this quasi-imprisonment for about a year before he was released; then, in 1811, he made his fourth trip to Missouri, this time to look into the state of his two Missouri stores. Of the St. Louis establishment nothing remained; young John

SIMON KENTON

FROM AN OIL PAINTING BY LOUIS MORGAN, 1836, PRESENTED BY WALTER D. McKINNEY TO THE OHIO STATE ARCHEOLOGICAL AND HISTORICAL SOCIETY, OCTOBER, 1924.

had sold it out and with the proceeds had bought "one hundred traps" for a fur-hunting trip up the Missouri. He was robbed by the Indians, lost all his belongings, and narrowly escaped with his life. In a brief letter home he "said he would never return till he had made as much as he lost, and started for Santa Fe." Kenton never saw his son again. Some years later he learned that the boy had gone on to Mexico, joined a revolutionary party there, and lost his life in storming a Spanish fort.

At St. Charles affairs were as bad; too many people had been "trusted," and the whole stock was squandered—Kenton's entire eighteen-thousand-dollar investment was gone.

And then at the end of the year came the earthquake which changed channels and made them and which put much of Kenton's Missouri holdings under water.

And then came the War of 1812. In September the first of the Kentucky troops passed through Urbana to join Harrison on the frontier, and from that time on Kenton's home was an inn where the guests did not pay. "His house was a home to the sick and afflicted," one of his granddaughters wrote to Dr. Draper. "He visited the camps, and if any needed assistance he gave it without wishing any recompense. In short, his family was almost servants for them from the time Hull came through until peace was made. One stormy evening and a deep snow on the ground, he was up in Town where he saw a company of Packhorsemen that could not get shelter. There was one of them sick and he took them all to his house."

At some time during the first year of the war Kenton was again imprisoned—on the same Kentucky claim. He was offered the bounds and bondsmen again but refused them, saying they had put him there and he would stay there till honestly released—and then he would come out with flying colors. His thoughts were on the war: "I could march to Canada now as quick as the next man," he said. His family was living in a house "about 20 rods away" and his wife and children and friends visited him freely. He was discharged half an hour after going into court.

His Urbana home was described to Dr. Draper by one of the Kentucky soldiers who saw it then, as "a log house of the most primitive style, with a dirt floor and a stump left standing in the center, which, properly dug out, formed the then necessary appendage of a hominy mortar." This was probably the family room of a "double cabin," the other being ten or twelve feet behind it and divided into sleeping chambers with sleeping lofts above. It can be imagined what these cabins were like when to Kenton's large family were added old friends, sick soldiers, and pack horse men from Kentucky to be bedded and fed.

Kenton was a sergeant under McArthur on the expedition that left Urbana for the relief of Fort Meigs in May, 1813—his first military service in this war. Hospital and commissary services he had been performing "on his own hook" all along, with that concern for the comfort and safety of individuals which had characterized all his border work.

He had another taste of "raising a party and pursuing" when word reached Urbana of the Thomas murders by British Indians near Solomon's Town on

August 9th. About thirty men went out under his command. His old "boy," Christopher Wood, was recruiting at Urbana then and joined in an old-time scout along the Miami.

"Went to Round Head's Town in Wyandott nation," he told Dr. Draper, "then turned and struck the Big Miami near Lewistown: Some 9 or 10 miles above Lewistown, at the Big Indian Lake, through the main Miami river; it was reported currently that the hostile Indians were going to waylay that spot for Ward and Kenton's party: Just below the Lake, east side, were small open spots of ground, and then very thicketty and so alternately. Kenton was a good deal afraid of it; didn't like the idea of losing a man—but the party dashed through this spot, and scoured all through it; but found none."

Major D. F. Heaton's narrative of this scout lies in the Kenton Papers. He was along and says that three Indians from Lewistown, a friendly Indian camp, followed Kenton's party and offered to guide them to a camp of British Indians, supposedly the party they wanted; that Kenton put them in front of him and never lost sight of them or the trail which crossed others several times; that when they had passed the "thicketty" spaces and came to a high bluff, Gillawa and the other Indians gave three whoops which aroused Kenton's suspicions afresh; that he bade the party halt and cover the opposite shore with their rifles while he and a few others crossed the river and scouted; that on their return Kenton addressed the whole party, saying openly that they had been pursuing hostile Indians who all day had been watching them through their spies, "looking dignifiedly at Gillawa and the other Indians"; that the Indians were now in ambush, probably within hearing of the spies's whoops; that they would have the first fire on ground chosen by themselves, and that he advised a quick return; that to some wishing to continue the pursuit and charging him with "over caution" he said: "'It is not my life which is now well nigh spent that I seek to save, it is your own, and let those who do not believe me—take up the line of march and pursue the enemy beyond the hearing of the war whoop, and they will never return.' General Fyffe, who was along, corroborates this story by saying that "Kenton remarked, if any of them wished to have something to do, they had only to cross over to the other side of the stream. None went."

After his return from this scout Kenton's nostrils dilated daily with the smell of war and when Governor Shelby came through Urbana on his way to the Thames, with hundreds of Kenton's old friends among his troops, he simply joined in.

There are no military records of his services on this campaign, for once again he went "on his own hook." Shelby urged him to go along as counselor and adviser, but Kenton's family, getting wind of it, objected vehemently. He was fifty-eight years old; he had a leg broken; he could not stand the hardships and exposures of a long campaign.

So Kenton, always amiable and considerate and always averse to "contrary talk" when his own mind was made up, saw Shelby's forces off without tears. His family sighed with relief when the last company marched out of Urbana; they thought the whole matter settled—and so it was. A few hours later Simon saddled his horse, flung a blanket and a sack of corn across it, mounted it, and rode casually off, presumably to the neighborhood mill. Falling in with a neighbor a few miles out on his journey, he sent back word to his family that he was on his way to Proctor's Mill. He went there indeed. He easily caught up with Shelby's troops and marched on to the Thames "simply on his own hook," says his son, "messed with his old friends whenever he pleased," and went about from company to company as he wished, a privileged member of Governor Shelby's military family.

By the time they reached Canada, Proctor had fled; then came the forced march to overtake him. Kenton was present "when Tecumseh was killed," and because of his long acquaintance with him was one of those sent for to identify the body. He always asserted that the Indian displayed as the great dead chief was not Tecumseh; said he had seen him too often and knew him too well to be mistaken. Kenton had known him under many circumstances—in war on the Little Miami and Paint Creek, in private treaty making for Ohio lands, in council at Springfield, and in play, when Tecumseh, as he told Judge James, "would wrestle and exercise in the snow at Jarboe's." He insisted that the Indians, with their reverence for the dead, would never have left the body of their chief behind them in their flight; that another body was substituted, and he implied that the victors were well enough content with a careless identification.

On the day of the great battle he was spying some

two hundred yards in advance of the army, and his criticisms of the British at close range were many. He said they "shot among the tree tops clear over our heads—were poor marksmen at best; and when they shot and found their lines broken, they called for quarter;" that "most of the British regulars were mostly Irishmen—threw down their arms—made no resistance—would not fight—did not intend to—and as soon as their officers fled, they threw down their arms." He did not like Harrison; he himself and Clark likewise had suffered from deserters, had gone after them, dragged them back, and freely cursed them out, but had never dreamed of shooting them; that savored too much of murder. But Harrison had some deserters shot at sunrise, "which Kenton disapproved and never liked Harrison afterwards."

When he got back from Proctor's Mill on the Thames he found young Simon Junior returned from his privateer service, who, landing at New Orleans, had made his way home through the Louisiana country. About his other son, Simon Ruth, Kenton was satisfied too; his long unknown fate after Hull's surrender had been a strong inducement for his going out on the Thames campaign. Taken with Hull's men, Simon Ruth had broken his parole, which later lost him his pension; he had volunteered and served in two other companies, and had been taken by Indians while guarding a party of sick and wounded from one fort to another. "Tom Johnson is taken," he called to his fellow captives, who took the warning and refrained from calling him by his own name. This bit of quick wit undoubtedly saved his life, for they were sold at Detroit, where the British would have made short work of him as Simon Ruth Kenton. "He was as brave a man as his father," a friend of the Kentons wrote Dr. Draper," and that is saying enough on that score."

Kenton's fighting days ended with this campaign. For forty-two years he had lived on the border with his gun in his hand. Now the border lay not northward but to the west. And never again would it be so concentrated along one little space of a great waterway where holding it meant holding all. The British had been driven north beyond the Great Lakes; the Indians were retreating tribe by tribe across the Mississippi; civilization was sweeping westward from the East, changing forests to fields and prairies to orchards. Simon Kenton's work in blazing the long trail was done; it had taken all his youth and all his middle years.

Chapter XIII

THE UNFORTUNATE YEARS
1814–1826

"MR. JAMES, I have had some people in my time that were very fond of me; I had a good deal of property, and may be they saw my weak parts enough to know how to use me."

So Simon Kenton, sitting in his old chair before his comfortable fire in the little cabin built for him in his daughter's side yard, summed up the simple causes of his catastrophes. Of the hundreds of thousands of dollars and the hundreds of thousands of acres that had passed through his hands he had few left of either in 1832. In these days with Judge James he had gone over his life, had seen his "weak parts," had accepted the consequences of them which he had suffered from impersonal land speculators, impersonal courts, and impersonal law. But the realization that he had been used by his friends still hurt him a little.

Unfortunately Kenton believed that white men were honest; he trusted them too much, put too much faith in a verbal agreement. He was no fool in his verbal business dealings, and he knew the values of the goods or the lands that he dealt in. His shrewdness in land trades was notable; he was seldom if ever cheated in one. The agreement made, "as man to man," his shrewdness vanished and he went into the realm of illusion. With some paper signed and some money laid down, the particular matter was ended and he went vitally on to the next project. He was careless about law, careless about taxes, failed to figure on payments due far enough in advance to meet them easily, and because he himself would not take advantage of lapsed payments to foreclose and buy in the land of another, he never took into account the fact that others would.

His brother John mismanaged the Kentucky property left him in trust; Kenton's obligations were met, but by the time the property was reconveyed to him a large amount, says his son, had been thriftlessly squandered. His son John lost him his two Missouri trading stores with their valuable stocks. His Missouri lands went by earthquake and default. The great part of his Ohio lands vanished with the collapse of the Symmes purchase. But for years he believed himself a man rich enough in lands held in partnership with Colonel William Ward.

Colonel Ward is one of the figures in Kenton's life about which one walks wonderingly. He came into it in the latter Kentucky days—about 1793—and from then on for nearly a quarter of a century their association in business and—on Kenton's part at least—in friendship was close. The two men were about the same age; both had been in the Dunmore war, and seen together they must have presented the strongest of contrasts—Kenton in his easy frontiersman's garb moving like an Indian beside the gentleman from Greenbriar County, Virginia. In Ohio they were close neighbors for years, for their homes near Springfield adjoined. After Urbana was settled and Kenton moved there Ward continued to live at his first home, riding up to Urbana when business called him there. Thus he passed the McBeth farm almost daily, and years later a child's impression of him then was set down by the child grown man. In 1866 James R. McBeth wrote it down for his nephew, John Quincy Adams Ward, grandson of William—"as strongly impressed on my mind this day as any I have seen within the last year." Perhaps the child's image of him may serve for Simon Kenton's too:

> In person he was taller than most of his sons, slender and lithe, shoulders broad, high cheek bones, keen penetrating eyes, dark auburn hair tied with a black ribbon in a que, which hung gracefully down his back—erect in person and particularly neat in his dress. He wore but one style of hat—black felt, moderately high, straight crown, and rather broad brim, sticking straight out and never turned up at the sides. . . . His coats were generally of black cloth of the frock or surtout style. He rode on horseback with green flannel wrappers or leggins as they were called, tied round . . . below the knee; and when on horseback he kept up a constant kicking movement of the feet, which kept time exactly with the movement of the horse.
>
> He was haughty, high-toned, impatient of a contradiction or restraint, and arbitrary in his manners as many of the old Virginians were, who had been used to slaves obeying their orders without hesitation or question. Some thought him tyrranical and exacting; but this was by no means the case. He was gentlemanly in his manners, kind as a neighbor, and liberal to those in need; but you had to receive his offers of liberality just as he offered it, or his arbitrary will would show itself, as the following anecdote will illustrate:
>
> When our family moved to Ohio, the country was new and produce scarce. But few farmers had any supplies to spare, and it was a matter of importance to secure something to eat until a crop could be raised. After enquiring for potatoes in various places without success, my mother stopped the colonel when he was riding by and asked if he had any potatotes to sell. His prompt reply was, "No, madame—none to sell—but plenty to give away to new settlers." Then if I send a boy down will you give me a bag full? "No Madame, I will not; but send a

cart or a wagon and I will fill that," adding, "Your family is large, you will need them for seed and for table use—send and get them."

So Simon Kenton in Kentucky used to give away his corn—share it rather.

Before Kenton moved to Ohio, Ward was his constant companion on land trips across the river. He signed with Kenton—and probably wrote—the letter on the Indian troubles of 1799. He was with Kenton on various Indian missions, and Christopher Wood says that on the Thomas scout after Indians in 1813, Kenton, chosen commander, "declined in favor of Ward as being more active." No other old campaigner recalls this, however. Ward was never known as an Indian fighter; he came to Kentucky too late for that. But he was with Kenton on Indian missions as on land trips.

In the old reminiscences of Kenton's misfortunes Ward is almost invariably mentioned as an agent. Dr. Draper made a very determined effort to get at the truth of "partnership" between the two men and of the suit which Kenton finally brought against him, and the Ward correspondence in the Kenton papers is as interesting as any part of them. A letter from John Quincy Adams Ward gives the only family statement of the matter:

> If the same papers I saw at home when a boy [he wrote Dr. Draper from New York, December 17, 1883] are still in existence, I think they would be of some value in tracing his [Kenton's] career and experience, especially after the years 1798 and 1810. This relationship with my grandfather, Col. Wm. Ward, was peculiar.
>
> Kenton accused him of sharp-dealing or wronging him of valuable lands and possessions.

Kenton's knowledge of the Territory of Ohio made his assistance valuable in selecting land. Ward associated with him in the occupation or purchase of large tracts—in some sections they were partners.

Kenton's lack of business habits and great disinclination to the forms of business, together with his roving nature, soon placed his interests in danger. He failed to meet his engagements, both in Kentucky and Ohio. Ward's financial safety lay in his ability to protect his claims too—so that he was obliged to carry all.

After many years of worry and annoyance, Ward assumed all and sought discharge from Kenton's claims—in the meantime much valuable property was lost by Kenton's inability and incapableness.

Then came the cry of wronged innocence—this is the substance of the transactions.

Much stress has been laid, I believe, upon Kenton's financial wrongs, but it is only the old story of a brave romantic frontiersman in love with the wild free life of the woods, caught in the snares of civilization—always a piteous sight, this childlike mind, unable to understand the machinery of State or Society—law, duty or service to the State is to them oppressive, and the attendant forms foolishness and silly confusion.

The papers above referred to cover this entire transaction, and contained many facts, incidents and points that would be worth your while looking over. It is thirty-five years nearly since I read them.

Some papers were thoughtlessly destroyed a few years since. But I hope those relating to Kenton are still in existence and it will give me great pleasure on my next visit to Urbana to look them over and give you the benefit of their contents.

Search for these Kenton-Ward papers proved fruitless for several years, but in 1889 Mr. Ward wrote the persistent Dr. Draper that he had at last found the papers bearing on the two men's business transactions

which in the latter part of their lives was in the nature of Law-suits. . . . The papers as I feared are not complete, having been carelessly treated perhaps by childish and thoughtless inmates of the house.

Then he asked certain questions: was Dr. Draper intending to try the case over in his own mind and arrive at a just conclusion as an historian searching for facts, or had he already formed an opinion and did he wish to select from the documents only those that would sustain it?

> . . . in either case if you read the papers at all you must read them carefully to know whether Kenton was wronged or whether from his carelesssness and "shiftlessness" and ignorance he lost that which he did not value so much, until after his family had grown up and themselves very poor they filled his mind with the idea that he had been robbed and urged him to try and recover what he had once claimed. It seemed to be very easy for him to find three lawyers (?)—Parish, Scott, and Ore, I believe, who entered into an agreement to divide the spoils in case of success; in fact, there was quite a little conspiracy to get spoils from grandfather.

The correspondence ends here; evidently the old papers were never sent on. The long association between Kenton and Ward was definitely broken in 1818, when Kenton brought suit against Ward for his share of certain Champaign County lands. The suit was decided against him and no proof exists that he was "cheated and defrauded" by Ward.[1]

[1]"He [Kenton] also owned several tracts of land in Ohio together with Colonel William Ward; in the division of which and exchange for other property, Kenton claimed that he was entitled to a half section adjoining Urbana. It is easy to conceive how an unlettered man in the sale or exchange of property might be overreached, but it is as easily conceivable that his memory might be treacherous, or misunderstandings exist. Colonel Ward was also interested in certain lands in Kentucky, which Kenton was supposed to hold in fee simple. It is claimed that Ward furnished some capital and his knowledge of land titles and conveyances. Kenton was familiar with the country and knew of choice locations. To the latter was entrusted the payment of taxes, which Ward claimed he neglected, involving loss to him, and that he closed his

But the belief that he was Ward's victim was strong not only among Kenton's children but among his friends. Kenton's son William says flatly that Colonel Ward "lived on Kenton" in Mason County, "kept store" for him there, and followed him to Ohio where he grew richer as Kenton became poorer and poorer; that "Col. Ward always by his suavity exerted a winning and overpowering influence over General Kenton." Judge Wood asserts that "it was common fame that Col. Ward took advantage of Kenton." In fact few of Kenton's friends who speak of this "partnership" between the two men fail to assert or imply that a large amount of his Ohio property was unjustly taken from him by Ward. John Arrowsmith, Kenton's grandnephew, relates a conversation between his uncle Mark and the younger Colonel William Ward "on the low lands east of Mad River where their lands joined," in which "Ward said that he was well satisfied that Gen. Kenton was wronged by his father and it was not in his power to make matters right."

Certainly Kenton's knowledge of land was at Ward's disposal and there was a partnership in some lands at least. It is clear that Kenton's understanding of the extent of the partnership was broader than Ward's. Incapable himself of taking advantage of entirely legal procedure to increase his wealth at the

---

partnership with Kenton by written articles. The consequence was that Ward was accused of cheating Kenton, but there is no evidence to confirm the charge, and on the other hand, Kenton, well-meaning, honest, and upright, was nevertheless known to be careless and shiftless in business matters, and as to his business ventures with Ward he was always reticent." *History of Champaign County*, John W. Ogden, 1881, p. 306.

expense of others—particularly of a friend—it never occurred to him that a friend could take such advantage. He himself could not have grown richer as his partner became poorer. But poorer and poorer he grew. Gone were the days of his thousand-acre farm worked by tenant farmers; gone the days of corn cribs filled to overflowing, of trading stores on which he and his friends could draw without ceasing and without accounting, of the fine brick house and the plenitude of slaves and horses and comfortably bedded guests. His first child was born to riches; his last, Ruth Jane, in 1816, to the plainest of pioneer living. What farming was done, Simon Junior did; what stock Kenton had, Simon Junior raised.

His Urbana neighbors say he was "always hard run to make ends meet." Once, going back to Kentucky on some of his interminable business there, he was forced to ask Zephaniah Luce to furnish his family with what they would need in his absence—he "would try to make it good on his return." Luce, himself the father of thirteen, cheerfully assented and was soon paid off. Kenton's looseness in business dealings appears to have centered in his tangled land operations and their nice questions of law; there is nowhere any indication that he did not meet his daily living expenses and his other obligations to his neighbors and friends.

When times were at their hardest, he would go off on an emergency land-trading trip—these grew frequent—during which he would sell lands by quitclaim deeds and take in exchange horses, cattle, wagons, cotton yarns, and the like, bring them back to Urbana by wagon, "sometimes by sleds," and then for a time "all live well by prudence and common sense."

On the occasion of President Monroe's visit to Louisville in 1817, Kenton was at Colonel Anderson's home on Bear Grass engaged in searching land records for his host, then surveyor-general of the district. In celebration of the President's almost completed circle of the northern states to inspect personally the fortifications, arsenals, naval depots, and garrisons along the new northern border from Maine to Michigan, a great dinner was given for him at Louisville—and a great chance missed by its patrons. How better emphasize the miracle of the quarter-century expansion northward from the Ohio to the Great Lakes than by having as one of their guests the man whose single-handed services in holding the Ohio could never have been commandeered or bought! "I do not think there is anything in Kenton's absence from the dinner," one of Anderson's sons wrote Dr. Draper. "He was always a modest man and was not then a notoriety." This is probably correct, that he was simply not thought of, so swiftly had a little time obliterated the memory of a service always so private.

It was at a reception given by Colonel Anderson to the President and his staff that Kenton met his old friend Andrew Jackson, late hero of New Orleans and soon himself to be President. Nearly forty years had passed since the Danville and Crow Station days. "I thought he looked shy at me," said Kenton, "but I never said Crow's Station to him once."

Clark died early in 1818—it was the first great historic break in Kenton's life with the old times. He knew that Boone could not survive much longer. His own years were sixty-three. Here is a little pen portrait of him in that year—another child's impression of a "figure" in its life, put down on paper many years later.

In the summer of 1818 [Thomas Cowgill wrote Dr. Draper], when about six years old, in company with my sister, three years older than I, were hunting our cows in the woods one evening before sunset. On the path we met an old man, riding a poor horse, with his coat hung on one arm, in his shirt sleeves, wearing an old low-crowned, broad brimmed hat flopped down over his shoulders. He spoke kindly to us, said, "Well, children, how do you do." My father had a blacksmith shop near our new home in the woods. The old man stopped and talked with my father. When we went home with the cows, father told us that was Simon Kenton.

It may have been in this year of Clark's death that Kenton had his wife take down his recollections of Clark. He talked much about him from then on, quoted Clark as saying to him once, when abused and vilified, that if he were only a dog he should be happy, and considered him a great and a greatly wronged man. As late as 1833, when Frederick W. Thomas visited him, he was very much concerned over Clark's lack of fame and very anxious that his life should be written, for Clark, he said, "had done more to save Kentucky from the Indians than any other man." He sent word then to Judge James to come to see him again. "I am mighty anxious to tell what I know about Clark, you may depend he was a brave man and did much."

Other breaks with the past came this year. His break with Ward culminated in the suit against him which Kenton lost. His son Simon's marriage took away the only prop he had at home, for his son William was still but a boy. And his eldest daughter Nancy had died the year before.

But an old frayed thread drifted up from the past at which he clutched. The brick house at Washington, sold so many years before, had not been paid for; and he took in payment, instead of money, a sixteen-hundred-acre tract on Mad River about three miles above Zanesfield. He had grown a little weary of trusting himself or his creditors with land in his own name; this tract was deeded to Simon Junior in trust. Intended for all of his children—there were seven left—it was portioned out equally and divided among them by lot, to be deeded to them by their brother as each should come of age. But with all these precautions, this too "soon went, little by little, to liquidate old debts." Only one share was held by his daughter Matilda—the place where he died.

About this same time he bought sixty-five acres in Isaac Zane's tract at Zanesfield for himself and his wife, "and after for me," says his son William. But this too was deeded in trust to Matilda's husband, John Parkison.

To this smaller place, within sight of his old gauntlet race track at Wappatomika, Simon Kenton moved early in 1820 with his wife and the four children still living at home, Mary, William, Elizabeth, and Ruth Jane. The idea that "had flashed in his mind that he would one day own some of that fine country" had had a history of fulfillment much like the Indians' story of his escape. He had been in dream possession of most of the state, but "the Great Spirit" had taken it from him little by little, and finally almost entirely away. The three-thousand-acre tract of land on Machachack prairie, near the site of another of his gauntlet races, which he had always intended for his permanent home, had vanished like the rest of the dream. Sixty-five acres at last was enough.

There was a partly finished cabin on the place, in which they lived while it was slowly completed. "The cabin was low, with one window of four panes, 8 x 10 inch glass on the north side—a door of common size, one window of the same size on the south side." It was about eighteen-feet square, and stood in a cleared space of fifteen or twenty acres. A fine sugar camp of several hundred maple trees adjoined it, and near by it grew apple trees grown from seeds the Indians had planted. For this was the very site of the Indian village where Simon Girty had found and rescued him.

There is a recurrent tradition that within a few yards of this Zanesfield home he had built Logan's last cabin during his captivity; it turns up everywhere in the casual sketches of him. But it is a myth—he did not meet Logan here; Logan awaited him in the little winter camp on the Scioto. But there were Indian cabins on his Zanesfield acres, for his retinue of Indians followed him here.

Kenton's Kentucky imprisonment began this year, and through a trick. He was sent for to testify in a land case there; no sooner had he landed in Kentucky than the execution against his body was served and it committed, with a raging spirit all on fire within it, to the Mason County Jail. The old debtor's law had seized on him again. Kenton and his friends were furious, both at the deception practised on him and at the general injustice of the whole case. There are a dozen stories of the affair, but the clearest statement comes from the Honorable Adam Beatty, in a letter to Dr. Draper, dated the 9th of August, 1855:

> At an early period [he wrote], when lands in Kentucky were of but little value, Gen. Kenton made a present of a tract of land to a friend, and executed a general warranty deed, which renders the executor liable for the value of the land at the time it shall be lost by an adverse title. At a late period, when the grantee was dead and land greatly increased in value, it was recovered from the heirs under a better adverse title. The heirs sued upon the warranty deed of their ancestor and recovered judgment in the Bourbon county court. Upon this judgment a *casa* was issued directed to the sheriff of Mason, by which the body of the debtor was liable to be taken in execution, and, in case the debt was not paid, was liable to be imprisoned, until the party should either pay his debt or obtain his discharge by taking the benefit of the insolvent laws—giving a schedule of his property and surrendering it for the benefit of his creditors.

Kenton's family and a number of his friends say that this gift of land—really a deed of gift but not so expressed—was made to one McConnell; that McConnell settled on it and there raised his family, that he advised his children before his death to let it go as it was a gift and not a purchase from Kenton, that after his death his children pressed the claim through one of his sons whom Kenton "had educated for the bar," in full knowledge of all the circumstances.

Kenton absolutely refused to pay or to allow his friends to pay for him, even though a number stood ready to supply the sum needed. He insisted that it was unjust, an outrage of law, and that he *would* not pay. At first he refused prison bounds, as he had once before in Ohio, but this his friends would not allow—they simply went his security that he would keep them, and so after a few weeks he left the jail and its small back yard for the wider freedom of "ten acres." Not until, however, in his state of rage against the world, he had all on his own removed the shackles from his companion in the jail yard—one Mike McGraw, an insane man with whom Kenton talked and whom he pronounced harmless. Mike "talked quite sensibly sometimes—would speak of villages as being the finest smelling places he ever knew," and followed Kenton about like a dog.

Strange, the chance that Kenton's jailer this time should be not himself but Thomas Williams, the man with whom he had came down the Ohio in 1775; with whom he landed at Limestone where the cane-lands began; with whom he took "planting possession" of Mason County; with whom he first heard from Michael Stoner of "Daniel Schpoon!" With whom he heard, too, jailed and jailer together, of Boone's death when word of it reached Washington from far off Missouri! O pioneers!

By some friendly machinations the prison bounds were extended during the year of Kenton's imprisonment—from the first ten acres about the jail to the town limits and finally to the county boundaries. He had to report to Williams at night and was supposed to sleep in the debtor's cell. Williams's table was his also, but as a matter of fact he ate where he wished and often slept out. His wife made several trips to Kentucky during the year, going down on horseback with William. On one of these trips the boy was left to "companion" his father, live with his uncle John, and go to school with the sons and grandsons of his father's old friends.

Kenton's first biography was planned at this time; John Bickley and Thomas Pickett had many long talks with him, took their copious notes, and issued a formal prospectus for subscribers. It was to contain about two hundred pages and would cost the subscribers one dollar a copy. But the signers were few; the notes remained notes; the book never appeared. Ten years later the papers were turned over to John Taylor for his use in writing Kenton's life; when his manuscript vanished the old notes vanished with it; all that remains of them is contained in McClung's brief sketch.

The anger of Kenton's friends did not die down as the months went on, and the general injustice of his imprisonment furnished one of them with all the ammunition he needed for a renewed attack on his particular detestation, the debtor's law. William Worthington was reëlected a member of the Kentucky legislature from Mason County on this single ground and in the first session after fought again for its repeal. He was successful. Imprisonment for debt was abolished forever in Kentucky and on December 17, 1821, Kenton walked out of jail, a free man. He had said he would never pay a cent of the claim and he never did.

He seems to have remained in Kentucky for nearly two years after this, trying to save what little land remained to him there; no "fine lands," these lingering tracts; they were mostly mountain wastes. In his pressing need for money to pay his taxes on them, he resorted to boring for salt on some Greenup County acres but without success. In May, 1822, his brother William died, full of years. The following December Colonel Ward died, and the next spring Kenton himself fell ill with "dropsey in the legs of which he was two or three months laid up" at his brother John's, "where he expected to die for twelve days." And again his wife, accompanied by William, came down from Ohio on horseback to care for him.

During his convalescence he had a letter written for him to Colonel Ward's son which he sent back to Ohio by William: "Coln[l] Ward and myself ware a makeing arrangements to settle our busyness if it had been permitted us to of seen each other again. . . . I am at this time very low in health." He asked that certain "busyness" be left untouched until he could get back to Ohio, but by then the muddle was complete, and Kenton's health kept him in Kentucky several months after his family's departure. His depression was great. He was outliving his period. "When I first saw this region," he said to friends he was visiting near Washington, "those tall yellow poplars were mere saplings. Now see them—many of them two feet through and some dying—and here am I yet."

He was cheered during the summer by word that, thanks to influence exerted, William had been appointed to a cadetship by President Monroe. The boy went to West Point before his father returned, "where he excelled in the drill and manual of arms and all athletic sports and exercises, but with books he failed." West Point was then an institution primitive enough, but the routine irked him, and within the year he resigned and came home, to find his father again in court difficulties.

For Kenton had no sooner returned to Ohio than he found the claimants responsible for his Kentucky—and probably the Ohio—imprisonment at work to imprison him again. He was in the Urbana Jail for a short time—he would probably have stayed in for life before he would have paid this debt—but "Lawyer Henry Bacon cleared Kenton of this case." He was safer now in Kentucky than in Ohio, for Ohio still had the debtor's law on its statutes.

Back in Kentucky in the summer of 1824 as witness in an important land suit there, he made one of his most interesting depositions at "Abner Hord's Tavern, Washington, Ky, June 5, 1824," in which he discoursed freely on "war roads" and "buffalo traces," old "geography" and the famous "powder route" followed in 1777. Then he went on to Falmouth, where he fell in with John W. McCann, also attending court there, and McCann's account of the meeting gives one of the most vivid pictures we have of Kenton at this time.

> As to Simon Kenton [he wrote Dr. Draper, May 19, 1865], I never saw him but once. He was the most remarkable *natural* man I ever saw or talked with. I met him for the first and last time at Falmouth where I was attending court in July, 1824, where he had been summoned as a witness in an important land suit. He and the renowned George M. Bibb, a very learned judge . . . were my room mates. I was richly entertained by them —was then a student of law—and appreciated everything they said and did. I had *panted* for years to see Simon Kenton and considered it the happiest day of my life. He at that time was in the 71 year [he was sixty-nine years old] but still a stout, athletick man—perfectly a child of nature, but was thus in possession of a vigorous organism mentally and physically.

Court Troubles in Ohio

Land suits, sheriffs' writs, and court orders continued to beset the old pioneer. But both courts and friends were kindly. One day David Smith, an Urbana constable, followed him to Ezekiel Arrowsmith's and coming into the living room said, "Father Kenton, among all the things I ever had to do this hurts my feelings the most"; then served him with a summons to appear before "Squire Markley" to answer to a suit brought by Buckley White, the Urbana jailor, for board and lodging furnished him while in jail two years before. Kenton affirmed he had paid what he thought sufficient when he left, and that more was too much. John Parkison, his son-in-law, and John Arrowsmith, his nephew, went on his bail, and when the case came to trial there was one question and one answer only before the squire summed up. "Squire Markley asked White, Did General Kenton go voluntarily to you and seek board and lodging: No, he was brought there by others, and incarcerated. Then, said the Squire, you must have recourse to those who brought him there, and discharged him from custody."

But often he did not reach the courts; friends gaily aided him in avoiding service. Major James Galloway about this time had need of some testimony from Kenton to use in a case of his own, and went over from Xenia to Zanesfield to get it. Hearing from Mrs. Kenton that her husband was not at home and suspecting that he was "hid out," Major Galloway prevailed with her to get Kenton in from his retreat, and he soon appeared. When the major found that Kenton, for good reasons, did not want to appear in open court and testify—thus exposing himself to service and trouble—he proposed that the two of them ride off together to Sandusky, out of jurisdiction, where Kenton's deposition could be taken and used in lieu of his testimony. It was on this ride that Kenton astonished his friend by his memory of old locations, old Indian villages, and old gauntlet race tracks; for it had been along this old Sandusky trail he had marched his hopeless way in captivity forty-eight years before.

Fielding Belt, another old friend of Kenton's, told Dr. Draper another incident of this same period which shows the friendliness of friends and process servers alike. Kenton was stopping with him in Kentucky, and at night, after all lights were out, the sheriff of Fleming County rode up and called out to know if General Kenton was there. "Knowing the object and knowing too full well that there was neither justice nor patriotism in these trumped up cases, Belt resolved in an instant that he would not be a party to annoying the old pioneer." So he said no, that the general had gone to visit a friend in another county. The sheriff, "himself the son of a distinguished pioneer and compatriot of Kenton's, was secretly not sorry that the good-hearted old pioneer, whom he knew well, was beyond his reach," and asked to be lodged over night. His host took him directly past Kenton's door to the furthermost room, and then softly entered Kenton's chamber and whispered "the situation." A word was enough; the hunted guest dressed and in his stocking feet, with his saddle-bags in his hand, made his way down the stairs to the yard where Belt had his horse waiting. Kenton appeared at davbreak next morning in another county, before the door of another friend—who was ready to do the same thing over again.

And even when sheriffs reached him with court papers to serve on him, the story often ended just there. One of Dr. Draper's correspondents wrote him that many a court order was returned with the notation, "too dangerous to serve."

Those mountain lands which Kenton had tried to save after his release from his Kentucky imprisonment had gone—some eighty thousand. The state had sold them for taxes, and the state had bid them in. In the late fall of 1826 Kenton made up his mind to ask a favor of Kentucky—to ask her to release those mountain wastes and give them back to him. None of them belonged in his original holdings—he knew land too well to make locations of his own such as these; he had taken area after area for bad debts, the best he could make of bad pieces of business. He placed little value on them, and was afterward able to sell but a small part of them—"and that at some 20 cents per acre," says his son.

A tolerable amount of verbal tears have been shed over this visit of Kenton's to Kentucky—his poverty, his tattered clothes, his starved horse, and his total indigence have been piteously dwelt on. He entered Frankfort a stranger, unrecognized, so runs the myth, so old and bent, so tattered and torn, that not one ever remembered to have seen him before until General Thomas Fletcher somehow pierced the wall of years and said, "This must be Simon Kenton"; then took him to be fitted for new clothes, introduced him as "Kentucky's pioneer," went with him to the capitol and seated him in the presiding officer's chair.

This would be all very well, if Kenton had not been in and out of Kentucky and all over Kentucky without ceasing ever since he left it in 1798—he was known from end to end of the state and had never been forgotten. He was neither bent with age nor clothed in tattered garments; he had been harassed with debts, but he had never been indigent; he had been imprisoned for debt, but he had gone to prison because he would not pay, not because he could not. He came down to Kentucky not to beg but to demand that an act of justice be done him.

He made this trip in fact a sort of holiday; took it in leisurely fashion; visited friends and relatives all along the road to the Ohio, and took in not only most of Ohio but a part of Illinois on his journey. Mason Arrowsmith, a great-nephew, accompanied him. He says his uncle's avowed purpose was to settle up all his business so as not to "have to go there agin." They went on horseback, and went well equipped—Simon by now was wearing "green spectacles."

One of the first visits on the journey was paid to General Whiteman near Clifton, Ohio, where Kenton found this "youngster" of the Kenton Station days ill from the effects of "old exposures in early Indian warfare." Whiteman told Dr. Draper that after Kenton had expressed his sorrow and sympathy, he, having his old commander's special case in mind, said: "I am sorry myself. If I had anticipated this, I would probably never have exposed my life and health for an ungrateful country.—that with my present knowledge of human nature and the world, I believe I would not under similar circumstances do it over again."

KENTON AND FLETCHER

FROM HARPER'S MAGAZINE, FEBRUARY, 1864

Kenton had buried his face in his hands, resting on the head of his cane, and was so long silent that his host thought he had fallen asleep. But suddenly he sprang to his feet and said: "'I have known you, Ben, from a youth, and thought I knew you better than either of my own children, but if these are the honest expressions of your feeling, I repeat, I never knew you. 'But,' added Kenton, with affectionate fervor, 'I cannot help believing, if the test could come and you were young again, you would be as ready as ever to shoulder your rifle and serve your country.'"

When Kenton arrived in Frankfort he sought out James Ward, senator of Mason County, who was ready to present his petition to the legislature, praying that his lands in Kentucky forfeited for non-payment of taxes might be relinquished to him. It was reported January 4, 1827, passed the Senate without opposition twelve days later, and passed the House on the 23d by a vote of sixty-seven to seventeen. There was an impromptu reception on the senate floor at the end of a session, and Kenton was seated in the speaker's chair, all of which was good indirect "influence" for the senate's unanimous passing of his petition. But General Fletcher, the mythical Good Samaritan who supposedly engineered the whole proceeding, was not a member of either House at the time. It was a planned piece of work by Kenton and his Kentucky friends, and was very largely incited by his long and unjust imprisonment a few years before. Which makes it on the whole, though less dramatic and far less "pathetic," a better bit of justice, better done.

Chapter XIV

THE LATTER YEARS
1827–1836

MORE justice was asked for Simon Kenton, immediately after the release of his Kentucky lands; both in Kentucky and Ohio a concerted movement began to obtain a pension for him. But this took a long time to accomplish, and meantime Kenton kept up his busy peregrinations between the two states. During the next few years his age began to show perceptibly; in 1829 Colonel John S. Williams met him on the road between Ohio and Kentucky and wrote that "he didn't say much, and appeared as if there was not much left of him."

Certainly there was not much left of his fortune. His brother John had died in April and Kenton had gone down to find out what remained, if anything, of certain properties so long since given in trust and never accounted for. Those were the days of loose business dealings; records were few and muddled, and of money or land there was none.

His biographers and would-be biographers began writing about him and visiting him in 1830 and from then on. John D. Taylor dates his unfinished and later "lost" manuscript, 1830. The Reverend John McClung used the Bickley and Pickett Notes and the Taylor Manuscript for his sketch of Kenton and visited him this year also for more material. Colonel

John McDonald and the Reverend Thomas S. Hinde came to talk with and to take notes from a man who had seen the whole panorama of Western history unfold before his eyes, who held in his memory the story of a period. If only they had taken down his story as he told it!

He was growing old. In this year he gave up the management of all his affairs to William. At last he could take his ease. On twenty dollars a month he could live well. For "An Act for the Relief of General Simon Kenton" had at last been approved and signed by the old friend of Crow Station days half a century gone—President Andrew Jackson.

Joseph Vance had sponsored this bill in the house since 1827; a year later Judge Burnet, just elected Senator from Ohio, began to push it in the senate. There had been many difficulties, for the Western records of Revolutionary service were loose. When it came on the senate calendar it stood below so many orders as to stand no chance whatever of passing in that session. But Judge Burnet moved that all bills preceding it be postponed and that it be taken up in a Committee of the Whole. This fortunately was carried, and it was then insisted that Simon Kenton's case did not come under the provisions of any pension law and that the passage of this bill would be a dangerous precedent.

This opposition, however [says Judge Burnet] was overcome by a full exhibition of the services and sufferings of the applicant. It was shown that his life had been a succession of exposures and privations in defending the frontier settlements from the desperate battle of Point Pleasant in 1774 to the last victory of Harrison on the Thames. The friends of the measure contended that if Kenton's case should become a precedent, it could not be a dangerous one, because it was *sui generis*, and without a parallel; but that if there were other cases of equal heroism and suffering, they would form a new class, as meritorious as any of those which had been provided for by law.

The bill passed by a large majority; and as it referred back to the date of the first application, and provided that the pension be paid from that date, the long waiting had not been time wasted.

And so at last a life of ease. He went to the little Zanesfield church on Sundays: "his wife walked a few feet behind him, which was the custom of some old married people of that day.

On week days that were "mill days" his pony could be seen ambling down the road to the mill with a bushel of corn in a sack on its back and Simon on top. On other days he visited, rain or shine. It was a regular formula of his when he appeared at certain houses: "Ye know I like hominy—have ye got hominy? Well—then, I'll stay." And by the fire if it were winter, placidly poking it up with the charred top of his staff, or under the trees in summer, he would sit, ruminative, contemplative, often silent for hours together. It was Uncle Simon's fashion—his way of visiting; and the work of the households went on about him as comfortably as if he were a member of them.

And then a life of greater ease. Shortly before William's marriage in 1832 the Zanesfield cabin was surrendered to him, and Kenton and his wife moved to the Parkison farm four miles north of the little town, where a new cabin had been built for them in their daughter Matilda's side yard. His own home was his no longer; he was an old man making his last stand in his last cabin. But he still talked of "going West." William was planning to move to Indiana and his married sisters likewise. Their father "ardently desired that they would go, he thought it would be the best thing that they could do—as for his part, he would be just as well contented on the road moving as at any other place."

Judge James visited him here for two entranced days and conceived then the idea of writing "his Life and Times in his own racy dialect." He took then the notes which preserve more of Kenton's terse and graphic speech, archaic style, and markedly peculiar utterance than anything we have. Kenton's diction interested him extremely; he had an eccentricity of rhythm and intonation that was all his own. He said "A-prile" and "dis-sip-lined," but he was wont not only to separate syllables but to run several single words into one. His common salutation was "Well-with-thee, John?" or whoever, and this habitual intoning of common speech, more perhaps than the actual quality of his voice, is the reason why so many of his old friends speak of his voice and utterance as "soft and musical."

Except in battle; then his voice rolled high and clear over his men. He could give the Indian yells as though he were one of them; could imitate their imitations of animal cries to the last inflection—and could detect the imitation from the real.

His laugh was characteristic also. He never laughed heartily, "except a frequent repetition of a quiet inward convulsion." And both speech and laughter were punctuated by odd snufflings of his nose, perhaps induced by his habitual snuff taking—his only indulgence. Thanks to all this, he was slow and measured in conversation, emphatic also. He always spoke well, sometimes with great power and eloquence, and he did not use speech trivially; when he spoke he always had a point to make and he always made it.

He was an old man. For the date of the Fifty Year Meeting was drawing near. For years letters had been passing among the survivors of Clark's campaign of 1782, each reminding the others of "the day"; each congratulating the other on "lasting this long"; each wondering if "this time next year," let pass the next year and the years after that, he would still be above sod.

By May word of the projected November meeting had reached the East—but only as a reunion meeting of unnamed officers who had served under an unnamed commander "on a Western campaign." The fifty years had gone so quickly for the rest of the world that the memorial year was commemorating no more than a shadow of something that happened "once upon a time." So swift had been the tread of development that it had obliterated the name of the man who had thrown the country open for it.

But Clark's name led the call Simon Kenton sent out in June. Not more than twenty survivors had been found in Kentucky of those who had taken the vow of reunion. In Ohio the situation was worse—Kenton and Galloway knew of not one survivor but themselves in all the state. So he addressed his call to "The Citizens of the Western Country" and the reunion gathering was widened to include not only the survivors but all the old pioneers, citizen-soldiers, and those of the regular service who had aided in the conquest of the West. The celebration would be held on the 4th of November, at old Fort Washington, site of Cincinnati. "I propose that we meet at Covington, Kentucky, on the 3rd: the 4th, being sabbath, to attend divine service; on Monday meet our friends on the ground where the old fort stood; and then take a final adieu, to meet no more, until we shall all meet in a world of spirits!"

The call was addressed not only to those who had shared in the conquest of the country, but those who were profiting by it. Innkeepers, captains of steam boats, owners of stages were called on to make generous provision for the journeys of their old fathers of the West.

One day in July Parson James Crow came out from Zanesfield to Kenton's cabin with a letter he had just received from Kentucky. Another important land suit was pending there in which Kenton's deposition was absolutely necessary and his presence likewise, to "find a corner" and establish a claim. If he would come to Mason County and give his deposition in person, he would "be paid fifty dollars and expenses both ways—and more, if that were not enough."

So in the early fall Simon Kenton and his wife Elizabeth set out together on their last visit to Kentucky, Kenton in his surtout and broad-brimmed hat, his wife in "brown cassamere with green spots and a green silk or satin bonnet." Not now the long trip on horseback over Kenton's Trace so long disused that the forest was growing over it again. They were driven by carriage—strange new luxury that was superseding the horseback and wagon days—to Dayton; thence by stage to Cincinnati; and from there by steamboat to old Limestone and Washington. As if fortune smiled on this fiftieth year and were determined to emphasize it, another party left Ohio when Simon Kenton began his memorial journey—the Ohio Shawanese. The last of the old enemy were leaving the old battle grounds on their way to their new reservation in Kansas.

Recollections of more than fifty years rose in Kenton's mind when he made his deposition at Washington. For it concerned the identity of John Todd's only heir at law—his daughter Mary. "The said deponent knew her well when a child . . . and played with this child . . . and feels satisfied that Mary Owen Wickliffe . . . is his only child and heir at law."

But there is much more to the deposition than this; the rest forms part of his Manuscript Statement. For in tracing his friendship with John Todd, slain in the battle of the Blue Licks which was the very cause for Clark's campaign of 1782, memories of Clark so filled his heart that the deposition became a little early history of the great general, whose memory the Western country was about to celebrate. It is as if he talked it out on the long journey and his wife set it down, that she then made a fair copy of his talk, and that it was accepted without further form except an oath to its truth. There are legal phrases at the beginning and end; the rest is Simon Kenton.

When he went out to "establish the land" for the child of his old friend, Washington and most of Mason County celebrated. "Gen. Kenton," says his son, "said hosts of men were present to witness the identification of the corner, describing an encampment where he had shot at a mark—found the encampment where Kenton and others had stopped when early locating the land—and some fifty rods off he pointed out the tree which formed the mark at which they shot—cut and scraped off till they found the leaden bullet: This was proved triumphantly—in Mason county—near May's Lick."

Only one shadow appears to have fallen over the Kentucky visit—the resentment of the living subject against its biographer! McClung's *Sketches of Western Adventure* had just appeared with his brief life of Simon Kenton. Kenton first encountered the volume in Kentucky, and F. W. Thomas, one of his interested visitors the next year, gives Kenton's reaction to a question on the "truth" of the sketch:

"'Well, I'll tell you,' said he, 'not true: the book says that when Blackfish the Ingin warrior asked me, when they had taken me prisoner, if Col. Boone had sent me to steal their horses, that I said "No sir." (Here he looked indignant and rose from his chair.) I tell you I never said *sir* to an Ingin in my life: I scarcely ever say it to a white man.' Here Mrs. Kenton who was engaged in some domestic occupation at the table turned round and remarked that when they were last in Kentucky, some one gave her the book to read to him, and that when she came to that part he would not let her read any further."

His indignation over this word and its misuse was profound. He never lost a chance to deny the libelous allegation.

Preparations for the Fifty Year Meeting were going briskly on. Newport and Covington were preparing to entertain the pioneers and Cincinnati was in the way of celebrating its semi-centennial as well, for from Clarks' two block houses built there in 1782 had sprung the city on a hill. Many names came in of men who were planning to make the journey, but of Clark's fourteen hundred pioneers, hardly more than fifteen were coming. Death had carried off most of them; others were too far away or too infirm to attend.

And then came an enemy which neither the pioneers nor their sons' sons could fight—the Asiatic cholera. It swept through the country. It stopped for a space at Cincinnati and the citizens fled before it; except for the sick and dying and a few who took care of them the town was left desolate. Plans to come into the danger zone were given up over night; the long-planned Fifty Year Meeting died before it was born. Kenton and his wife and General Whiteman left Maysville for Newport in the same boat late in October. They crossed to Cincinnati where they were the guests of "Mr. Farrar the engineer," and "at a hotel took a corporation dinner." But they did not linger, for the scene was too depressing and the danger too great; while Kenton was there "he saw a coffin with a cholera subject handed out of a window in the house opposite the one where he stopped."

So the trip back home began, "by stage from Cincinnati to Xenia," where they stopped over night with Major Galloway—and discussed perhaps the strange ways of Providence in giving and taking away. Some of the multitudinous Kentons met them there and took them to Chillicothe Old Town—scene fifty-four years before of Kenton's taking of horses from the

Indian pound and of his first gauntlet race. Here a great reception awaited him; all the old ground was retraced and the old action rehearsed. Then the two old people were taken to Springfield and from there made the last stage of their journey alone.

But not unobserved. A young man making his first trip through the Mad River country was going north that same day from Springfield, and he chanced to set down his impressions of that part of his journey, so interesting was it:

When I entered the two-horse hack for Urbana, in the morning [wrote Richard McNesmar, later editor of the Springfield *Republic*], I found already seated there a very elderly and dignified gentleman, who at the first glance commanded my respect. By his side sat a lady much younger in appearance, with an animated countenance, and intelligent eye and pleasing manners. We three formed the load. As we wheeled by the residence of the late Maddox Fisher . . . on Limestone street, the lady directed my attention to it as the most beautiful place in the town and the one she always most admired. This led into a running conversation, and I found her to be a very agreeable and companionable traveler. Among other facts, she told me that Springfield was so named at her suggestion, on account of the many delightful and valuable springs within and around the place located for the town.

While we chatted about as freely as strangers generally do on first meeting, the old gentleman sat in silence, and as his appearance was not of a character to invite to conversation a young and bashful man, I had to be content for the while with looking at him and wondering who he was. At last, however, when we came into the neighborhood of Maj. Wm. Hunt's, I ventured to ask him if he were "going far north?" He said no. The lady then said they were going to their home near Zanesfield, in Logan county. This question happened to break the ice a little, and the gentleman became somewhat talkative—in a slow way. He told me he had been at Newport, Ky., to attend a meeting of pioneers appointed fifty years before, but that the cholera had thwarted the meeting.

He pointed out along the verge of the road nearly opposite the Half Way House, the path along which the Indians had once escorted him, a prisoner, on the way to Zanesfield, to make him run the gauntlet, and gave me sundry snatches of detail as to his early hardships in the backwoods, and adventures with the Indians, so that by the time we came to Urbana, we had all become quite free talkers. At the time I did not take any hint as to who he was, though I tried hard to study him out, and though I had been somewhat familiar with his history from my boyhood.

When we landed at Urbana, at the house kept by Daniel Harr Esq., the people collected pretty freely around the hack, all anxious to see and speak to, who I now became convinced was a man of eminent distinction. On eager inquiry I soon learned that I had been traveling with whom I had till then known only in history—the celebrated pioneer, Simon Kenton, and his excellent lady.

So ended the long-thought-of, long-planned-for Fifty Year Meeting, in disappointment and failure. The day of glory passed in mourning, and the old pioneers sank once again into the oblivion from which they had so briefly emerged.

But the comfortable routine of life began again in the little two-roomed cabin on the Parkison farm. When Ruth Jane left them, Matilda's daughter Judith took her place, came over from her parents' home not a hundred yards away to live with her grandparents. William and his wife left the following year for Indiana—he was the apple of his mother's eye, but the newer country called him and his answer was like his father's before him. Simon and his wife attended their last "camp meeting" that year, a great gathering of several counties, where he saw many of his old friends for the last time. General Workman was there, returned from his journey with the Shawanese to Kansas. He had passed through Missouri, and he brought

Kenton word from Governor William Clark, younger brother of George Rogers, that his memory was as good as it had been forty years before, and that "he had vivid remembrances of the streams, vallies and face of the country along the Miami and Mad rivers as they had appeared during the period when they served together under Mad Anthony." Several native Wyandotte preachers were here, and Kenton was placed among them on the stand. As if that were not drama enough, one of them, Rhon-con-ess, who had been preaching through an interpreter, suddenly swept that unnecesary aid aside, left him standing on the platform, and descending to the ground in front of it, on a level with his audience, told the six-hundred word story of the crucifixion with pantomime so vivid that the audience was hushed and awed. And then he spoke of peace on earth, of himself and Kenton, once enemies, now friends, and still the audience followed him through his vivid pantomime to the final embrace of Indian and old Indian fighter.

Frederick W. Thomas visited Kenton two months later—in October, 1833. His story of his trip is one of the submerged little documents on Kenton which is full of meat. For one thing it answers all the questions of the comfort or discomfort of Kenton's last days, about which so many needless tears have been shed; it disposes forever of the "miserable cabin" and the "poverty" in which he died. Dr. Draper, too, visited the cabin in 1852, "and am well convinced," he says, "it was in Kenton's day a very comfortable two-roomed house, built precisely as he himself devised and planned it. Nor could he have wanted for any of the comforts of life. His pension was $20 a month." Kenton's "poverty" was never actual lack of money to live on so much as lack of money with which to swing his large land operations. His great fortune, like most of the fortunes of those days, was in the future solely—a dream fortune, with dream profits and dream losses. When he gave up the dream he lived in the practical world comfortably enough.

The house was comfortable and large for one of the kind [said Thomas]; on stopping, a son-in-law of the old worthy met us at the bars, and though he knew us not, with the hospitality of the country, he insisted upon putting up our horses, which we were obliged to decline, as we could not tarry long. As we advanced toward it, I observed that everything about the house wore the air of frugal comfort. We ascended two or three steps and entered a room in which there was a matron who we learned was the wife of the Pioneer; seated by the fire was the old worthy himself. He rose as we entered; advancing toward him we told him that we were strangers who had read often of him and his adventures, and that being in his neighborhood, we had taken the liberty to call and see him as we were anxious to know him. The old gentleman was gratified and touched by our remark, and after an effort to suppress his emotions, he said—"Take seats, take seats, I'm right glad to see you." We sat down and immediately entered into conversation with him. He conversed in a desultory manner, and often had to make an effort to recollect himself, but when he did recollect, his memory seemed perfectly to call up the events alluded to: when asked anything, "well, I'll tell you," he would say, and after a pause he would narrate it.

Kenton was already failing, and his mind was troubled with efforts to remember, yet in the details of the interview Thomas wrote out, evidently as nearly as possible in Kenton's own words, the old man's efforts to recollect resulted in clear recollection. He seems to have been conscious of his failing powers, to have felt the need and to have supplied the force to gather up all his remaining abilities for expressing the truth that still lay in his memory.

And physically he was still strong.

Kenton's form [said Thomas], even under the weight of seventy-nine years, is striking and must have been a model of manly strength and ability. His eye is blue, mild, and yet penetrating in its glance. The forehead projects very much at the eyebrows (which are well defined), and then it recedes and is not very high or very broad—his hair was light, now it is nearly all grey—the nose straight and well shaped—and his mouth before he lost his teeth must have been expressive and handsome. I observed he had one tooth left, which taking into consideration his character and manner of conversation, was continually reminding one of Leatherstocking. The whole face is remarkably expressive, not of turbulence or excitement, but rather of rumination and self-possession. Simplicity, frankness, honesty, and a strict regard to truth, appeared the prominent traits of his character.

Nothing in this visit impressed Thomas more than Kenton's innate courtesy and delicacy of feeling, which he gives in an incident. They had been talking of Kenton's injuries and of his remarkable strength to endure.

"Yes," he said, he believed that he might say that he was once an active man, "but," continued he, taking my crutch in his hand as I sat beside him and holding it together with his staff—I could trace the association of his ideas—"I am old now." I observed from his manner that he wanted to ask me about my crutch, but that he felt a delicacy in doing so. I explained it to him; after observing the fashion of it for some time, he looked at me for a moment and said with much emotion, showing me his own staff, "You see, I have to use one too, you are young and I am old, but I tell you we all have to come to it at last." Many in their courtesy have tried to reconcile me to a crutch, but no one ever did it with so bland a spirit as this blunt backwoodsman, who never said "sir to an Ingin in his life and scarcely ever to a white man." True politeness is from the heart, and from the abundance of the heart it speaketh, the rest is but imitation, and at best the automaton, *fashioned* to act like a man.

Old age descended swiftly on him after this. One of his neighbors, in a painfully written letter to Dr. Draper, says that he knew Kenton only in his latter years, when "the Gen. had become old and fretful, done nothing much but scold his wife and pound the floor with his staff." John Arrowsmith saw him last in June, 1835. "His mind was much impaired. He could no longer give a connected account of any incident of his life. He was anxious to talk about scenes that he had passed through, but could no longer make anything intelligible, would get several incidents mixed all together. I have often thought that the fracture of his skull injured his memory towards the end of his life. It was then, at his request that I should take hold of his head and see where the Indians had stuck the tomahawk in. The sunken places in his head were visible, one about two inches long, sunk about half the thickness of my finger; the other was not quite so deep."

And yet he was placid when the effort to recall old scenes rested from its ineffectual work and became passive. He moved slowly along the paths to his nearest neighbors and in some old chair not his own slept a while and roused to play with some child lingering near, and then slept again. And then slowly home, to sit under the trees or by the fire, to sleep, to dream, to rouse again and begin his slow pacing of some familiar path whose "sign" he watched and the lay of its land with the horizon as intently as he had watched the trails of sixty years ago. And finally he surrendered his walks and sat all day in his fireside chair.

Four weeks before his death there came a Sunday when two clergymen carried him from his cabin across the yard to his daughter's house, where service was held for the neighborhood. He was carried back that afternoon and never left his cabin again. The rest was simply "running down." On the day of his death he said to his good wife, "I have fought my last battle, and it has been the hardest of them all." He lay after that in restful peace, quietly dying through the day, but recognizing the friends and neighbors who came in and out, and in the evening of April 29, 1836, he breathed his last, "like a candle going out."

Chapter XV

THE PORTRAITS AND THE MAN

ART—PORTRAITURE, that is, in painting, drawing, and sculpture—did not flourish greatly in the Middle West during the pioneer days, and when it did it mostly passed the pioneers by. The artists of the period were not interested in a good subject nearly so much as in a good name to write under their portraits, and the silhouette makers who began to traverse the country with "traveling museums" in covered wagons did more than the portrait painters then abroad in the land to perpetuate the features of the pioneers. For only a penny or two, while the self-conscious subject sat in straight profile before him, the silhouette artist made his profile in half a dozen flashes of his scissors; and good or bad, and always frail, it was often the only memorial of what many an old backwoodsman even faintly resembled.

Yet this was Simon Kenton's odd fate; if his first portrait was done by a silhouette cutter traveling through the forests of Ohio, his last portrait was made by Jean François Millet in the forest of Fontainebleau.

The silhouette was cut in 1812; it "hung with the rest of the Family" on the cabin walls at Urbana, at the Zanesfield home, and in the last cabin on the

Parkison farm. But the silhouette reproduced for this volume is not the "solid" but the outline, somehow thriftily picked up by some member of the family as the portrait was cut and later basted on a bit of black calico—the stitches and stray threads can be plainly seen. It came into Dr. Draper's possession in 1860, sent him by Kenton's daughter Elizabeth through William—"a profile of her father taken when she was one year old (born May 29, 1811)."

The Hinde pencil sketch was made in 1832—by the Reverend Thomas S. Hinde who, saturated with the conviction that some general presentment of Simon Kenton's features should be preserved for posterity, did his best. "I visited Kenton in 1830, and saw him again in 1832 and '33—by accident sketched a good likeness of him in the 78th year of his age. He was a tall, spare, raw-bone—thin visage, light complexioned, brown hair and light blue eyes. He was slow of speech, and quite meditative and contemplative in his turn." So much for the amateur artist's impression of his subject. Hinde made his drawing on a very thin, almost transparent paper which, given the hard pencil he used, resulted in the faintest of sketches.

Four years later Louis Morgan, then a rising young artist of the East, presented himself at Kenton's home on a commission to paint his portrait for the *National Portrait Gallery of Distinguished Americans.* This was an enterprise sponsored in Philadelphia, the first ambitious attempt to collect portraits of Americans painted by American artists. Boone's portrait had been already painted for this collection, but Boone's name had been a familiar one since 1784, not only in America and England but also in France and Germany where translations of Filson's so-called *Autobiography* had appeared. Byron had written of him—as he might have written of Kenton had accident made him instead of Boone the first autobiographed Kentucky pioneer. As it is, in the early Kenton sketches we often come on references to his wild colt ride as the theme of Byron's "Mazeppa"! McClung's brief sketch of him had but lately appeared, however; had it not been for this, it is doubtful that the editors of the *Portrait Gallery* would have known of his existence—this man almost unknown outside of the two states he had helped to found and preserve, whose services were so great just exactly because they were so private.

Judge Noah McCulloch went up from Zanesfield with the "gentlemanly young man" just arrived from Louisville to introduce him to Kenton and to prepare the old man for the ordeal. But Mrs. Kenton was the troubled one. Judge McCulloch says that she was greatly concerned over her husband's lack of proper attire for a portrait, and was not at all consoled by Morgan's assertion that he "cared nothing for that." Kenton himself was pleased and interested, and the painter, having arranged all to his liking, settled down for a week's stay at the Parkisons'.

He was evidently charmed with his subject, for he made not one but three portraits. He did them all in Kenton's characteristic posture before the fire, with his old staff in his hand—its charred end can be seen. As he painted, the old man talked, retold the stories of the past, and so reanimated himself that the painter had little work to do in entertaining the sitter

—he was himself the entertained.[1] This was just three months before Kenton's death.

When Morgan returned to Louisville he sent on one of the three portraits to James Longacre, editor and publisher of the *Gallery*. R. W. Hodson made the engraving; then the portrait was exhibited at the Philadelphia Academy of Fine Arts, and was unfortunately "skyed." But Felix Darley—old famous art critic—saw it, approved it, had it rehung, and it became the success of the exhibition.

Another of the portraits passed into the possession of the late Colonel R. T. Durrett of Louisville and was for years one of the prizes in his fine collection of early Kentucky papers and pictures. In 1913, after his death, this collection was purchased by the University of Chicago.

The third had a checkered history and rather a

---

[1]Chester Harding painted Boone's portrait for this same *Gallery*—on an ordinary table oilcloth, in 1819. In his *My Egotistiography* he tells of his trip from St. Louis to St. Charles on this mission; of how the nearer he got to Boone's home the vaguer the directions became—when within two miles of the house he found people who "did not know any such man."

"I found the object of my search engaged in cooking his dinner. He was lying in his bunk, near the fire, and had a long strip of venison wound around his ramrod, and was busy turning it before a brisk fire, and using salt and pepper to season his meat. I at once told him the object of my visit. I found that he hardly knew what I meant. I explained the matter to him, and he agreed to sit. He was ninety years old and rather infirm; his memory of passing events was much impaired, yet he amused me every day by his anecdotes of his earlier life. I asked him one day, just after his description of one of his long hunts, if he never got lost, having no compass. 'No,' he said, 'I can't say as ever I was lost, but I was *bewildered* once for three days.'

"He was much astonished at seeing the likeness. He had a very large progeny; one grand daughter had eighteen children, all at home near the old man's cabin; they were even more astonished at the picture than was the old man himself."

hard one, as its present battered state clearly shows. Morgan evidently hoped to sell it to Kentucky and kept it in his studio for some years as he moved about from Louisville to Frankfort to Lexington. But no appropriation for its purchase was made by any legislature, and finally he turned it over to Thomas W. Cridland, his frame maker, in payment for some debt. Cridland also attempted to sell it to Kentucky but failed, and when he left Kentucky for Ohio, in 1852, he took the portrait with him. In 1890 it passed into the possession of his eldest son, Thomas H. Cridland, who held it until his death in 1924. Then his nephew, Walter C. McKinney, presented it to the Ohio State Archeological and Historical Society at Columbus. "Five generations of the Cridland family," he said his in presentation speech, "have looked upon this portrait, and for many years the face of 'Uncle Simon' hung on the wall in my room, the first to greet me in the morning, and the last to bid me good night. He comforted me and guarded me as a boy and young man, until I left my grandfather's home." And then he added what seems inseparable from any reminiscence of Kenton, what so many had said before him in the Kenton Papers, "Simon Kenton, however, is something more to me than a portrait. He was the pioneer guide and personal friend of my father's people."

From the forests of Ohio to the forest of Fontainebleau—the distance is no greater than the space Jean François Millet spanned when he turned for an interval from his French peasants—his Sower, the praying figure in his Angelus—to American Indians and American pioneers. At Fontainebleau he made his "portrait" of Simon Kenton perhaps a dozen years after Kenton's death. But Millet had never heard of Simon Kenton; he labeled his work "Simon Butler," and later, "Mazeppa américain."

Like most stories, the story of "Mazeppa américain" begins, too, far back.

When Karl Bodmer, great Swiss artist, set out for the new world in 1832 with Maximilian, Prince of Neuwied, to illustrate the book his royal companion purposed writing, he knew neither Millet nor the American Indians. Of the latter he was to know enough during the next three years. They delighted him; he drew them in dress, full dress and undress; he lived when he could in their wigwams, smoked with them, talked with them, danced with them, even fought with them—for he and Maximilian were at Fort McKenzie in western Montana when it was attacked in August, 1833, by the Assiniboins in full war array. What his eye caught his pencil set down—his illustrations for Maximilian's *Travels in the Interior of North America.* 1832–1834 show what he saw—they are a joy. He heard the legends of the country, absorbed them, read Cooper, and conceived the splendid idea of illustrating a French edition of the Leatherstocking Tales.

He met Millet after he returned to France, and for years to come the two men lived side by side at Fontainebleau. He interested Millet in the Indians, told him the classic tales of the American frontier, told him of Simon Butler's Mazeppa ride. Millet began to make drawings of the Indians in crayon and charcoal and finally he and Bodmer collaborated in a series of lithographs which were published in 1852; one of these was "Mazeppa américain." It was an odd and an interesting collaboration, Bodmer doing the landscapes and horses, Millet the figures—Indians as well as white men.[1]

As for the other imaginary portraits of Simon Kenton reproduced here, they are taken from old border books and old magazines of the border literature period. They pretend to no portraiture, to nothing but "action," and since that is their aim they fulfill their purpose. Doubtless some reader will relive a day of childhood's dreaming as his eye falls for the first time in years on "Kenton's First Victory," "Kenton and Logan," and the like.

Honors came slowly after Kenton's death. He had wished for no military rites, and so quickly did his funeral follow his death that no more than thirty people were present when he was buried at the foot of the little hill where his cabin stood "on the Sandusky road," a spot he had himself selected. Four years after his death Kenton County, Kentucky, was organized. Two years later the town of Kenton, Ohio, was founded. In 1849 the citizens of Maysville—old Limestone—provided for a new cemetery with a mound in the center designed for Kenton's grave when his body should be brought "back home" from Ohio. In 1854 the Ohio legislature appropriated $1000 for a monument to be erected over his grave after it had been removed to "some suitable place," and from then until the close of the Civil War the two states contested briefly from time to time for his body, and different cities of these states as well. It

[1]For the sake of a larger reproduction of this very large lithograph, it is shown in the lining papers at the front of this book.

was a little fragment of the Civil War—this contest between Southern state and Northern, so sharply divided now by the Ohio. At the outbreak of the war Kentucky had claimed him—had established Camp Kenton in Mason County near his old station site where the grandsons of his "Kentucky boys" gathered to train for civil warfare. But by now most of the Kentons were "Yankees." and from Ohio, Illinois, and Indiana sixteen of his grandsons marched against Kentucky and the South. One wonders on which side Simon Kenton would have found himself—could have found himself—in the terrible conflict.

Finally, spurred to action by Kentucky's provision in January, 1865, for the removal of his remains to Frankfort, the Ohio legislature passed a bill appropriating five thousand dollars for a monument over his permanent resting place at Urbana, and there his remains were reinterred on November 30, 1865. But the monument appropriation lapsed; not until 1884 was a monument erected—John Quincy Adams Ward, early American sculptor and grandson of Kenton's old friend and partner, made the design "without charge." Over twenty years before he had come to Columbus with a model for a statue of Simon Kenton, hoping to get a commission from the state. But the state failed him.

Few border books were written for fifty years after Kenton's death without some chapter devoted to him—to his exploits, rather, both real and mythical. He began to appear in border fiction very early. In 1837 Robert Bird's *Nick of the Woods, Or, The Jibbenainosay. A Story of Kentucky*, came out in London, with an introduction by Harrison Ainsworth. Roaring

Ralph Stackpole was identified from the beginning with Simon Kenton—his name sufficiently indicates the dare-devil recklessness of the character, and Ainsworth pronounced him a figure limned from life. James Weir's *Simon Kenton, Or, The Scout's Revenge* and its sequel, *The Winter Lodge,* are magnificent examples of the loose and easy in romantic historical novels of the period. Unfortunately for the hard facts in the case, the author based his plot and all of his conflicts on the supposed war to the death between the great scout and "his old enemy, Simon Girty."

Would-be biographers contemplated his life, but where was his record? It occurred to no one but Dr. Draper to go straight to the source—the memories of Kenton's contemporaries and the old records of the land itself.

Historians, it would seem, never considered Kenton. It is an incredible fact that in the American Commonwealth series—histories of the separate states—the historian of Kentucky does not mention him; the historian of Ohio takes a page or two to relate the story of his captivity. Not until William Hayden English went to the Draper collection of manuscripts for his *Conquest of the Country North West of the River Ohio* and Theodore Roosevelt worked with the same papers for his *Winning of the West* did any material on Simon Kenton as a real force in the development of the West swim into an historian's ken. Both of these men devoted pages to Kenton. But neither went to the source of his story—the verbal and written memories of the people who knew him as he was.

He was a man made for danger; it was ever-present

peril that brought out the total man. He could fear death as whole-heartedly for a friend or a stranger as for himself, and with no moment to plan could act on the second as instinctively right, as naturally directed, as grass grows or water runs.

For the clear bright sense of danger inspired him; at ease he was at loss. It was as if Nature had fashioned him like clay to the seal for her purpose—a brief rôle in a brief act of an endless drama; his part played, he was like an old actor out of work, his play never more to be revived and he unfitted by very virtue of his nature to play any character but his own. The drama went on with other actors and his old eyes saw the panorama of their period unfold behind them, war giving way to peace, forests to fields, tree trails to traveled roads, secret settlements to cities, with two million people living in the fertile land whose white men he had once counted along the fingers of one hand. But the comfortable background was not his background; he had been fashioned against the time of trouble, against the day of battle and war.

He was a natural man who breathed danger like air—it was his life; when the dangerous days were ended, almost he began to die. He was a man "on his own hook," framed to swim in his own sea; when it drained away he was left without the right lungs to breathe the new air. But in his own waters—his own time—he was leviathan.

BIBLIOGRAPHY

THE only authentic material for a life of Simon Kenton is in the Draper Manuscripts in the archives of the State Historical Society of Wisconsin. For access to the Kenton Papers and associated manuscripts and for unfailingly kind and courteous assistance in working with them the author is deeply indebted to Dr. Joseph Schafer, Miss Annie Nunns, and Miss Louise Phelps Kellogg of the State Historical Library staff.

The Kenton Papers in thirteen volumes, the Clark Papers for the years 1776-1782, the Kentucky Papers and the thirty-three volumes of Draper's Notes are the four series of manuscripts in which most of the biographical material lies.

The brief bibliography given below makes no pretence of including all of the multitudinous sketches of Kenton's life, most of which are derived directly from McClung and McDonald. It lists only the most valuable material which has been published; it includes also a few of the more important Draper Manuscripts.

ARROWSMITH, JOHN, Biographical Sketch of Simon Kenton, 1862. Draper MSS.—10BB16.

——Letters to Dr. Draper, 1862–1863. Draper MSS.—10BB17–22.

BEMAN, IRVING, Two Interesting Traditions. (In Magazine of Western History, Vol. III, March, 1886, pp. 484–488.)

BROWN, T. J., Kenton's Chilicothes. (In Ohio Archæological and Historical Quarterly, Vol. XII, July, 1903, pp.322–323).

——Kenton's Gauntlet at Chilicothe. (In Ohio Archæological and Historical Quarterly, Vol. XIII, October, 1904, pp. 483–484).

BURNET, JACOB, Notes on the Early Settlement of the North-Western Territory. Cincinnati, 1847, pp. 460–468.

CATTERMOLE. E. G. Famous Frontiersmen, Pioneers and Scouts. Chicago, 18—. (Contains a sketch of "Gen. Simon Kenton, alias Butler," pp. 169–202).

COLEMAN, ROBERT T., Simon Kenton. (In Harper's Magazine, Vol. XXVIII, February, 1864, pp. 289–304).

COLLINS, LEWIS, and RICHARD, The History of Kentucky. Louisville, 1874. 2 vols. (Contains a sketch of Simon Kenton by John A. McClung, Vol. II, pp. 442–450, and many references.)

ELLET, ELIZABETH FRIES, Pioneer Women of the West. New York, 1852. (Contains a sketch of Elizabeth Kenton, pp. 428–434.)

ENGLISH, WILLIAM HAYDEN, The Conquest of the Country North-West of the River Ohio. Indianapolis, 1896.

FINLEY, JAMES B., Autobiography. Cincinnati, 1853. (Contains a sketch of Simon Kenton, pp. 26–33.)

FROST, JOHN, Border Wars of the West. Cincinnati, 1853.

GRAHAM, CHRISTOPHER C., Simon Kenton. (In the Louisville Monthly Magazine, Vol. I, March, 1879, pp. 127–132.)

HARTLEY, CECIL B., Life and Adventures of Lewis Wetzel. New York, 1860. (Contains a sketch of Simon Kenton pp. 113–170.)

HOWE, HENRY, Historical collections of Ohio. Cincinnati, 1847. 1 vol. Another edition, Columbus, 1891, 3 vols.

JAMES, JOHN H., Notes on Conversations with General Simon Kenton. February 13, 1832. Transcript in Draper MSS.—5BB97–125.

JILLSON, WILLARD ROUSE, Old Kentucky Entries and Deeds. Filson Club Publications, No. 34. Louisville, 1926.

——Old Kentucky Land Grants. Filson Club Publications, No. 33. Louisville, 1925.

Bibliography

KENTON, SIMON, Manuscript Statement: Recollections of General George Rogers Clark. Taken down by Mrs. Simon Kenton (n.d.). Transcript in Draper MSS.—1BB72–79.

——Pension Statement. Transcript in Draper MSS.—1BB84–86.

——Letter to Samuel H. Sanders, March 18, 1834. Transcript in Draper MSS.—8S5–7.

——Depositions of, Transcripts in Draper MSS.—6BB18–29, 33, 108; 4J33–34.

——Letter to General Robert Poague, August 16, 1821. Transscript in Draper MSS.—4J31–32.

KENTON, WILLIAM, Letters to Dr. Draper, 1847–1863. Draper MSS.—8BB200–216.

McCLUNG, JOHN ALEXANDER, Sketches of Western Adventure. Maysville, Ky., 1832. (Contains a sketch of Simon Kenton, pp. 93–125; addenda, 212–220.)

——Simon Kenton. (In history of Kentucky, Lewis and Richard Collins, Louisville, 1874. Vol. II, pp. 442–450.)

McDONALD, JOHN, Biographical Sketches of General Nathaniel Massie, General Duncan McArthur, Captain William Wells and General Simon Kenton. Cincinnati, 1838.
(The sketch of Simon Kenton, pp. 197–267, and the other three likewise, appeared originally in the Western Christian Advocate in 1835.)

McFARLAND, ROBERT W., Simon Kenton. (In Ohio Archæological and Historical Quarterly, Vol. XIII, January, 1904, pp. 1–39.)

——Simon Kenton—Supplementary Note. (In Ohio Archæological and Historical Quarterly, Vol. XIII, April, 1904, p. 281.)

McKINNEY, WALTER D., Simon Kenton—Thomas W. Cridland, Pioneers. (In Ohio Archæological and Historical Quarterly, Vol. XXXIV, January, 1925, pp. 117–131).

MARSHALL, HUMPHREY, History of Kentucky. Frankfort, 1812. (Contains the first published sketch of Simon Kenton, pp. 214–220.)

OWEN, ASAL, Narrative of Simon Kenton. Draper MSS.—7BB63

PATRICK, WILLIAM, Sketch of Simon Kenton. (In History of Champaign County, Ohio, compiled by Joshua Antrim, n. p., 1872, pp. 60–62.)

PRICE, SAMUEL W., The Old Masters of the Blue Grass. Filson Club Publications, No. 17. Louisville, 1902.

ROBERTSON, JAMES ROOD, Petitions of the Early Inhabitants of Kentucky to the General Assembly of Virginia. Filson Club Publications, No. 27. Louisville, 1914.

ROOSEVELT, THEODORE, The Winning of the West. New York, 1889–1896. 6 Vols.

SMITH, DE COST, Jean François Millet's Drawings of American Indians. (In Century Magazine, Vol. LXXX, May, 1910, pp. 77–84).

TAYLOR, JOHN D., Fragments of a Biography of Simon Kenton. Draper MSS.—6BB1–17.

THOMAS, FREDERICK WILLIAM, Sketches of Character. Louisville, 1849. (Contains "A Day's Ramble in the Interior: A Visit to Simon Kenton." This sketch appeared originally in the Cincinnati Mirror, December 7, 1833.)

WILLSON, ANNIE, E., A Pioneer in his Corn-Patch. (In Magazine of American History, Vol. XXIII, June, 1890, pp. 450–459.)

Index

Index

Index

Index

Index

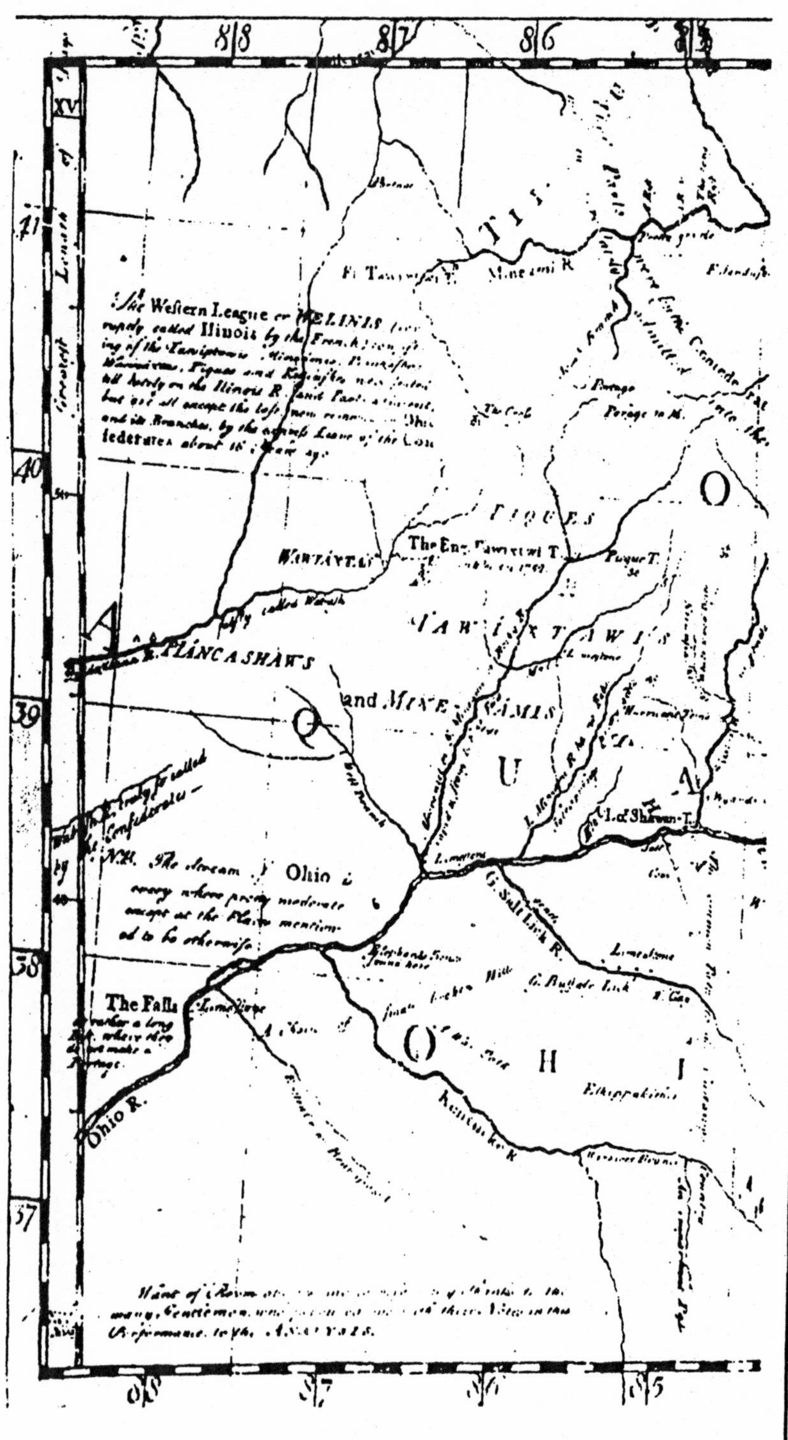

The Western League or WELINIS
The Falls
Ohio R.
G. Salt Lick R.
Kentucke R.

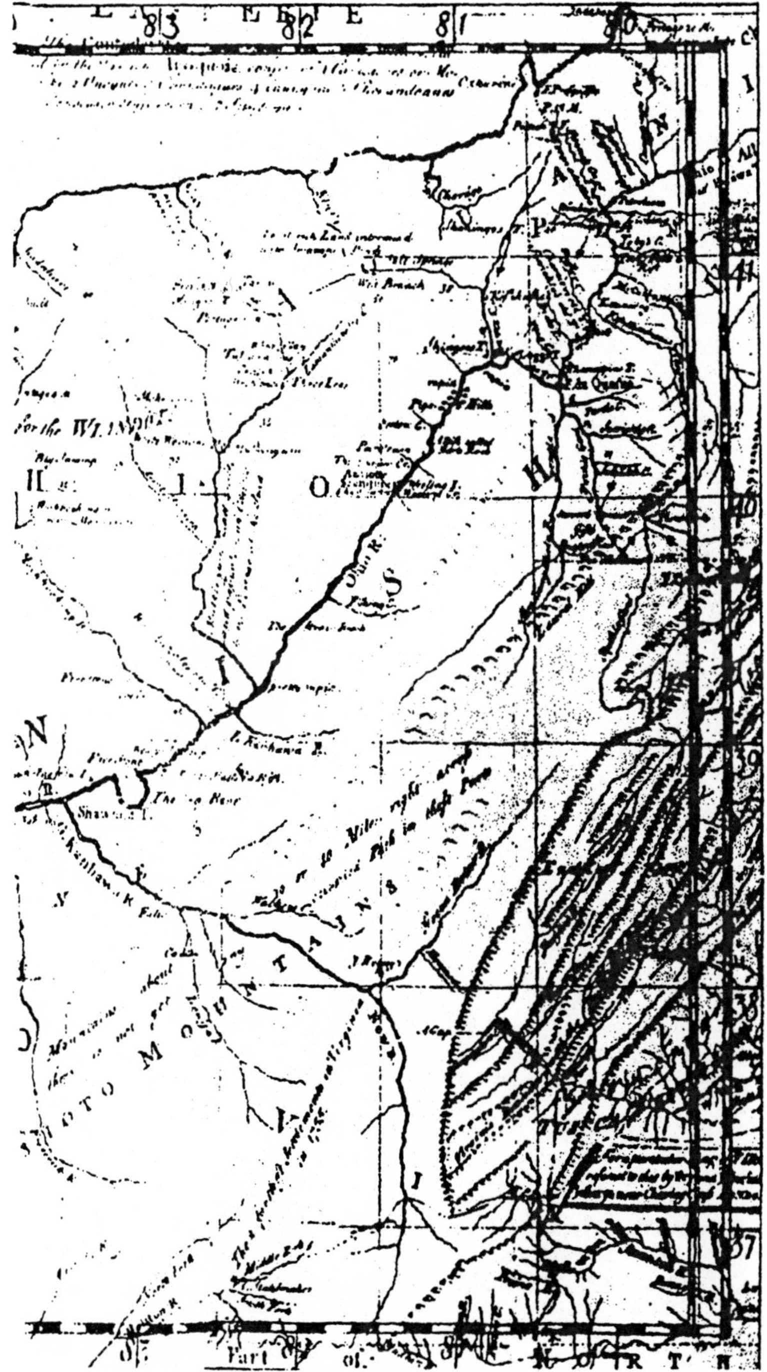

for the WIANDOTS
Ohio R.
Shawanoe I.
Ouasioto Mountains
Mountains about 20 or 30 Miles right across

Index

Index

Index

Index

Index

Index

Index

The First American Frontier

the Ayer Company collection

Agnew, Daniel.
A History of the Region of Pennsylvania North of the Allegheny River. 1887.

Alden, George H.
New Government West of the Alleghenies Before 1780. 1897.

Barrett, Jay Amos.
Evolution of the Ordinance of 1787. 1891.

Billon, Frederick.
Annals of St. Louis in its Early Days Under the French and Spanish Dominations. 1886.

Billon, Frederick.
Annals of St. Louis in its Territorial Days, 1804-1821. 1888.

Littel, William.
Political Transactions in and Concerning Kentucky. 1926.

Bowles, William Augustus.
Authentic Memoirs of William Augustus Bowles. 1916.

Bradley, A. G.
The Fight with France for North America. 1900.

Brannan, John, ed.
Official Letters of the Military and Naval Officers of the War, 1812-1815. 1823.

Brown, John P.
Old Frontiers. 1938.

Brown, Samuel R.
The Western Gazetteer. 1817.

Cist, Charles.

Cincinnati Miscellany of Antiquities of the West and Pioneer History. (2 volumes in one). 1845-6.

Claiborne, Nathaniel Herbert.

Notes on the War in the South with Biographical Sketches of the Lives of Montgomery, Jackson, Sevier, and Others. 1819.

Clark, Daniel.

Proofs of the Corruption of Gen. James Wilkinson. 1809.

Clark, George Rogers.

Colonel George Rogers Clark's Sketch of His Campaign in the Illinois in 1778-9. 1869.

Collins, Lewis.

Historical Sketches of Kentucky. 1847.

Cruikshank, Ernest, ed,

Documents Relating to Invasion of Canada and the Surrender of Detroit. 1912.

Cruikshank, Ernest, ed,

The Documentary History of the Campaign on the Niagara Frontier, 1812-1814. (4 volumes). 1896-1909.

Cutler, Jervis.

A Topographical Description of the State of Ohio, Indian Territory, and Louisiana. 1812.

Cutler, Julia P.

The Life and Times of Ephraim Cutler. 1890.

Darlington, Mary C.

History of Col. Henry Bouquet and the Western Frontiers of Pennsylvania. 1920.

Darlington, Mary C.

Fort Pitt and Letters From the Frontier. 1892.

De Schweinitz, Edmund.

The Life and Times of David Zeisberger. 1870.

Dillon, John B.

History of Indiana. 1859.

Eaton, John Henry.
Life of Andrew Jackson. 1824.

English, William Hayden.
Conquest of the Country Northwest of the Ohio. (2 volumes in one). 1896.

Flint, Timothy.
Indian Wars of the West. 1833.

Forbes, John.
Writings of General John Forbes Relating to His Service in North America. 1938.

Forman, Samuel S.
Narrative of a Journey Down the Ohio and Mississippi in 1789-90. 1888.

Haywood, John.
Civil and Political History of the State of Tennessee to 1796. 1823.

Heckewelder, John.
History, Manners and Customs of the Indian Nations. 1876.

Heckewelder, John.
Narrative of the Mission of the United Brethren. 1820.

Hildreth, Samuel P.
Pioneer History. 1848.

Houck, Louis.
The Boundaries of the Louisiana Purchase: A Historical Study. 1901.

Houck, Louis.
History of Missouri. (3 volumes in one). 1908.

Houck, Louis.
The Spanish Regime in Missouri. (2 volumes in one). 1909.

Jacob, John J.
A Biographical Sketch of the Life of the Late Capt. Michael Cresap. 1826.

Jones, David.

A Journal of Two Visits Made to Some Nations of Indians on the West Side of the River Ohio, in the Years 1772 and 1773. 1774.

Kenton, Edna.

Simon Kenton. 1930.

Loudon, Archibald.

Selection of Some of the Most Interesting Narratives of Outrages. (2 volumes in one). **1808-1811.**

Monette, J. W.

History, Discovery and Settlement of the Mississippi Valley. (2 volumes in one). 1846.

Morse, Jedediah.

American Gazetteer. 1797.

Pickett, Albert James.

History of Alabama. (2 volumes in one). 1851.

Pope, John.

A Tour Through the Southern and Western Territories. 1792.

Putnam, Albigence Waldo.

History of Middle Tennessee. 1859.

Ramsey, James G. M.

Annals of Tennessee. 1853.

Ranck, George W.

Boonesborough. 1901.

Robertson, James Rood, ed.

Petitions of the Early Inhabitants of Kentucky to the Gen. Assembly of Virginia. 1914.

Royce, Charles.

Indian Land Cessions. 1899.

Rupp, I. Daniel.

History of Northampton, Lehigh, Monroe, Carbon and Schuykill Counties. 1845.

Safford, William H.

The Blennerhasset Papers. 1864.

St. Clair, Arthur.
A Narrative of the Manner in which the Campaign Against the Indians, in the Year 1791 was Conducted. 1812.

Sargent, Winthrop, ed.
A History of an Expedition Against Fort DuQuesne in 1755. 1855.

Severance, Frank H.
An Old Frontier of France. (2 volumes in one). 1917.

Sipe, C. Hale.
Fort Ligonier and Its Times. 1932.

Stevens, Henry N.
Lewis Evans: His Map of the Middle British Colonies in America. 1920.

Timberlake, Henry.
The Memoirs of Lieut. Henry Timberlake. 1927.

Tome, Philip.
Pioneer Life: Or Thirty Years a Hunter. 1854.

Trent, William.
Journal of Captain William Trent From Logstown to Pickawillany. 1871.

Walton, Joseph S.
Conrad Weiser and the Indian Policy of Colonial Pennsylvania. 1900.

Withers, Alexander Scott.
Chronicles of Border Warfare. 1895.

Printed in the United States
154347LV00006B/35/A

9 781432 519131